Water in Buildings

Water in Buildings

An Architect's Guide
to Moisture and Mold

WILLIAM B. ROSE

WILEY

JOHN WILEY & SONS, INC.

Library of Congress Cataloging-in-Publication Data:
Rose, William B. (William Browning), 1947–
  Water in Buildings : an architect's guide to moisture and mold / by William B. Rose.
     p. cm.
  Includes bibliographical references and index.
  ISBN 0-471-46850-9 (cloth)
     1. Waterproofing. 2. Dampness in buildings. 3. Molds (Funji)—Control.
  I. Title.
  TH9031.R67 2005
  693.8′92—dc22   2004014937

Printed in the United States of America

10 9 8 7 6 5 4 3 2

For Claudine

Contents

Preface

This book began several years ago. I was on the staff of the Small Homes Council at the University of Illinois, a small group of researchers and educators working on residential construction. We answered questions for homeowners, architects, and builders on any matters related to design and construction. Many of the questions had to do with water and moisture and humidity, and the old researchers on staff handed the task of answering these nettlesome questions to me. The same questions recurred: about vapor retarders and attic ventilation and wet basements and crawl spaces. I looked for a handbook on moisture control, found none, and promised to write one. This book is the product of that resolution. In writing this book I try to recall the voices of those callers to try to find the right balance between completeness and complexity.

I was granted generous funding by CertainTeed Corporation to conduct research in attic and wall performance. I measured the conditions of heat and moisture in attics and walls with a wide variety of design conditions: with and without vapor retarders, with and without ventilation, with and without a hole through the interior finish. It became quite easy for me to predict what the temperature profile and the moisture profile for an attic might be for any set of conditions. Then the realization hit that this ability is a far cry from being able to advise designers, builders, and owners what to do. So A is drier than B—so what? Always do A? Never do B? The building code says explicitly to do C—the very specific and prescriptive moisture control regulations regarding attics, walls, and crawl spaces. Does that mean that C always works, or that not doing C dooms a building? My research showed otherwise: that C could be effective, ineffective, or detrimental, depending on other factors.

So I went to the library of documents from the era when moisture control regulations such as C arose—the 1930s and 1940s. The directors, staff, and librarians of the Small Homes Council deserve much credit for hanging onto archival material from that time. I was able to trace the source of these regulations and to assess the strength of the research on which they were based. I concluded that the basis was weak. The dean of moisture control in 1952, Tyler Stewart Rogers, said in a conference that he expected the prescriptions to last a year, or six months, and he encouraged other researchers to provide the necessary updates. This book picks up that charge from over 50 years ago.

Research gives answers to questions, but the answers are probabilistic and full of qualifications and limitations. Designers and builders need to know what to do now. Advice to designers and builders must convert probabilistic and qualified findings into deterministic, unqualified advice—and someone has to make that conversion. That is the basis of this book: to lay out the process by which building science, messy and immature as it is, provides guidance to designers and builders. The natural tendency of any reader is to jump to the results and bypass the process. But someone, somewhere, must address the process: thus this book.

ACKNOWLEDGMENTS

The citizens of Illinois have provided generous support for building research for over 50 years; I hope this book begins to repay our debt to them. My interest in water and its effects comes from two cherished mentors, Michael Kim and Seichi Konzo. Anton TenWolde is the phantom coauthor of this book; he had no hand in its preparation (so he cannot be blamed for its flaws), but the direction and scope of the material arose in our many discussions.

I am grateful for the contributions of many friends and colleagues. E. Lawrence Broggini introduced me at an early age to humidity and dew point. Henry Cobb, Urs Gauchat, and Masami Takayama helped direct my architecture education. Don Brotherson godfathered my early research efforts. Jeffrey Gordon has maintained the gold standard in research and writing clarity. Joseph Lstiburek bulldozed the path for a new generation of building scientists. J. P. Brown expressed the truths we hold self-evident. Hugo Hens has provided the educational and organizational backbone of international building science. Heinz Trechsel and Gordon Tully, who reviewed an early version of this text, both get my vote for lifetime achievement in building science.

This book is written in loving memory of my father.

W. B. Rose

Introduction

AIM

This book describes water, buildings, and the range of effects that water has on buildings. The objective of the book is to bring understanding of this intersection of two difficult topics to people who are responsible for delivering buildings that must be dry, durable, and healthful. At a practical level it is about rain and snow, water in the soil, humidity in the air, building foundations, walls, windows, roofs, mechanical systems, and mold. At a technical level the book is about the physics, chemistry, biology, and engineering of the interaction of water with building materials and equipment. Let's look first at what the book is not.

The book is not a digest of the building code. Building codes are fine instruments without which the building stock would very likely be in a sorry state. They were originally designed to prevent conflagrations from passing from one building to another and to prevent building collapse under wind, seismic, live, and dead loads. In Chapter 3 we will see how moisture control snuck into building codes in the 1940s. Ever since that time, architects and builders turn to building codes for direction to ensure dryness in buildings. Building codes have never been a good source of that information. The information in this book may help future writers of building codes to ensure that their moisture control provisions are effective. Or it may illustrate a complexity far beyond the ability of building codes to capture. In any case, architects and builders who are accustomed to turning to building codes for "official" information may not find much of that in these pages. For information on building codes, contact your local building code official.

The book is not a reference handbook on moisture control. It is a "how-come" book, not a "how-to" book. Those who read the book in the usual book order, front to back, are likely to gain some understanding. Those who read the roof part when they're designing or installing a roof, or those who turn to the foundations part when the basement springs a leak, may not find the book quite so helpful. The book aims to prompt interest and learning rather than immediate action. I've heard some say: "Don't tell me how to build a watch—tell me the time" as a way of expressing their need for prompt action with minimum reflection. Fine, it's 7 p.m., October 19, 2003. I'm offering no description of how that time was determined, of how accurately it is represented, nor in which zone the reading was taken. That information loses its helpfulness rather quickly; incidentally it's no longer 7 p.m. This book is for watch builders, not watch readers. It does not tell you what to do, it tells you what water does; you may do as you wish armed with that knowledge. There are other books available that give specific answers to questions, and some are quite excellent. See the list of suggested references at the end of the book. In particular, Christine Beall's (1999) *Thermal and Moisture Protection Manual* provides an excellent compilation of recommendations and practices that are currently in use in much of the United States. The best guides for current practice in residential construction are Lstiburek's (1999; Building Science Corporation) *Builder's Guides*. Alan Oliver's (1997) *Dampness in Buildings* provides excellent scientific information on wetness, particularly for British construction.

This book is not a textbook. If the science in this book were a mature science, if the material in the book had been vetted for completeness and linear presentation in semester-long modules, and if school curricula were designed around the content of building science, a textbook would certainly have a place. This book may be considered a precursor to a textbook in building science or building hygrothermal studies. It aims to test the scope and content for future texts, syllabuses, and curricula. Is there a population that wishes to advance its knowledge in the field? I'm sure my publisher will let me know the answer to that question and to the question of the need for a textbook. There is an excellent textbook in English for Canadian climates: Neil Hutcheon and Gus Handegord's (1989) *Building Science for a Cold Climate*. Other textbooks are in preparation.

This book aims to provoke interest in a scientific study of water in buildings. If the adjective *scientific* makes the artists within architecture uncomfortable, think of this material and its presentation as systematic and orderly.[1] The aim is to help readers and users of this book to think through design for water, building for water management, and solving water problems in buildings.

---

[1] Northrop Frye tries to put literary criticism on a scientific footing: "The presence of science in any subject changes its character from the casual to the causal, from the random and intuitive to the systematic, as well as safeguarding the integrity of that subject from external invasions. However, if there are any readers for whom the word 'scientific' conveys emotional overtones of unimaginative barbarism, they may substitute 'systematic' or 'progressive' instead" (Frye, 1973, pp. 7–8).

The book is a polemic in a sense. It argues that early researchers jumped too quickly from observations and research into design recommendations. The consequence of this is that we have a set of design recommendations that have become quite outdated, but we have great difficulty bringing the complexity of nature back to design. It is human nature to prefer an imperfect simplicity over complexity. The problem is, however, that out-of-date prescriptions do not improve with time, they degrade. Sooner or later, the professions involved in construction must take a second look. The out-of-date prescriptions are in flux and under review at this time. Readers of this book should be able to understand those changes and, who knows, perhaps participate in them.

AUDIENCE

Somebody, somewhere, in the delivery system of design and construction must know water management in order to deliver dry buildings. It may be the architect. It may be someone working in the architecture office, usually someone who opted to become expert in technology over "design" and whose job it is to inspire confidence in the client rather than inspiration (or apoplexy). It may be a consultant; there are several tiers of consultants in a large job and varying levels of involvement for each tier. It may be the builder who is expected to make it work. It may be a subcontractor: roofer, plumber, or insulation installer. It may be a product manufacturer—no one should ever underestimate the teaching function supplied (for better or worse) by product literature. It may, for that matter, be the janitor, who wonders why they don't fix the leak instead of requiring continually that it be mopped up. It may be the building owner. It is not the lawyer.

Many architects do deliver dry buildings. Those who design buildings with simple roof systems, or who site buildings up high, generally do quite well. (We're getting ahead of ourselves.) Architecture offices usually house one or more persons that the office turns to for technical expertise. Max Abramovitz, architect of the United Nations headquarters in New York City, described their importance this way:

> Actually, I am very concerned that the science of building is going to disappear. I wonder if you realize how very few men are left today who are expert in building science. They are very rare and they are passed around among the large offices. You have to dig them out of their holes and revive them. One of them in our office is eighty years old. He passed out the other day and we had to pump stuff into him to get him going again because we couldn't spare him. It sounds like a joke, but we also have one who gets drunk every third day, but we can't fire him.

One would think we would know whether we can build a marble wall that will not crack and let water in. That sounds very simple. After all they've been doing it for three thousand years. Well, right now we're having a hot argument about it on the United Nations building. We can't find anyone who will say "I am sure it can be done this way", or "I am sure it cannot be done." We've asked old builders who have repaired the marble columns in St. Patrick's Cathedral. . . . I am sure many other architects are doing the same thing and that all of us are probably repeating each other's mistakes. If one of us finds the answer, the rest won't know about it. Yet, even if you've created a fine piece of architecture, it's a terrific black mark against your reputation when a simple thing like a leak occurs. (Abramovitz et al., 1949, p. 134)

The intended audience of this book is that group of people (drunken octogenarians or not) who wish to bring technical expertise to the problem of delivering dry, durable, healthful buildings. It is for those who believe that these technical matters deserve study and for those who recognize that not every answer is a good answer.

Like others involved in construction delivery, architects are busy people. They often do not want to have to learn more than necessary to get through a particular project or a particular problem on a project. How much building science is too much, not enough, and just the right amount? One attempt at the answer is this, the present volume, although whether it's a correct answer remains to be seen by the readers. For those who want the answer right now, those who want the answer to jump off the page at them, may be disappointed by the lack of immediacy in this volume. But if the material contained here has the right scope and depth, another book, a few years from now, should be able to make the material leap from the page into the hands of the busy designer. But first we have to get the scope and depth right.

The material contained here is not a simple restatement of moisture control advice that has accumulated over the last 50 years or so of building science investigations. Instead, it challenges much of that material and attempts to provide a different response structure to the questions of how to deliver dry buildings. Those who have lived by some of the tenets of moisture control over the last few decades may find some discomfort at how once-simple decisions look more and more complex. My response is this—don't blame me if building science isn't simple. No science is simple. Do you need a vapor retarder in the wall? If the question were actually as simple as that, it would have been answered long ago. The fact that the question continues to haunt us means, to me at least, that we have to probe more deeply.

What Abramovitz seems to be telling his audience is this: (1) keeping buildings dry is absolutely important; (2) keeping buildings dry is the job of building scientists; and (3) building science, like its practitioners, works at the margins of architecture. Why this odd relationship between building science and architecture? Are any of the other parts of the construction delivery system—contractors, building code officials, engineers, product manufacturers, consultants, and so on—more likely candidates for a scientific approach to buildings? We answer those questions in Chapter 1.

Most of the people who make on-the-spot decisions about buildings do not make those decisions scientifically. They make decisions using other methods, such as grandpappy-said-so and look-it-up-in-the-code, but science is quite a newcomer to the building construction process. When we build we usually build according to conventions, using conventional materials, following conventional techniques, governed by conventional wisdom. Even unconventional designs and unconventional construction are, in a way, conventional in that they are rarely designed or built with a lot of science. A theme of this book will be the confrontation between conventional wisdom and science.

SOURCES

The physical centerpiece of this book is water. My experience with water comes from camping outdoors, swimming, study of physics and engineering, as well as design and construction of buildings. I imagine (with some slight dread) this book in the hands of readers whose familiarity with water far exceeds my own. Sailors, hydrologists, urologists, meteorologists, oceanographers, chemists, and designers of water supply and waste systems will all be able to test my presentation of water in this book. Others who might have a bone to pick are fishermen, plumbers, landscapers, swimmers, and farmers as well as launderers, janitors, and bartenders. I bow to the expertise that all of these professions and trades have brought to the study and recognize that there aren't enough lifetimes to put together a sufficiently comprehensive view of water. Let's not forget poets, especially Neruda and Coleridge, or artists such as Turner or Escher.

I trust that after reading this book you will be able to do a better job of managing water and its effects in the buildings you care about. But you must be asking yourself: On what authority is this material based? Before answering, let's meet the candidates.

Pure Science. Water is composed of hydrogen and oxygen, and those two hydrogen molecules situate themselves around the oxygen molecule with 105 degrees separating them. Perhaps some physicist can derive from this fact how water adheres to surfaces, how it remains a liquid at room temperature, how it chills the surfaces from which it evaporates, and so on. Explaining why water creates the often beautiful effects it does by referring to first principles of physics and chemistry is one of the most exciting tasks an author of a book like this can have, but also one of the most frustrating, because the effects are rarely attributable to single factors. This is not intended as a science book. It uses science. In fact, you probably won't get far in it without allowing yourself some recall of high school chemistry, physics, and mathematics. If it prompts you toward a refresher, fine. But you should be able to make it through regardless of your level of science mastery.

Applied Science. This is a work of applied science. Pure science provides definite answers, and applied science provides approximate and fuzzy answers. I happen to like approximation—it leaves room for improvement. Often, the best source of information is other works of applied science. Unfortunately, applied science often seems like a stepchild, not really welcomed by either parent—theory or experience. In this cosmology of theory (good and pure) and experience (impure, less good), applied science has no home. What I hope you will read here is that the cosmology has become somewhat unraveled, and applied science makes quite a cozy home for itself. The world is not divided into left-brainers and right-brainers; rather, it is divided into those who use their brains and those who don't. Please do.

Design. This is a book about buildings, and we often say that buildings are "designed." Design, of course, simply means putting parts together in a way that is part rational and part intuitive. It is deductive and inductive. Some designers stress the importance of functionality in design, others stress image. Design means making thousands of decisions—design decisions. Some will be made rationally ("Run the numbers.") some will be made intuitively ("It worked the last time.") and some may made magically ("Here goes nothin'.") The first two sound suspiciously like applied science, but there is a distinctly nonscientific element in design as it is taught in architecture schools. There is no room for magic or hocus-pocus or voodoo, at least not in my book. If design chooses to ignore the science that underlies water effects and acts at the prompting of mystical voices, well, it is not the job of building science to man the bilge pumps of the design *Titanic*.

Construction. We learn from experience. Want to know about roofs? Install roofs. Want to know about pipes? Install plumbing. There is a sort of wisdom that comes only with grime. Unfortunately, the grime does not always bring wisdom with it. The construction industry is characterized by terrible social stratification, with those at the top (architects, brokers, bankers) rarely engaged with those at the bottom (the trades) in honest conversation about building failures. This is an accident of history, 300 years old, and some day that story will be told by a writer better predisposed in sociology (see Gutman, 1988). Meanwhile, this book relies heavily on construction experience, and its faults will no doubt be most apparent to the roofers and plumbers who read it.

History. We learn from experience, but to do that may involve more than citing references in a refereed journal or learning tricks of the construction trade from grandfather. The things we know best are those that are the product of a narrative, starting at a beginning point somewhere, passing through several learning events, to get to the present time. Where can we start? I like to start way back at the beginning. Western civilization could be said to have arisen with the notion of causation, with the explanation of the world being the way it is for reasons other than the caprice of the gods. When was that? Before Aristotle, before Plato and Socrates, back to the pre-Socratic philosophers, and back to the very first of those, Thales of Miletus. Around 650 B.C. he was the first to propose an alternative to caprice and chaos, and he did it with the first recorded utterance of causation in Western civilization: All things are made of water. For the first time ever, effects and their causes are seen to inhabit not two worlds but one. This was directly contrary to the world of the Mycenean civilization, the world of the *Iliad* and the *Odyssey,* the two worlds of humans and their puppet masters, the gods and goddesses. By noting that all things are made of water, Thales of Miletus prompted observation over speculation, and scientific thinking was jump-started. It was pretty smart on Thales's part to make water the centerpiece of causation. Its effects are never perfectly clear; it operates indirectly, some would say poetically. Anyhow, the subject of water in buildings, the subject of this book, has a fine but distant pedigree.

In this book we trace the history of certain moisture control practices. We must turn to history when current practices are opened to question. The past, better than the present, helps us to answer the question "why?"

They don't make 'em like they used to, so they say. It is widely held that old buildings stand up better than today's buildings. If you've done any work on old buildings, you know that some of the work back then was real schlock. The impression we have of high-quality work back then is to some extent the product of time erasing the weaker examples and leaving the better for us to admire. But they did have better materials, from virgin woodlands and quarries. The design was better, too, so they say. I'm not so sure. The roofs of the Edwardian and Victorian period were almost unflashable. John Ruskin believed the workmen of his day to be the saints of that era—the roofs were so complex I suspect they may have needed divine intervention to keep the water out. More on roofs and roof flashing in Chapter 4.

But there is one regard in which I believe old architects had it over their present-day counterparts—use of the ruling pen (Figure I-1). Architects

Figure I-1
Ruling pen.

today design on computers, and their drawings look that way. Old architects used ruling pens. A ruling pen is made of two steel nibs. The distance between the points of the nibs can be varied using a finger screw. Ink goes into the reservoir between the nibs either by dipping then wiping, or by filling using a hooked filler in the cap of the ink bottle. The ink adheres to the steel surfaces (more on surface energy, surface tension, and contact angles in Chapter 2) more strongly than it coheres together in a liquid mass. The ink molecule that is right at the steel grabs on tightly and is difficult even to wipe off; molecules in the middle of the mass cohere together with weaker bonds, and they can be shaken off by a careless wrist movement. So the draftsman using a ruling pen had a working understanding of the attraction of liquids for surfaces and the competition between surface adhesion and cohesion, a competition that is won by the steel surface. But not all surfaces are the same. The attractive forces between ink and paper or linen are even greater than those between ink and steel; or, with fibrous materials there are simply many more surfaces to attract those first few strong monomolecular coatings. Ink flows from the pen to the paper. Ink fills the small capillary spaces where fibers touch one another and is absorbed into the tight spaces between the surfaces (Figure I-2). Capillary attraction always tends to take fluids from larger to smaller capillaries, never from smaller to larger. Throughout this book we refer to this rule—call it the *Rule of Capillarity.* The nibs compress the paper or linen, so ink tends to flow from the middle of the line out to the edges, where the fibers are compressed. But it stops at those edges. It cannot flow from the tighter capillaries out to the looser, uncompressed paper. The result is a tight, well-defined line, all thanks to the draftsman's innate understanding of adhesion,

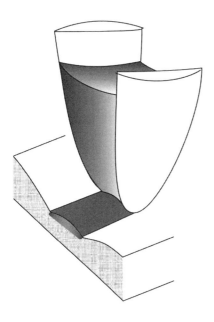

Figure I-2
The nibs of a ruling pen compress the fibers of the paper. Fluids migrate from large pores to smaller pores, never the other way. This illustrates the rule of capillarity.

cohesion, and adsorption. You can't get that know-how from the pixels on a computer screen.

LANGUAGE

The language of moisture control in buildings is very interesting. Let's begin with an example: "A building's got to breathe." People breathe. People live in buildings, so buildings have to allow air to get to the people and living things inside; otherwise, they suffocate. Building scientists—who are people, too—agree wholeheartedly and may pay particularly close attention to where and how fresh air is supplied to a building.

But that is only part of the "breathing" story. The conventional wisdom is also saying that the building itself has to breathe, not just deliver fresh air to the occupants. Behind the statement "A building's got to breathe" is *animism*, an attribution of living qualities to the inanimate assemblies that are our buildings. Without allowance for the building to breathe, moisture will get "trapped" inside. Trapped moisture suggests some very nonscientific trepidation, some frightening, noxious, vengeful fluid, worse if allowed to stagnate in the dark cavities of our walls, attics, and crawl spaces. Send Edgar Allen Poe down to the crawl space, not me. The words for buildings—"sick," "toxic," "dry rot"—are chilling and stupefying. So if someone proposes a barrier or a vent, those are greeted with relief, a toning down of the fearsomeness of the environment we built around ourselves. Or so the conventional wisdom goes.

Building science has quite a task ahead of it if it is to address these fears. If my computer program says that everything should be okay, but a homeowner is frightened, how much consolation can computer code offer? Fear of the environment is normal, I suppose. There are many physical forces that affect water flow—gravity, adhesion, capillary suction, phase change, convection, diffusion, just to give you a foretaste of the effects described in this book—and to feel comfortable with them may be a daunting prospect. So the first rule in talking about moisture is this: Identify the undercurrents of superstition. Then find the kernel of truth and dump the rest. There is usually a kernel of truth in even the most preposterous statements about building science. (That may hold true for more issues than building science.)

People say: "You don't want to trap that moisture in there, you need a vapor barrier." The key here is the word "you." Scientists use the passive voice. They do not say "you." Parents say "you" when speaking to children. "You" (singular or plural) is the word common to all admonishment. If the parent admonishes, the child asks why, and the parent responds, "Because I say so, that's why." Parenting is not a science; water management in buildings is, or should be. There is a widespread perception that building science says what a person should do. This book, in contrast, holds the point of view that building science describes what nature does, and it expects designers to respond to that.

I often hear that owners or managers of buildings—clients for design or construction—do not want their building used as an "experiment." If they only knew the extent to which every design decision and every field decision is an experiment. The same building hasn't been built twice. Communities such as Levittown are excellent examples of how change affects similar buildings differently. Where similar designs are used, both nature and nurture conspire toward nonuniformity. Recognition of the inevitable experimental nature of construction is one of the rewards of building science.

Technical people often ask about the correct use of the term *vapor barrier*. In Chapter 3 will describe the history of how this building envelope component came about in the late 1930s. The term persisted until a court ruling in Pennsylvania in the 1970s which held that (in the mind of the presiding judge, in any case) a "barrier" implies absolute impossibility of water vapor penetration. In response to this ruling, ASTM and ASHRAE undertook an effort to change the wording from *vapor barrier* to *vapor retarder*. Up to now, formal usage generally requires *retarder*, while *barrier* is in common usage. Several excellent building scientists are proponents, with good reasons on their part, of enforcement of formal usage of terms. The trades, however, rarely use *retarder*. There is a move afoot to use both *vapor barrier* and *vapor retarder* but to apply *barrier* to materials with a very low permeance (less than 1 perm) and *retarder* to materials with a permeance below 10 perms. Nothing is resolved on this matter at the moment.

In my opinion, the terminology dissension since 1970 has not as yet borne fruit. As this book aims to show, permeances of barriers or retarders or whatever play minor roles, not major roles, in the long-term durability of building envelope assemblies. I believe our squabbles should be proportional to the criticality of what we're squabbling about. I prefer to set the matter aside and get on with the treatment of the physics, engineering, and design. This book contains much historical material that uses the term *vapor barrier*, which I have left intact. For a discussion of current use, I've opted to use *vapor retarder*. I consider these two terms to be interchangeable, for now at any rate.

UNITS

In any science book, some housekeeping needs to be done at the outset regarding units. Most of the world has accepted the metric system, or Système International (SI). Only two countries have not (so I've been told): the United States and Burma. In this book, I sometimes use metric units, particularly when discussing research results or practice overseas. Most of the time I will use nonmetric [i.e., "imperial" or "inch-pound" (I-P)] units, certainly when referring to observations or assemblies that refer to U.S. construction practice. The international building science community prefers metric, but most readers of this book, I suppose, favor I-P. The ASHRAE *Handbook* issues two versions, one in SI and one in I-P.

The metric unit for mass is the gram. In inch-pounds it is the slug. More recently, it is the pound-mass, or the mass of an object that weighs 1 pound at the standard acceleration of Earth's gravity. You might think that this is a trivial distinction, requiring lunar travel to find the exceptions. Wrong. Mass times acceleration is force, so the pound is really a measure of force. Pressure is force applied over an area, and a commonly used unit of pressure is pound per square inch (psi). Several times I've reviewed articles in building science where the pound (mass) is used in concentration calculations and the pound (force) per square inch is used in pressure calculations, and the result is not pretty.

Perhaps a resolution to these matters is under way in the United States, though very slowly. Some parameters are strongly resistant to metrification: the 2×4 or the layout of repeated members such as studs or joists in light-frame construction. Others are already mostly metric, such as the use of the pascal (Pa), at least for air pressure measurements. The familiarity with Celsius units is growing, except in units such as *R*-value, where degrees Fahrenheit are strongly embedded. Any U.S. building scientist must now be familiar with metric and nonmetric units, so I propose here a mongrel approach of using both. If the two systems of units are to find some common ground at some time in the future, familiarity with both seems to me to be a prerequisite. Unit conversions are presented in Appendix C.

Some more housekeeping: The approach used in this book is the engineering approach. The engineering approach uses:

- *Design loads*, which represent a realistic input values for engineering calculations
- *Design/analysis tools*, which take the input loads and produce a certain output
- *Design criteria*, which allow the output to be judged and determine whether or not it is acceptable

All three of these involve some guesswork, imprecision, approximation. Committees set design input loads and often haggle over factors of safety. The analysis tools turn inputs into outputs, which can impress the uninitiated. True engineers are quite aware of the limitations of their tools even as they market their services as having and using the "latest, state-of-the-art" analytic devices, and design criteria are intended to turn the murky, contingent, and probabilistic inputs into single, sharp, incontrovertible design decisions—to put it in or leave it out. How this is done cannot be explained in a book but rather, constitutes the life and work of design engineers. The engineering approach—loads, analysis, and criteria—will be implicit in each chapter of this book but will be detailed explicitly in the final chapters for use in particular applications of foundations, walls, windows, and attic/roof structures.

SUMMARIES OF CHAPTERS

The book presents the history of some of the building practices in use, including drainage. Henry French of Exeter New Hampshire wrote the first edition of *Farm Drainage* in 1865 (our term *French drain* comes straight from the techniques recommended by French). I turn to him also to describe the suspense of authorship:

> With an earnest endeavor to clip the wings of imagination, and to keep not only on the earth, but to burrow, like a mole or a subsoiler, *in* it, with a painful apprehension lest some technical term in Chemistry or Philosophy should falsely indicate that we make pretensions to the character of a scientific farmer, or some odd phrase of law-Latin should betray that we know something besides agriculture, and so, are not worthy of the confidence of practical men, we have, nevertheless, by some means, got together more than a bookfull of matter upon our subject. Our publisher says our book must be so large, and no larger—and we all know that an author is but a grasshopper in the hands of his publisher, and ought to be

very thankful to be allowed to publish his book at all. So we have only to say, that if there is any chapter in this book not sufficiently elaborate, or any subject akin to that of drainage, that ought to have been embraced in our plan and is not, it is because we have not space for further expansion. The reader has our heartfelt sympathy, if it should happen that the very topic which most interests him is entirely omitted, or imperfectly treated; and we can only advise him to write a book himself, by way of showing proper resentment, and to put into it everything that everybody desires most to know. A book that shall contain all that we do *not* know on the subject of drainage, would be a valuable acquisition to agricultural literature, and we bespeak an early copy of it when published.

The science of water in buildings is both deductive and inductive. A deductive science structure begins with the elementary and moves to the complex and applied. An inductive science structure begins with observations and moves toward classification and explanation of those observations. In this book we have some of both. In the first three chapters we present fundamentals of hygrothermal building science. In the remaining chapters we trace water movement at, around, and through building assemblies. The trace follows a raindrop's path: roof, exteriors of walls, soils, foundations, building interior, walls, and attics. This sequence reflects a diminishing change in quantity of water: from greatest at the roof to least as water vapor inside the building. The book closes with a chapter on mold.

Building Science

DEFINITION

Building science is the systematic study of the physical performance of buildings under natural conditions. It is an applied science that draws on the more fundamental sciences of physics, chemistry, and biology. Building science provides the base of knowledge and understanding that permits designers, builders, product manufacturers, and building code officials to deliver buildings that are durable, useful, sturdy, healthful, and comfortable.

That is what building science would be if it were a mature science. It isn't. Building science has survived at the margins of architectural and construction activity for several decades without ever popping through to prominence. Presently in the United States there are no degrees, curricula, courses, or for that matter, textbooks in building science.

Building science does not have a well-defined scope at this point. It certainly includes the study of hygrothermal performance of buildings, that is, how heat and water act in, around, and through buildings. It may also include acoustics, lighting, fire behavior, structures, and indeed, any other scientific study associated with buildings. No one polices use of the term *building science*. Many countries in Europe, especially Germany and Belgium, use the term *building physics* to describe heat, air, and moisture movement in buildings and building envelopes. In North America, the term *building science* has been used in both the broad sense, encompassing all physical elements of building, and in the narrow sense of heat and moisture performance of buildings. In this book, *building science* is used in its narrow sense of hygrothermal performance of buildings. No offense is meant toward colleagues in acoustics, lighting, or structures.

The output of building science is understanding. It is not new or fancy ways of doing things, not new designs, and certainly not buildings themselves. Building science seeks to deliver understandings. These understandings will, if luck holds, eventually show up in our cities and towns as better buildings. As the science matures, the understandings will seem less haphazard and can be organized into a "body of knowledge."

The incentives for building science are curiosity as well as a desire for improvement in the human condition. What propels the fascination with building science, mine anyway, is quest for discovery. We may adopt images of discovery from sixteenth-century exploration or from the characters in Poe's story, who are obliged to feel the surfaces of their unlit dungeons. Humans seek patterns, and the patterns of moisture—telltale spots, the way that mold grows, lines on a hygrothermograph—are the raw materials of building science understanding.

Designers want guidelines for practice, and they expect building scientists to provide those guidelines. But building scientists know that practice recommendations come loaded with qualifications that describe a tightly defined idealized world in which those recommendations can be sure to pertain. The farther from the research setup that they are applied, the chancier the outcome. Practice guidelines and recommendations from building scientists should come with an expiration date, a sunset provision, which states that in a matter of years, the assumptions on which this work is based will start to appear out of date. In the meantime, building scientists cross their fingers, hope for the best, and write guidelines and recommendations.

The perplexity of building science is that most people are surprised to find that building science is so underdeveloped. Building code provisions are tough pronouncements that make big differences in money and lives. It takes only a few years in the construction industry to learn that many provisions reflect biases, interests, and assumptions at least as much as scientific findings.

The model for building science might be something like the science of nutrition. We all eat, as we all find shelter. The materials, preparation, and effects of food affect our lives. Nutrition does not lend itself to linearization. Instead, there are many ways to outline the subject matter. Specialists tend toward focus areas where the interest (or funding) lies. Since the field is essentially nonlinear, even the best people in the field can benefit from revisiting established understandings. Also, there is a certain job security in mastering a field such as food or shelter.

BACKGROUND: BUILDING SCIENCE INSTITUTIONS

Building science (hygrothermal building science, to be precise) began, we might say, with the introduction of insulation into buildings. Fiberglass insulation was invented in Germany as a replacement for asbestos, which was in short supply during and after World War I. Building physics (*bauphysik*) became an established discipline in Germany during the 1930s, and its spread to other parts of Europe was due, in part, to German occupation. In the United States, during the 1930s, painters noticed that insulated buildings could not hold paint, and peeling was widespread. The story of why that happens and what the insulation companies and paint companies did about it is told in greater detail in Chapter 4. The leading researchers were Larry Teesdale from the Forest Products Laboratory of the U.S. Forest Service and Frank Rowley from the University of Minnesota. Seichi Konzo and his colleagues at the University of Illinois brought mechanical engineering to residential construction. We refer to these early researchers at several points in this book. The Division of Building Research of the National Bureau of Standards did outstanding work, much of it related to the performance of building products. This division became the Center for Building Technology of the National Bureau of Standards (NBS) and is now the Center for Building and Fire Research of what is now the National Institute for Standards and Technology (NIST) (see Dorothy Nelkin, 1971). Canada has a deeper history of work in building science. The National Research Council of Canada (NRC) held a central role in the construction industry ever since the 1930s. Neil Hutcheon led the effort since the 1940s. NRC publications on construction for the Canadian climate remain classics. We might explain Canada's advancement in building science by the severity of their climate, but I suspect it has more to do with a social commitment to the value of science in the construction industry.

Despite these efforts, building science did not mature into a full curriculum within architecture in the United States. Following World War II, the National Academy of Science sought to coordinate research on buildings and held conferences on building science and building technology. The Building Research Advisory Board was created to coordinate building science research. It continued work for two decades, although only one coordinator position was funded; the remaining effort was voluntary. Figure 1-1 shows the early idea that U.S. building science could be composed of several contributing streams of scientific knowledge. In 1974 the National Institute of Building Science was formed to carry on the tradition of coordinating research, particularly through the Building Environment and Thermal Envelope Council. To see building scientists at their social best, the triennial U.S. Department of Energy Clearwater Conferences have been very important. The proceedings of those conferences deserve to be made more widely available.

Throughout the period of building science development, ASHRAE (the American Society of Heating, Refrigerating, and Air-Conditioning Engineers) has been a gathering point for researchers and information on hygrothermal building science. The fundamental knowledge in building science, although not always the most up to date, is maintained in the ASHRAE *Handbook—Fundamentals*. The present book relies to a great extent on the material contained in ASHRAE *Handbook—Fundamentals* (2001), particularly Chapters 6, 23, 24, and 25.

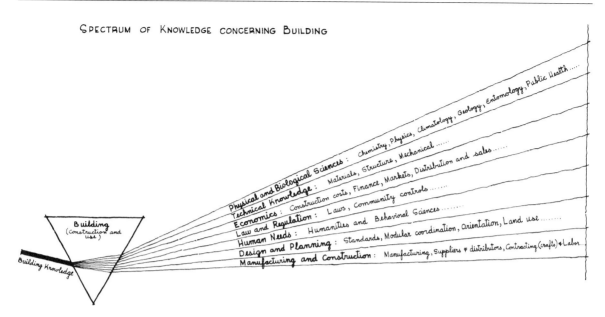

SPECTRUM OF KNOWLEDGE CONCERNING BUILDING

Figure 1-1
Building Research Advisory Board outline, showing an early idea of the makeup of building science for the
United States. (From NAS, 1960.)

Building science serves the building delivery system—the entire process
from conception through documentation, planning, construction, and punch
list—the construction ecosystem. Close inspection will probably reveal that
there is not much science along the way. The players in the delivery system
are clients, architects, engineers, contractors, and subcontractors, as well as
bankers, brokers, appraisers, and government officials. All of the parties—
architects, engineers, contractors, subcontractors, product manufacturers,
code officials—have good reason to support the scientific approach to the
construction industry. No building science has yet been done in a courtroom.

BUILDING SCIENCE AND ARCHITECTURE

Compare the delivery of buildings to the delivery of dental services. Teeth
should be tough, useful for their intended purpose, and look spiffy. That is,
they should meet Vitruvius's three criteria for buildings of *firmitas, utilitas*,
and *venustas*. Suppose now that dental work was divided into two professions. Patients have to go first to a dental designer, who might seek inspiration from the patient's mouth, and then go on to develop schematics and
construction documents to describe the work. Then these documents would
be shopped out to dental contractors, and the lowest of three bidders would
be invited to do the work. The patient would hope for the best, but if the

project begins to go sour and to encounter difficulties, disputes would risk falling into the rancorous middle ground between the dental designers and dental contractors. The patient may not smile.

Of course, architects must argue that the dental analogy fails to appreciate the art imperative—the need for singularity in our buildings. Perhaps that is so, but the analogy does highlight the difference between one profession taking responsibility for what is done in our buildings, and two professions. The division of building design services from building construction services is supported by tradition and by the status quo in both fields. Nowadays, it is being challenged by alternative delivery methods such as design–build. It has its roots, I believe, in seventeenth-century France, when Colbert sought to undercut the power of the construction guilds and moved a handful of architects to the Académie de Beaux-Arts. I picture how the masons of the time must have resented this. But that's another story. Architects design buildings, and contractors deliver on the construction documents. Who gets the building science and the mandate to deliver dry buildings? When water comes in the buildings, it may be argued, it comes in through the crack between the design and the construction professions.

The public expects buildings to be dry and healthful. Building science holds out the promise of building performance, the promise of delivering dry buildings. A dry, healthful building seems to be fundamental expectation; it seems to go directly to the meaning of the term *shelter*. Delivering a dry, healthful building would be one of the implicit minimal conditions of habitability, and of competence among everyone involved in the delivery process. Architects and builders must be competent. Walter Gropius, however, said somewhere that architects must strive to go "beyond competence." We can all imagine what he means, and most architects would nod almost reflexively in agreement. However, if the architect not only strives but succeeds at going beyond competence, the nagging public might demand to know what happens to competence in all this striving beyond. Is a building that has passed beyond competence one that has retained competence or lost it? Will an architecture student who is directed to go beyond competence be likely to develop a level of competence in personal practice? Or is such a student likely to set aside competence as a criterion in design and thereby make all the more unmistakable their commitment to the state of being beyond competence? We do not solve that problem in this book, of course. Delivering dry, healthful buildings should be a hallmark of competence in architecture.

BUILDING SCIENCE AND CONSTRUCTION

The construction trades work in a tradition. Tradition and science actually have quite a bit in common, as we learn from advances in cognitive science. Humans are pattern-seeking animals (Shermer, 2002). Things that work and things that don't work are captured in memory. Once a pattern or form or template is established, we formulate our finding: "Stand downwind of prey" or "Hit the circuit breaker before changing the receptacle." Some formulations are truer than others, at least in the sense that some provide more rewards in results. These become templates that become hardwired into our survival know-how. When something is believed it is held very deeply and for a long time. As long as the world remains essentially the same from generation to generation, traditions and beliefs provide essential aid. But constancy is not the hallmark of the world in which building construction is practiced today. Some builders build from tradition and may get undone when the materials, specifications, or conditions change too quickly. Or they may avoid traditions and thereby have trouble taking the next steps in construction. Builders may formulate their own rules for how to build and pass on that knowledge. Or the finding may institutionalize itself as a requirement in a building code.

But there is a downside to a belief engine: that formulations that sound like tenets of a belief may worm their way just as deeply into our beliefs as if they were supportable. Something may sound true, may have a kernel of truth, but may miss the mark by a wide margin—which brings us to the role of building science. As it encounters traditions, it has great difficulty. Traditions are wired into the survival brain at the back. Building science works at the front. Those who have studied human motivation know that the back brain wins. Despite the apparent difficulty, building science lives and is practiced most productively in the community of builders and subcontractors. Builders carry on traditions. Lessons learned are often learned for a lifetime.

BUILDING SCIENCE AND ENGINEERING

Engineers apply science to the problems of the world. In order to apply science, they must work daily with equations. The equations in this book are equations of science in that they can be derived from prior principles. One such equation is $PV = nRT$, the ideal gas law, which can be derived from Boyle's law showing the proportion of volume and pressure, and Charles's law, showing the proportion between volume and temperature. But there are other equations—equations of convention—that are not derived but rather, are negotiated. One example that is addressed here in detail is the attic ventilation requirement: NFA = 1/300 × HPRA, where NFA is the net free area of the vent device and HPRA is the horizontally projected roof area. This and the ideal gas law both use the same equation sign, but they are very different in origin and in use. Engineers use both equations of science and equations of convention. It is hoped that they recognize the difference.

Most engineers work in the mature areas of building technology. In structural engineering, for example, there is a broad convergence among the science of structural engineering, its practice by engineers, and its expression and enforcement in the building code. Hygrothermal building science is not quite so mature. The scope and methods are still under discussion. The current code requirements for moisture control are shaky. Basic engineering practice provides the key to making progress, and basic engineering practice involves number crunching. Those who have actually crunched numbers know that real number-crunching skills are not simply computational, but involve having a "feel" for the numbers. Are these the right design input values? Are we using the right set of equations? Does the output have the right units, and is the magnitude reasonable? Can we stand behind the results? Don Fugler from the Canada Mortgage and Housing Corporation hopes that even if the answer is not too precise, and the order of magnitude might be off, at least we have the positive or negative sign right and we're headed in the right direction.

The lines are quite blurred between applied science, such as building science, and engineering. In fact, the relationship between the two should be recursive throughout a lifetime of practice or research. Learn, do, teach, learn, do, teach . . . not a bad sequence. The building science in this volume moves toward making design recommendations. All books for busy professionals must these days. But please recall the importance attached here to understanding for its own sake. If we also have good buildings as a result, that's fine.

BUILDING SCIENCE AND THE BUILDING CODES

As mentioned above, building codes perform a critical function for the community of people who build or inhabit buildings. In this book we are critical of present building code requirements in the area of moisture control in the context of overall satisfaction with the methods and content of building codes. Perhaps any building code requirement will appear unsatisfactory when scrutinized as deeply as is done here. Please note that the criticism directed at common code requirements here is not meant to diminish the confidence that the community should have in the code process, only to help ensure that code changes are made as necessary for the betterment of all.

The public presumes that there is a mature building science out there somewhere. The public presumes that the requirements found in the building code were worked out on paper and that chances are that complying with the requirements of the code will lead to good performance. They have not taken any peeks behind the curtain recently. If they did, they would find that many building code provisions have a life of their own. In one case regarding the ventilation of crawl spaces in the southern United States, one building code organization justified its ventilation requirement by noting that 20 years previously, the subject was studied, so now the matter is closed. That is bad policy—building code requirements are based on assumptions, and those assumptions change over time. Building code requirements, at least prescriptive building code requirements, should recognize how ephemeral are the assumptions used in formulating building code provisions.

Compliance and performance may inhabit parallel universes, with sometimes little in common. A code-complying building may perform poorly; a building that is dry, energy conserving, and comfortable may not be in compliance with code provisions at all. This puts architects and builders in quite a predicament, of course. But as with all professions, the principal duty is to the health and welfare of the client, so a conscientious professional must deliver buildings with good performance: thus the need for building science.

Code language is prescriptive, that is, it tells a designer or builder what to do, and those actions must be verifiable in the course of construction. Building technology may very well do what it is told. But building science is more skeptical. It adopts testing in order to gain predictability. It challenges rules of thumb and tradition ways of construction. Building science then, is building technology for skeptics.

Ideally, building codes would have a basis in building science. However, the findings of building science are often probabilistic, whereas the requirements of building codes have outcomes that appear deterministic. Building science says that good things will probably occur if certain actions are taken; building codes say to do certain things, and leave the impression that the outcome will, of necessity, be welcome. Building codes were begun primarily to avoid conflagration and structural catastrophe and to permit egress in case these occur. Preventing moisture damage is a latecomer to building codes, and it has an uneasy fit. When catastrophe strikes, the particulars of building codes are often revisited. But moisture damage to buildings is rarely catastrophic. So the original rationales for building code requirements are subject to less scrutiny and may thereby inspire less confidence.

THE METHODS OF BUILDING SCIENCE

The methods of building science are typical of applied science, not pure science. Pure science discovers laws governing the behavior of things. Applied science applies those laws, but that is not the main task of an applied science. Rather, that job is observation and induction.

The methods are primarily inductive. That is, they rely first and foremost on observation of phenomena around us. Observations of the world lead to patterns being recognized. Then science seeks to explain the patterns. Most statements in the science take the form: These are the patterns we observe, and we can explain these patterns this way. Once this approach becomes more institutionalized and scholarly, once it is taught in the schools, we are likely to see an inversion, in which the explanations come first and the observations will be used to confirm the wisdom of the theorist. That will be unfortunate. Science is most challenging and satisfying at the beginning, while predispositions about what we will find are few. Building science is still full of surprises. Konrad Lorenz said that a good scientist must discard at least one pet hypothesis every morning before breakfast.

Case studies are the rawest of raw material for building science. They are usually presented with a predisposition toward an explanation. The observations are presented with evidence of a pet hypothesis. For a case study to be useful, the investigator would have to have a sense of several of the common hypotheses and would disprove the alternative hypotheses as a way of lending support to the preferred one. This illustrates one aspect of science that is often ignored—that it takes teamwork. Archimedes could spring from his tub saying *"Eureka"* only in a culture where questions and alternative hypotheses are in the air he breathes and are discussed on the street.

Next come laboratory benchtop demonstration studies. If a phenomenon is complex, it should be simplified and the parts studied independently. The setup usually takes some ingenuity. Benchtop studies are very helpful in refining measurement techniques. Standard measurement techniques need to be mastered of course, for temperature, humidity, weight, and so on. Some parameters, such as moisture content of materials, are hard to measure. Early in my research career I once complained to a stranger on an airplane about measurement difficulties. He said that with conventional measurement devices, all the interesting measurements have already been made; real science requires ingenious specific instruments.

Laboratory studies allow a precise set of conditions to be applied to the sample. We tried to study how much air moves through a weep hole in a brick wall and soon realized that first we had to study what conditions actually were applied in the field. To get a sense of the setup difficulties for full building assemblies, imagine what a test setup would be to examine solar vapor drive (i.e., the inward drive of moisture in wetted masonry or stucco due to direct sunshine following a driving rain). First you wet the sample with a spray unit, somehow evacuating the excess water, then blast radiant heat against the wall surface but remove the steambath effect rapidly, the way the wind does outdoors.

Test cells are like laboratory samples set up outdoors. These are excellent setups to study phenomena, but the researcher must be patient. The effect that we wish to study will occur when it pleases, not on an accelerated schedule that is needed by most of the clients who pay for research. The good clients will invest in long-term studies. One benefit of such a study is that it may provide validation data for modeling studies (see below). The material properties need to be very well characterized, and those properties may change over time. Nowadays it is common for funding agencies to combine research and demonstration. There is an inherent contradiction here of course, because demonstration implies that we have the answer and research presumes that we do not. But beyond that, how do we do a demonstration of building durability? Won't the interested parties be retired when the results come in?

Field studies involve examinations in the field at different sites. Researchers must respect privacy—institutional review boards see to that—so these studies are usually done only after a phenomenon becomes something that occupants or building users wish to participate in. Field studies involve great difficulty. We hoped to do a field study to see if solving moisture problems made improvements in occupants' health. This involved tracking humidity before and after remediation. Winters could only be compared to winters, of course, so the term of the study was 18 months, whereas the average length of stay by the occupants was eight months.

Modeling studies have become popular, and exciting. As you will see in this book, the recent advances in building science could not have been made without the computer. Many research reports describe a computer model that replicates a physical phenomenon. The convergence criteria are assessed and all the factors that might affect the outcome are accounted for. Then, for the last 5% of the paper, the modeled data are compared to a set of measured data to demonstrate validation. In my opinion, the percentages are backward. The baseline remains the measured data, and if it can be modeled, that's fine. My colleague J. P. Brown warns modelers against what he calls the *Nintendo effect* in which the results of modeling appear more real than what happens in the building itself. We are not concerned with what is happening at the monitor—we want to see what happens in the building.

Modeling done by applying first principles of physics and thermodynamics to the inputs, *direct modeling*, has the advantage of being "correct"; its major disadvantage is that it usually provides answers that are wide of the mark. Some modelers try *reverse modeling*, finding out what happens in building performance and making the calculation tool trace curves that are as close as possible to the data measured in the field. Is reverse modeling useful? When reverse modeling is applied to economics to predict future booms and busts, the results are uninspiring.

Modeling and experiment are both approaches to the testing of hypotheses. In good science the working hypothesis is made explicit, and the research design is able to prove or disprove that hypothesis, given the limitations. Good science and good testing both also make explicit use of statistics. We should learn to distrust results that report, say, an average value of x; we need to expect results reported as a mean of x, $\pm y$, to a $z\%$ level of confidence. We shall see in Chapter 9 how important this is.

Modeling is the key to linking building science to design. Once we have a working model, one that accepts a wide variety of inputs (building assembly, material properties, indoor climate, outdoor climate), and once that model has been validated in a range of cases, then building science can bring its goods to the design table. What happens next may be an influence on design of building science.

THE PREREQUISITES OF BUILDING SCIENCE

Math

Science uses mathematics. Architecture uses very little math. We will be using math. The following paragraphs do not provide math instruction. That requires a math teacher. These paragraphs are provided because they indicate what math should be known or at least recoverable from algebra and calculus courses long past.

Algebra uses *variables*—letters or symbols that stand in for numerical values. Variables of the same unit may use subscripts to distinguish different instances. For example, we may use T_i for indoor temperature and T_o for outdoor temperature. Symbols that appear as superscripts, such as the x in e^x, are called *exponents*. The *Avogadro number*, which represents the number of molecules in a mole, is 6.02×10^{23}, or $6.02 \cdot 10^{23}$. The dot between 6.02 and 10 represents multiplication; an $\times$ may be confused with a variable, and an asterisk appears too literary. This is expressed in engineering notation as 6.02E23. Most spreadsheet programs accept engineering notation, or may accept this value represented in keystrokes as 6.02*10^23.

Relations are expressed by equations. At some point in the architect's education, a horror of equations seems to set in. All of the construction delivery system is a turf war, and equations mark the engineer's turf. If mastery of equations gives an edge to engineers, architects develop a caution that becomes an aversion. As Steven Vogel (1994) points out in his book *Life in Moving Fluids*, "for reasons that flatter neither the author nor most readers the mathematical niceties . . . will not loom large here." In this book equations are presented. They are bound to be the centerpiece of a future building science textbook. To soften the blow, equations are presented here softly, with explanatory material regarding where the equation originated, how it gets to its present form, and the meaning and significance of the values and expressions. We discuss the forms of various equations. Equations fit into families. If architects specialize at pattern recognition, perhaps they can begin to recognize the patterns that equations express. To jump the gun a bit, one prominent pattern is an exponential relationship. Air pressure varies exponentially with elevation, vapor pressure varies exponentially with temperature, and the pressure in a leaky tire varies exponentially with time.

That specialty of engineering textbooks—derivation—is not presented here, with one small exception because of its importance. There is an exquisite pleasure that is had only by mathematicians, scientists, and engineers that comes from a derivation. It is an exercise in absolute economy of expression. So it is natural they would want to share their pleasure with others. They fail to acknowledge the difference in experience between the person doing the derivation and the reader, much like the difference between having an exotic vacation and showing someone postcards of the visit. I don't follow all derivations. I'll work them through if I'll need to reconstruct the argument; otherwise, I often jump to the conclusion, telling the author in my mind, "Yes, I'm sure you had fun getting there."

Relations between two sets of values may be represented by plotting the coincident values on a chart. If the values are measured values, they are usually shown as points. If a numerical relation is established, it is usually shown as a line or a curve, representing a function. The independent variable is usually plotted on the x-axis (horizontal axis, called the *abscissa*, representing input values), the dependent variable on the y-axis (vertical axis, called the *ordinate*, representing output values). A *function* is any relationship in which an input value or set of input values produces a unique output value. A simple function takes the form $y = f(x)$. An inverse function is formed by flipping the independent and dependent variables, giving $x = g(y)$.

Data is a plural noun, plural of the singular *datum*. Some data suggest a *linear* relationship, such as the relationship between rainfall amount and the severity of the roof leak indoors. There are several ways to measure the spread of data. If the relationship is somewhat linear, a function of the form $y = mx + b$ can be used to express it. In this equation, m, the multiplier, is termed the *slope* of the linear equation. If $y = x$, the slope is 1 for this identity relation. If we wish to represent data by a linear equation called a *linear regression*, the closeness of the data can be represented by the R^2 function, for which the value zero shows no linearity and the value 1 represents perfect linearity.

If the function is linear, the slope is constant. If the function is not linear, the slope will vary. Smooth functions will have well-defined slopes at each point on the curve. Pointed functions will not have well-defined slopes at the points. For functions with varying slope, the slope at any point may be determined by focusing in on the function in a very small region, small enough that the function can be considered linear within it. The slope is the rise over the run (to adapt carpentry terminology to Cartesian coordinates). In x–y coordinates, the rise is written dy and the run dx. The incremental slope is dy/dx. The slope of the function of one independent variable can be seen as the output of a new function called the *derivative* of the original function. When plotted against a single independent variable, the slope of a function of several independent variables produces a differential of the function against that variable. The derivative of a function $f'(x)$ is expressed as $f'(x)$ or $df(x)/dx$.

The integral of a function $f(x)$ is defined as the function $g(x)$, which satisfies the equation $g'(x) = f(x)$. Finding the integral of $f(x)$ is equivalent to finding the equation $g(x)$ whose derivative is $f(x)$. Picture $f(x)$ as a curve in Cartesian coordinates. While the derivative of $f(x)$ expresses the slope of the function $f(x)$, the integral expresses the area under the curve.

Can a function be its own derivative? If a function *is* its own derivative, it would have to be its own integral. The function that meets this criterion is the *exponential function*, exp(x) or e^x. The number e equals approximately 2.718281828. The *natural logarithm* is the inverse function of the exponential function. If $y = e^x$, then $x = \ln(y)$. These functions appear in water studies because of a peculiar characteristic of the natural log function: For the function $f(x) = 1/x$, where x is greater than zero, the integral of $f(x)$ is the natural log of x. So any time that we take the integral with respect to a variable, say p, and p appears in the denominator of the function, the relationship will be logarithmic. The integral of $(1/p)\,dp$ is $\ln(p)$. Set that integral equal to another function, say a function of t, $f(t)$. Then

$$\ln(p) = f(t) \quad \text{so} \quad p = \exp(f(t)) = e^{f(t)}$$

We find several expressions for pressure that fit that form.

Physics

Physics uses units. The fundamental units that we will use are mass, length, time, and temperature (lowercase t for time, capital T for temperature). The other units we will use are composites of these four fundamental measures. If L is length, area is L^2 and volume is L^3. Density is mass per volume, $M \cdot L^{-3}$ or M/L^3. Speed is length per unit time, $L \cdot t^{-1}$ or L/t; acceleration change is speed over time, $L \cdot t^{-2}$ (L/t^2). Velocity is speed with direction. Momentum is mass times velocity.

The mindset that permits the United States to be a holdout in the area of metric conversion comes as no surprise to me. I was trained in the inch-pound (I-P) system, and when I practiced architecture in France, I had to learn dimensioning in the metric system; it took all of 10 minutes. The unit for mass in SI units is the kilogram. Mass is invariant—it is the sum of the masses of all the atomic particles contained in the material, and those masses do not change with location. The pound is a unit of weight. A pound of cheese at sea level weighs more than a pound on Mt. Everest or on the moon. Weight is a force. Mass is the expression of materiality unaffected by location or forces acting on it. The I-P system has no unit for mass, unless we count the slug or the pound-mass (lb_m). A pound-mass weighs 1 pound at sea-level Earth gravity. A pound-weight equals 1 pound-mass times 32 ft/sec^2, the acceleration of gravity. The acceleration of gravity in SI is 9.807 m/s^2. The grain, a unit found frequently in water studies, is 1/7000 of a pound. No one has been able to advise me whether that is 1/7000 of a pound-mass or of a pound-weight. The ounce may be a unit of weight or volume. I hope the imprecision in I-P units leads to another reconsideration of the adoption of metric.

In this book, both SI and I-P units will be used, depending on the context of the discussion. Scientists use SI; engineers in the United States use I-P, but elsewhere use SI. The ASHRAE handbooks are printed in both SI and I-P units. A kilogram is the SI unit for mass. A kilogram weighs 2.2 pounds and is the mass of water in a liter, which is slightly bigger than a quart. A gram of water occupies a cubic centimeter, about the volume of a sugar cube. A meter is slightly larger than a yard. I was surprised to find in French architectural practice a predisposition toward the units 30 cm and 90 cm, which correspond rather closely to the foot and the yard; perhaps that similarity represented a desire for building product manufacturers to serve two markets with a minimum of compromise, or perhaps there was something human in scale about these common dimensions. Celsius temperature units should be usable for most building professionals. Water freezes at 0°C and boils at 100°C; −40°C is the same temperature as −40°F, on the Fahrenheit scale; 22°C is room temperature; −273.15°C is absolute zero. Temperatures taken with absolute zero as the starting point, using the metric meaning for 1 degree, are called kelvin (K). The unit of force in SI is the newton (N), a small force, applied by 1 kg accelerating at 1 m·s^{-2}. Weight is a force. The acceleration that produces the weight is the acceleration of gravity.

A force applied to an area produces pressure, which is a central concept for this book and for building science. The force is considered applied normal to the plane of the area. The SI unit of pressure is the pascal (Pa), which is a force of 1 N applied over 1 m^2. A pascal is a small unit of pressure. Pressure may be positive (blowing) or negative (suction). The suction on a soda straw may be 1000 Pa. Standard atmospheric pressure is 101,325 Pa or 101.3 kPa or 1 atm. In SI, pressure measurements are quite simple. Not so in I-P. The units of pressure in I-P include:

Inches of water column	Atmospheric pressure is about 32 ft of water column.
Inches of mercury	Standard atmospheric pressure is 29.98 in. of mercury.
Pounds per square foot	This is 1/144 of the more common measure. . . .
Pounds per square inch	Atmospheric pressure applies 14.7 psi.

The simplest representation of pressure uses a manometer. Imagine a fluid in an open cylinder. The fluid has weight, which it applies to the circular base of the cylinder. Density (ρ, the Greek lowercase letter rho) of a fluid is its mass per volume. Volume is the area of the base times the height, so one representation of pressure is Bernoulli pressure, $p = \rho g h$, where h is the height of the fluid column. A manometer is a common instrument (if somewhat fragile and messy) for measuring pressure.

Note that the area term does not appear in a Bernoulli representation of pressure, so it doesn't matter how fat the tube is once it is beyond capillary thinness (more on that later). It may be as thin as a soda straw or as wide as a lake—the pressure at a given height will be the same. The manometer gives intuitive meaning to the first of the two I-P units of pressure cited above. Mercury is much denser than water, so higher pressures can be measured using a mercury manometer than a water manometer for the same height.

Forces may produce no active outcome. My weight on my chair produces no active outcome. Such a condition is called *static*, to contrast it with dynamic and kinetic. If a force acts on a distance, that is, it acts *dynamically*, it produces work. Pressure can produce work, too, if it effects a change in volume. Picture the pressure as tiny forces acting on tiny areas. If the pressure causes expansion, the tiny forces will have moved a distance and done work. A *potential* is any condition capable of driving work. A dynamic activity involves external translational or rotational movement. Work is dynamic. *Kinetic* activity relates to the internal goings-on in matter. Molecules are quite busy, particularly gas molecules, and kinetics concerns itself with their internal activities.

Most books on science, and this is no exception, begin with the *law of conservation of mass*. Stuff, big stuff, little stuff, any stuff, doesn't just go away and then reappear elsewhere. (We're ignoring black holes, the Einsteinian world of interchangeable mass and energy, and then maybe Utah's cold fusion.) This is a simple rule, but it is very helpful in the diagnosis of moisture problems. Some problems, such as erosion, require a lot of water. Others, such as corrosion, may require only a small amount, strategically placed. Most moisture problems can be diagnosed by looking at the condition and asking how much water it took to create that problem. Solving the problem amounts to asking where that amount of water could have come from and where it should go.

Chemistry

Matter is composed of *atoms*, the building blocks of elements. Atoms combine to form *molecules*, and molecules are the building blocks of compounds. Electronegative *electrons* surround a positive *nucleus* in atoms.

The *atomic number* of an element is determined by the number of protons in the nucleus, the *atomic mass* by the number of protons and neutrons. The atomic number of hydrogen is 1 and the atomic mass of hydrogen is 1.008. Most hydrogen atoms have no neutrons—the few that do (deuterium and tritium) add to the decimal atomic mass, which is greater than 1. Atoms with atypical numbers of neutrons are called *isotopes*. Oxygen has an atomic mass of 16.00. The molecular mass of water is thus 18.

A *mole* of any material has a mass equal to its atomic or molecular mass, expressed in grams. A mole of water has a mass of 18 g. A mole contains 6.02×10^{23} units, and for a chemist those units are usually atoms, molecules, or ions (atoms that carry a positive or negative electric charge as a result of having lost or gained one or more electrons). A molar solution contains a mole of solute in a liter of solution.

The completeness or incompleteness of successive electron shells around the atom determines the ability of elements to form compounds. Inert gases such as helium, neon, and argon have complete shells and so react only marginally with other atoms. Elements such as lithium, sodium, and potassium have only one electron in their outer shell, which they tend to give up readily; these are called *alkaline earth metals*. Elements that donate electrons are *metals*. Fluorine and chlorine lack one electron in their outermost shell, so they tend to welcome spare electrons from other atoms; they are called *halogens*. Elements that receive or borrow electrons to complete a shell are *nonmetals*. Atoms with shells that are almost complete, especially the active metals and halogens, form *ions* by finding or giving one or more electrons to complete the shell. Ions thus have unbalanced charges; the number of protons does not equal the number of electrons. Metal ions lose electrons to complete their shell, so they have a net positive charge. Ions with positive charges, which are drawn to negatively charged sites or cathodes, are called *cations*. Ions with net negative charges such as halogen ions that need to borrow an electron, leaving a net negative charge, are called *anions*.

When atoms share electrons, with both nuclei benefiting from the arrangement, the bond is called covalent. The hydrogen–oxygen bonds in water are typically covalent bonds. Elements that have shells half-filled or semi-filled tend to form shared or covalent bonds. Carbon and silicon each have 4 of eight electrons in their outer shells, so they are able to form bonds of great complexity. Hydrocarbons form the basis of organic building materials such as wood and plastics. Silicon-based materials, including sand and glass, form all or part of most of the inorganic building materials.

Water will also contain ionic units with one hydrogen and one oxygen atom called *hydroxyl ions* (OH^-). It may also contain hydronium (H_3O^+) ions, which are often considered as H^+ ions piggybacking on a complete water molecule. If the ionic charges in water are perfectly balanced, a liter of water will contain 1×10^{-7} moles each of OH^- and H^+ ions. Such water is said to have a *pH* of 7, the negative of the $\log_{10}$ of the number of moles per liter (L). If the concentration of H^+ increases, say to 1×10^{-6} mol/L, then the pH becomes 6 or another value below 7 representing the concentration. *Acid solutions* have high H^+ concentrations, so they have low pH. On the other hand, solutions poor in H^+ and thereby rich in OH^- are called alkaline *solutions*. Their pH varies between 7 and 14.

Elements and compounds react. Acids and bases may react to form salts. Limestone and marble building materials are alkaline. Polluted rain may be acidic. This reaction leads to surface erosion. Another reaction is combustion. Hydrocarbons used as fuel combine with oxygen to form water, carbon dioxide, and other by-products.

There are three phases of pure materials: *solid, liquid,* and *gas.* Solid salts are usually in crystal form. Water-soluble salts lose their crystal structure and become free ions in water. Water molecules bind by electrostatic forces to the unbalanced charges in ions. Water will also bind to hydrocarbons with hydroxyl (OH^-) radicals on the surface, such as alcohol. The similarity of hydroxyl radicals and the water molecule lends support to the rule of thumb in chemistry that "like dissolves like."

Cellulose is a large organic (carbon-based) molecule with several hydroxyl radicals on the surface. The attachment of water to surfaces is like the attachment of water to other materials in solutions, but unlike salt, the crystal structure of wood survives attachment by water molecules. The water that is attached to the surface cannot be considered to be in any of the three phases of pure materials. Instead, it is considered *bound water,* in a phase (or phases) of its own. Bound water is one of the central concepts of this book.

2 | Water

MOLECULAR STRUCTURE

Bernard Jaffe (1976), in his excellent history of chemistry, *Crucibles*, tells the story of Henry Cavendish, who discovered the makeup of the water molecule. Cavendish was the richest man in England in the early 1780s when he discovered and published his findings about water. According to Jaffe, Cavendish was possibly the wisest man in England at the time and also the strangest, owning only one suit of clothes at a time, all in the style of 100 years earlier. In the reading of his *Experiments on Air* before the Royal Society of England in January 1784, Cavendish made this remarkable claim: "Water consists of dephlogisticated air united with phlogiston." That may sound like an odd way to describe hydrogen and oxygen. It was not. For the preceding century, the study of chemistry had been the study of phlogiston. What are phlogiston and dephlogisticated air? Recall from Chapter 1 our comment that humans are believers by nature and that once a causal framework is proposed, it is not easily dislodged. In Cavendish's lifetime, alchemy had been providing techniques for purification of materials, but otherwise was contributing little to human understanding. The *phlogiston theory* was the first effort to make sense of some of the alchemical observations. According to Becher, who proposed it, phlogiston is the substance of fire. Two compounds may combine, give off heat, and the resulting ash may weigh less than the original components. The original components obviously contained phlogiston, and when it turned to fire, the results were *dephlogisticated*, and weighed less. Never mind that other reactions occasionally led, after fire, to a heavier result—phlogiston could have either a positive or a negative weight. The phlogiston theory governed natural science for more than a century, up through the publications of Cavendish and his contemporaries Priestly, a staunch believer in phlogiston, and Lavoisier, a skeptic. By the end of the 1780s it had been argued away by the Irishman Higgins and then by Dalton, who first proposed the *atomic theory*. To Cavendish, working without the benefit of the atomic theory, phlogiston was oxygen and dephlogisticated air was hydrogen.

Translated into the language of modern chemistry, Cavendish was informing his hearers that water was really a compound of two gases, hydrogen and oxygen, in the proportion two volumes of hydrogen to one volume of oxygen. That wonderful liquid was not the simple elementary substance all the savants of the world, from Thales of Miletus on, thought it to be. Rather, the masterpiece of creation was cobbled together out of two common invisible gases.

We have all seen the chemistry textbook image of water, Mickey Mouse with two hydrogen ears. Carbon dioxide has the same number of atoms, but the two oxygen atoms are on a single axis with the carbon atom at the center. The rules governing the spatial distribution of atoms in a molecule have to do with the number of electron pairs in the outer, *valence* shell of a molecular model. Carbon shares its four valence electrons with two oxygen atoms in a CO_2 molecule, leaving no other electron pairs that would need a place. Once it has shared an electron with each of the two hydrogen atoms, the oxygen atom at the heart of a water molecule still has two electron pairs needing a place around the central atom. The most uniform distribution of four atoms around the sphere of the central atom is a tetrahedral distribution. In the Mickey Mouse distribution of hydrogen atoms, what cannot be seen are the two pairs of electrons that are placekeepers in the tetrahedral distribution. The two hydrogen atoms and the two electron pairs try to distribute themselves evenly around the sphere of the atom model. In any tetrahedral arrangement of four items, any two items will be loaded to one side. Every water molecule winds up with a hydrogen (+)-rich side and an electron (−)-rich side, thanks to the valence electrons of oxygen (Figure 2-1). Thus, the water molecule is a *dipole,* or tiny magnet. This property of water makes all the difference. The polarity of the water molecule is what renders

Figure 2-1
Hydrogen atoms taking two of four places in a tetrahedral array around an oxygen atom. The resulting imbalance creates positive and negative ends of the molecule.

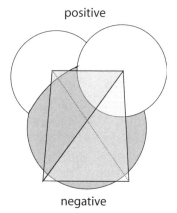

positive

negative

it endlessly interesting, interacting as it does with practically every other molecule on Earth.

HYDROGEN BONDS

Water molecules may bond to one another. The bonds are called *hydrogen bonds*, and the resulting force binding water molecules together is *cohesion*. Other molecules of roughly the same molecular weight are gases (e.g., methane). The cohesive hydrogen bonds provide the glue that holds the molecules in place, which otherwise would be as kinetic a gas as methane.

Ice is a crystal structure with molecules arranged in a lattice. The hydrogen bonds attach hydrogen sites to electronegative electron sites in the oxygen shell. There are several such lattices possible, but the most common one at normal pressures is called *ice I*. Kavanau (1964) describes ice I this way: "The oxygen atoms lie in layers with each layer consisting of a network of open, puckered, hexagonal rings. The oxygen atoms alternately are raised and lowered, each layer being the mirror image of adjacent layers. Water molecules retain their individuality but participate in four hydrogen bonds. Each oxygen atom is surrounded tetrahedrally at a distance of 2.76 Å [angstrom units] by the four other oxygen atoms to which it is hydrogen-bonded. The hydrogen atoms, however, are distributed asymmetrically, lying on lines connecting adjacent hydrogen-bonded oxygen atoms." Figure 2-2 shows these layers of puckered hexagonal rings, resulting in a tetrahedral arrangement of oxygen atoms.

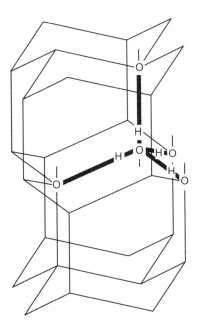

Figure 2-2
Arrangement of hydrogen and oxygen molecules in a crystal array of ice I, the most common form of ice.

At the molecular level, liquid water is not as simple as it seems. Kavanau (1964) describes some of the complexity found in liquid water: Röentgen, famous for x-rays, was the first to suggest that there were ice crystals in water. Samilov (see Kavanau, 1964) arrived at a general conclusion that the structure of water is merely a slightly distorted version of the structure of ice. But upon melting, some of the molecules move from their equilibrium positions and pass into neighboring interstitial spaces. The greater density of water, he holds, is due to these molecules floating within the remnants of the lattice. Frank and Wen (1957) proposed a *flickering cluster model,* in which icelike clusters of highly hydrogen-bonded water molecules gather together and break up in a time span of 10^{-10} to 10^{-11} s, 100 to 1000 times the period of a molecular vibration. The bonds in the clusters are quadruply bonded (as in the ice crystal lattice) and doubly bonded compact bodies. Unbonded water molecules fill the spaces between clusters. Linus Pauling proposed that water molecules might form dodecahedrons, 20 water molecules each at the corner of the 12 pentagons, with a twenty-first water molecule fitting neatly within the unobstructed interior. Critics of this point of view say that perhaps this is one of the possible cluster shapes that Frank and Wen mentioned earlier. The Pauling dodecahedra do represent a stable shape, but evidence in support of this theory is lacking.

In short, liquid water forms aggregate clusters, although we are not likely ever to see the variety of forms this may take. The ice I lattice keeps the molecules at arm's length, whereas the models for liquid water allow the arms to bend, to distort, and to fold the molecules in upon one another more closely, or to permit floaters within a fragmentary lattice structure. Whatever the speculation on structure, two physical phenomena are of utmost importance. First, the density of liquid water is greater than the density of ice, by about 8%. Mark Denny (1993) says that floating ice has important biological consequences, not just for ice skaters and hockey players, but for the many organisms that seek shelter from winter cold by burrowing in lake bottoms. Second, liquid water is most dense at 3.98°C (39.2°F), ensuring that lake bottoms tend to stay above freezing, making for interesting times during spring and fall when the water in lakes goes through a temperature inversion.

SURFACE TENSION

Regardless of the cluster aggregation, the hydrogen bonds acting on water molecules in liquid water act in all directions. But water volumes never extend forever, eventually they are bounded by a surface. Let's look at an air–water interface. A molecule at the surface is pulled to all sides and is pulled inward by hydrogen attraction. It takes work to keep the surface molecule at the surface. Of course, restless as these molecules are, no one molecule resides long at the surface. But the math remains the same; some molecules are always residing at the surface and it takes work to keep them there. That work is *surface tension*. Work is energy. All bodies tend toward the lowest-energy states, so water volumes—droplets, say—tend toward the smallest surface area for the volume.

The units of surface tension or surface energy are energy per unit area. (*Energy* is force times distance, so another set of units could just as well be force per unit length, and these units might sound more like tension units to a structural engineer.) The symbol commonly used for surface tension is gamma, γ. The surface energy of water is 0.0728 J/m^2.

We might imagine surface tension as being like a skin, such as a balloon, around an air or water volume. But this analogy is very limited. The tension in a balloon varies as the balloon is stretched, whereas surface tension does not. Still, the surface tension that surrounds a spherical droplet, for example, applies a pressure to the volume inside, and as with a balloon, that pressure may be greatest when the volume is smallest. (It is always hardest to get the first air into a balloon.) Let's see how this is true. Imagine a spherical droplet of radius r. The surface area A is $4\pi r^2$ and the volume V is $\frac{4}{3}\pi r^3$. If we wish to increase the surface area of the droplet slightly, by the amount dA, the energy required is $\gamma\,dA$. We can replace the derivative dA by $8\pi r\,dr$, so the energy required is $8\gamma\pi r\,dr$. Any action by pressure that changes a volume is *work*, and work is energy, so let's equate this amount of work—$p\,dV$—to the energy we just calculated. The result, after taking the derivative of the volume (V) above, is that the work $= 4p\pi r^2\,dr$. Setting the change in energy to the change in work gives as a result $p = 2\gamma/r$. The pressure inside a droplet or a bubble depends only on the surface tension and the radius.

The smaller the radius, the greater the pressure of the sphere within the tension surface, whether it is a droplet of water in air or a bubble of air in a beer glass. This raises a troubling question: How do bubbles or aerosol droplets begin? The pressure must be very high in a very small bubble or droplet. How great must the pressures be if the radius is very, very small? We'll come back to that, but for now, suffice it to say that forming bubbles or droplets out of pure media is exceptionally difficult and exceptionally rare. Anyone who has stared at a beer glass or champagne flute long enough knows that a tiny defect in the surface of the glass can sponsor a site where bubbles arise with precise regularity.

WATER VAPOR

All water molecules are energetic. Molecules in an ice lattice vibrate and pulse, but their energy is low enough that the energy is not *translational*— causing molecules to move. In liquid water, the molecular energy, including rotational energy, challenges the hydrogen bonds in the clusters. In any of the models, liquid water contains at least some free molecules with translational movement. This movement may lead to collisions. That leads to the probability that some of the molecules (a small number) will have the speed to get to the surface, break any remaining hydrogen bonds, including those yanking hard from below the surface without counterbalancing forces above (recall surface tension), and head on out. Those particularly energetic molecules, free of hydrogen bonds, become water vapor, the gas phase of water. *Evaporation* is the term used to describe a change from the liquid phase to the gas (vapor) phase. *Condensation is the term used to describe a change from the gas (vapor) phase to the liquid phase.* This definition will become *very* important later, as *condensation* is the most improperly used term in all of building science. If the author could wish for one thing from his readers, it is the precise and careful use of the term *condensation*. The importance of precision here will be clearly evident later in this chapter and in Chapter 3.

Different phases of water have different average energy levels. Energy is required to move material from one phase to another. The *heat of fusion* (or *enthalpy of fusion*) for water is 143.5 Btu/lb. The freezing–melting temperature of water is 32°F. It takes 143.5 Btu of energy (heat) to convert ice to water at that temperature. If water becomes ice, 143.5 Btu must be supplied. In Chapter 8 we will see how insulation on pipes helps prevent bursting, because the insulation retards the escape of this heat of fusion as water turns to ice. The *heat of vaporization* (or *enthalpy of vaporization*) of water is 970 Btu/lb. If water condenses, the surroundings must be heated this many Btu for every pound of condensate.

According to the kinetic theory of gases, gas molecules are in constant motion, whizzing past one another and colliding in almost purely elastic collisions (not generating heat or friction) and have been doing so ever since the Big Bang. Gas volumes with whizzing molecules have energy, calculated using $E = mv^2/2$. Knowing the mass and the velocities allows us to know the energy. We can figure the mass. Dry air is a mixture of several gases, the principal one being nitrogen (78% by volume). Nitrogen (N_2) gas has a molecular weight of 28. The molecular weight of air may vary slightly, but a commonly used value is 28.96. Oxygen (O_2) constitutes about 21% of air by volume, argon 1%, and the remaining 1% is composed of traces of carbon dioxide, neon, helium, methane, and other elements and compounds. The amount of water vapor in the air may vary considerably. You might take as a rough starting figure that one air molecule out of a hundred is a water vapor molecule.

Temperature is one measure of the energy of a gas volume. Good students may calculate the average speed of a gas molecule using the Boltzmann constant and the relation

$$T = \frac{m\langle u^2 \rangle}{3k} \qquad (2\text{-}1)$$

where temperature T is absolute temperature. In SI units, absolute temperature is expressed in kelvin, where K = °C + 273.15. In I-P units, absolute temperature is in degrees Rankine, where R = °F + 459.67. $\langle u^2 \rangle$ is the root-mean-square velocity, and k is the Boltzmann constant, 1.38054×10^{-23} J/K. The resulting average speed is around 500 m/s. That may appear at first to move individual molecules quickly away from their starting point, except for the fact that there are approximately 10^{12} collisions in any 1-s interval. As a result, an air molecule is likely to wind up about 1 cm away from where it started a second earlier.

Pressure in a gas container is the result of collisions between the whizzing molecules and the walls of the container. Each time one of the molecules in a gas collides with the side of a container, its velocity (at least that component of the velocity normal to the plane of the container wall) is changed from u to $-u$. That velocity change is an acceleration; and acceleration times the mass of the molecule represents a force. The sum of those forces, divided by the area of the container wall, is the pressure against that wall. If this were a building science textbook, we might derive the average speed of a molecule from the values of standard atmospheric pressure and air density. To reach this result you might make the assumption that the velocity vectors of all the molecules can be simplified to a set of six vectors pushing against each of the six sides of a square container. You are invited to do the math.

To get an idea of the kinetic activity of gases, recall what happens at the air valve of a bicycle or car tire. Assume inflation to 30 psi (a little low for a tire). Standard atmospheric pressure is 14.7 psi [1 atmosphere (atm) of pressure]. So 30 psi represents air pressure of about 2 atm over the ambient air pressure. If you depress the air valve, you feel the rush of air on your fingers. The momentum of the air molecules in the airstream is not caused accidentally by your intervention. Rather, the molecules flying past your fingers began simply as molecules within the tire, colliding as they usually do and escaping through the valve simply at the rate at which they would normally hit the closed valve. We only feel the rush of air as one air volume seeks equilibrium with an adjoining volume. The rush begins as kinetic energy (with a net translational effect of zero), and when the valve is opened the energy becomes mechanical, leading to mass movement in one general direction. Kinetic gas activity feels like nothing. Mechanical gas activity feels, well, cool.

Movement or transport by kinetic activity alone is called *diffusion*. Recall from above that molecules in gases (liquids, too) move with high speed but encounter many collisions. Their punch may be great, but their progress is often slow.

How active must a water molecule be to break free of a surface of liquid water? The whizzing molecules do not all move at the same speed. The range of speeds of gas molecules is given by the Maxwell–Boltzmann distribution, shown in Figure 2-3. The curves represent the probability of any molecule having any speed. The sum of all the probabilities is, of course, unity. Slower molecules get stuck into hydrogen-bonded lattices. Higher-energy molecules can subsist with the other jetsetters in the vapor phase. Some chemistry texts describe the conditions for vaporization as "having the energy necessary to break the bonds binding a liquid together" (Zumdahl, 1997). Energy is represented by the square of the speed, so some molecules reach *escape speed*. These texts paint a picture whereby the proportion of molecules in or out of the gas phase at a given temperature is determined by the probability number above or below the escape speed at that temperature. Higher-temperature distributions have a greater probability zone above the escape velocity.

Intriguing as this approach may be, it is does not generate handbook values for vapor pressure above liquid water. This is for several reasons. First, the escape velocity itself may vary with surface tension, which varies with temperature. So the escape velocity probably varies with temperature. Second, even in the vapor phase, the polarity of the water molecule and its tendency to form hydrogen bonds even with itself is never outside consideration. These secondary effects are strong and ensure that the behavior of water is far from "ideal."

So some molecules in a free water surface become water vapor molecules. This effect, the creation of equilibrium vapor pressure, is purely a

Figure 2-3

Maxwell distributions of the speeds of gas molecules at three different temperatures. Higher-speed molecules escape to the vapor phase. There are more high-speed molecules at higher temperatures.

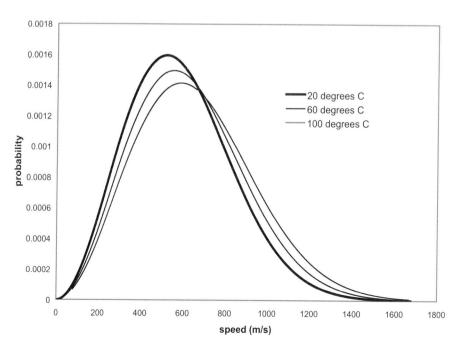

function of the temperature of the water surface that generates and sponsors the vapor pressure. Keep this in mind, particularly when you confront someone who says something like "warmer air holds more water." The quantity of water in the air is almost purely a function of the temperature and wetness of the bounding surfaces than it is of any characteristics of the air itself. It depends most strongly on what is happening at the boundary surfaces, not on the middle of the airspace. Imagine a room with five warm walls and one cold wall. The air temperature will tend toward the surface average of the six surface temperatures; that is, the temperature of the air can be averaged from the temperatures of the surrounding walls, although there will be gradients and convective loops. But the cold wall will call the shots when it comes to moisture—it will regulate the amount of moisture in the air. But we're getting ahead of ourselves.

A free water surface will sponsor a certain water vapor pressure in equilibrium with the liquid volume. Any gas or vapor pressure, you will recall, occurs as molecules collide with the sides of containers. The likelihood or frequency of collision is a function of the density of molecules in the gas volume. One way to determine the water vapor pressure is to imagine the use of a Torricelli barometer. (It is always easier to imagine the use of a Torricelli barometer than to actually use one—inverting tall tubes of liquids is quite a challenge; see Figure 2-4.) At standard temperature and pressure, a column of mercury will measure 29.98 in. in height, and any space above the mercury meniscus will be in a vacuum. (It will not be a pure vacuum. Mercury has a nonzero equilibrium vapor pressure at room temperature, although it is much smaller than the vapor pressure of water.) Now imag-

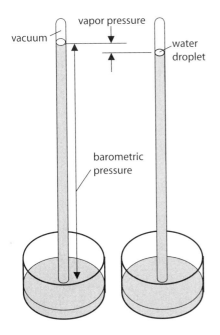

Figure 2-4

A Torricelli barometer contains a column of liquid in a closed tube, on the left. The liquid has the same weight as the column of air acting on the free liquid. If a small amount of water is injected into the vacuum space above the liquid as at the right, some will turn to vapor, creating a gas vapor pressure. That vapor pressure can be read as a height difference between the two liquid columns.

ine injecting a few drops of water into the vacuum area above the mercury. (Once again, imagining is much easier than doing). The free water surface created will sponsor a certain concentration of water vapor molecules into the otherwise vacuum area. The water vapor pressure at 70°F is 0.73966 in. of mercury (in.Hg). So the level of the mercury column would drop by about $\frac{3}{4}$ in. An easier way to make these measurements would be with a vacuum pump and bell jar. A good pump could create close to vacuum conditions, but with a pan of water in the bell jar, the lower limit of the air pressure in the jar is the vapor pressure of the water. By varying the water temperature, the associated vapor pressure could be calculated for the temperature range. A source of vapor pressure values for water of a wide range of temperatures is the ASHRAE *Handbook, Fundamentals,* Chapter 6 (see Table 2-1). Appendix A gives the formula provided by ASHRAE *Handbook—Fundamentals* to derive saturation vapor pressure from temperature.

A mole of an element or compound has a mass equal to the atomic or molecular mass in grams. As stated above, a mole is any collection of 6.022×10^{23} items. So moles of different things have different weights. Gas volumes, however, are special. A mole of any gas occupies the same volume as a mole of any other gas (with certain minor exceptions), regardless of whether it is a heavy gas or a light gas. A gas molecule could be pictured as having a fixed size regardless of its mass. At standard temperature and pressure (1 atm at 0°C) a gas mole occupies 22.4 L. A cubic foot contains about 30 L.

John Dalton proposed the law of partial pressures for gases. He claimed that the total pressure for a gas volume made up of a mixture of gases is the sum of the individual or partial pressures of the individual gases. The relative contribution depends on the number of moles of each gas, not on any of the mass or weight properties of the gas.

We have stated that the water vapor pressure in a volume that is in equilibrium with a free water surface is strictly a function of the water temperature. We just showed that if water is in equilibrium with an evacuated volume, water molecules fill the space up to the handbook value of the vapor pressure. On the other hand, if the volume contains air, the same amount of water vapor enters the volume, perhaps pushing the air aside. This contribution from the water to the adjoining volume is entirely independent of what gas (or none) is in the volume at the outset. As the water temperature rises, the water vapor pressure rises as well. When the water vapor pressure gets so high that it equals the air pressure against the water surface, the water boils. If the air pressure is lower than standard (sea level) pressure, as in Denver, for example, water still boils when the vapor pressure equals the air pressure but this time at a lower air pressure and a lower temperature.

We learned from Boyle that the volume of a gas varies inversely with the pressure. We learned from Charles (see Chapter 1) that the volume of a

Table 2-1   Representative values of water vapor pressure as a function of temperature

Temperature (°F)	Saturation Vapor Pressure (in.Hg)	Temperature (°C)	Saturation Vapor Pressure (kPa)
0	0.038	−20	0.103
5	0.049	−17	0.137
10	0.063	−14	0.181
15	0.081	−11	0.238
20	0.103	−8	0.310
25	0.130	−5	0.402
30	0.165	−2	0.518
35	0.204	1	0.657
40	0.248	4	0.813
45	0.300	7	1.002
50	0.363	10	1.228
55	0.436	13	1.498
60	0.522	16	1.818
65	0.622	19	2.198
70	0.740	22	2.645
75	0.876	25	3.169
80	1.033	28	3.782
85	1.214	31	4.496
90	1.423	34	5.324
95	1.662	37	6.281
100	1.935	40	7.383
105	2.246	43	8.649
110	2.599	46	10.097

gas varies directly with the temperature. We learned from Avogadro that the volume of a gas varies directly with the number of moles in the gas. Connect the dots, and we have the ideal gas law, usually expressed as, where P is the pressure, V the volume, n the number of moles, and T the absolute temperature. The constant that wraps the package together is R, the universal gas constant. In SI units the value of R is 0.08206 L·atm/(K·mol); in I-P the value is $R = 1545$ ft-(lb_f/lb_m)/(°R·mol). It so happens that the universal gas constant is equal to the product of the Avogadro number and the Boltzmann number, both given above (R may be expressed as 8.3145 J/K·mol). An ideal gas is any gas that can be imagined to comply with the pressure–volume–temperature relation expressed above. All gases deviate somewhat, and water vapor deviates quite strongly.

If we plot the vapor pressure of pure water against the temperature of that water, the resulting curve, called the *curve of saturation vapor pressure over pure water,* is as shown in Figure 2-5. Vapor pressure values are commonly less than the saturation vapor pressure value. Occasionally, they can be higher, as we shall see. Note, too, the repetition of the term *pure.* Sometimes the water is not pure; in fact, it is rarely pure. Later we will see the impact of water impurities.

The shape of the saturation vapor pressure curve is exponential. Exponential relationships occur in nature when an additive increase in one characteristic means a multiplicative increase in another. For example, take the interest paid on principal. If the interest is *simple* (i.e., it is taken on a principal amount that does not vary), the accumulation is by the same amount every year. *Compound* interest involves an adjustment to the system, in this case to the principal. When the system adjusts and the principal grows, the cumulative growth is no longer linear but is exponential. Or take, for example, fluid pressure as a function of height. Water is incompressible, so the water pressures vary linearly with depth. Water doesn't adjust to the load above. Air, on the other hand, does adjust through compression, and for each change in height, the change in pressure diminishes with height.

The heat of vaporization of pure water is 970 Btu/lb$_m$. That means that it requires 970 Btu (each Btu has about the heat of a kitchen match) to evaporate 1 pound of water: to convert it from liquid to gas. The relationship between heat and vapor pressure is expressed by the Clausius equation:

$$\frac{dp}{dT} = \frac{\Delta H}{T \, \Delta V} \tag{2-2}$$

where p is the pressure, T the temperature, ΔH the heat of vaporization, and ΔV the change in volume. As you can see, the change in pressure for a change in temperature involves T, seen on the right-hand side. So the relation must be exponential. The exponential relation is seen best in the Clausius–Clapeyron equation:

$$\frac{p}{p_0} = e^{-\Delta H/nRT} \tag{2-3}$$

where p_0 is any reference pressure. These two equations are derived from thermodynamics, which is beyond the scope of this book.

Is it possible for air to contain a higher water vapor pressure than the handbook value shown in Figure 2-5? Yes, indeed. Recall that the strongest determinant of the moisture quantity in the air is the temperature of the sur-

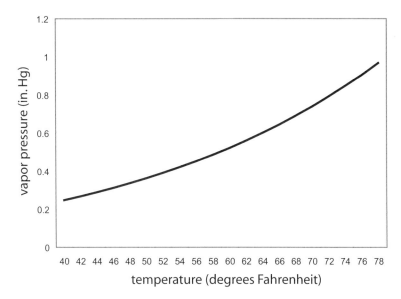

Figure 2-5
Curve of saturation water vapor pressure over a body of pure water.

rounding surfaces. In Figure 2-5 there is a presumption that the surfaces are in very close contact, freely exchanging molecules across the interface between the liquid and gas. But in the middle of the atmosphere, surfaces are hard to find, so the water vapor pressure may float much more widely. If the air is dirty or is seeded with solutes, those can act as surfaces and pull water vapor toward them. In clean air, the water vapor may be much higher than Figure 2-5 allows. When water vapor supersaturates cold air, some corrective events are likely to occur. The prettiest of these is the formation of snowflakes. Nakaya (1954) studied snowflakes through the duration of World War II on the island of Hokkaido. He discovered that in a certain range of air temperatures, and with a certain degree of supersaturation, dendritic (fernlike) snowflakes will form. Other conditions of supersaturation will lead to the formation of snowflakes of other geometries. Phase change requires nucleation, a peculiar condition (perhaps even a contaminant) that can catalyze the change. In Chapter 7 we solve the problem of pipe bursting under freezing conditions thanks to our understanding of supersaturation. The snowflake discussion illustrates an important point—that conditions for phase *change* are flexible, whereas conditions for coexistence of two phases are very precise. The formation of snowflakes or droplets may be affected by impurities in the air, but conditions at the surface between pure liquid water and air above can be defined with great precision. Those conditions are expressed in the psychrometric chart.

PSYCHROMETRICS

The plot of vapor pressure against temperature shown in Figure 2-5 is the basis of the psychrometric chart shown in Figure 2-6. Willis Carrier, the father

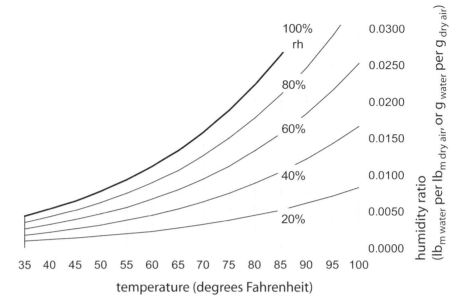

Figure 2-6
Psychrometric chart similar to that used by ASHRAE. Values for vapor pressure are derived from the calculations in Appendix A.

of air conditioning, adopted the term *psychrometrics* from the Greek words for "cold" and "measure," to describe the temperature and water vapor properties of air. The x-axis shows temperature. Temperature represents the kinetic activity of the molecules in the system. Several representations are possible on the y-axis. The most fundamental value that could be represented there is water vapor pressure, but the most useful is humidity ratio.

The values of *vapor pressure* (p_w) over water are available in Table 2-1 and can be calculated using Appendix A. Total air pressure (p) is the same as barometric pressure and is the sum of the pressures of the component gases (recall Dalton's law) or $p = p_w + p_{da}$, where p_{da} is the pressure of dry air. Dry air is a mixture of other gases, mostly nitrogen, and has a molecular mass of 28.96, close to that of N_2, which is 28. According to the ideal gas law, $PV = nRT$, pressure is proportional to the number of moles (n), assuming constant temperature and volume. In particular,

$$p_w V = n_w RT$$
$$p_{da} V = n_{da} RT \tag{2-4}$$
$$(p_w + p_{da})V = (n_w + n_{da})RT$$

From this we can deduce that

$$\frac{n_w}{n_{da}} = \frac{p_w}{p_{da}} = \frac{p_w}{p - p_w} \tag{2-5}$$

This allows us to calculate the *humidity ratio* (W), the ratio of the mass of water vapor molecules to the mass of dry air molecules in the sample. The mass (*M*) of any material is the product of the molecular mass and the number of moles. If the mass of a water vapor molecule were the same as the mass of an air molecule, the humidity ratio would simply be the ratio of water vapor pressure to the dry air pressure (total barometric air pressure – water vapor pressure). It isn't, as you recall. The molecular mass of water is 18. The molecular mass of dry air is 28.9. The mass of water vapor $M_w = 18n_w$ and $M_{da} = 28.9n_{da}$. So

$$W = \frac{M_w}{M_{da}} = \frac{18n_w}{28.9n_{da}} = \frac{0.62198p_w}{p - p_w} \qquad (2\text{-}6)$$

Note that in passing from vapor pressure to humidity ratio units for the psych chart, we needed to introduce the outdoor barometric pressure. But barometric pressure varies according to the weather and altitude. We do not have different psych charts for fair weather and foul, but there are different psych charts for altitude. The psych chart presented here is for standard atmospheric pressure.

The humidity ratio has no units. The humidity ratio in the comfort zone (we'll get to that) varies from about 0.003 to 0.012 (g_{water} per $g_{dry\ air}$, or lb_{water} per $lb_{dry\ air}$). If the number of decimal places seems unwieldy, the value is sometimes multiplied by 1000 and termed the *mixing ratio*, where the units might be considered g_{water} per $kg_{dry\ air}$. This is done only for convenience.

Imagine a sample of air in a closed jar. The concentration, expressed as a humidity ratio, does not change even if the air is subject to temperature change. The humidity ratio is one of the ways of expressing the humidity in the air in a way that is unaffected by temperature. The *y*-axis value of the sample in the jar does not change, even as the temperature (along the *x*-axis) is allowed to vary. Picky readers may note that we have to accommodate air pressure changes in the jar, not just for safety against jar explosions at high temperatures, but to adjust for changes in the total pressure in the equation.

Another way to express humidity in a way that is unaffected by temperature is by using *dew point temperature*. Take the jar and subject it to lowered temperatures. "Instrument" the surface of the inside of the jar for temperature. At the moment that condensation appears on the inside surface of the jar, the surface temperature will be the dew point temperature. If we actually tried this experiment, we might find that the surface temperature drops slightly below what the eventual dew point measurement will be. But the act of formation of condensation warms the surface back up to the temperature at which the vapor and the "dew" coexist and are in equilibrium. Wait too long and the instrumented surface will continue chilling below the dew point, extracting water vapor from the air. It is most correct to state that the dew point is the incipient temperature at which liquid and vapor coexist and are in equilibrium. To state that it is the temperature at which dew "forms" is not quite correct, since nucleation (described above regarding snowflakes) may affect the temperature at which the dew phenomenon first becomes visible.

The term *absolute humidity* means, precisely, the mass of water per volume of dry air (g_{water} per m^3_{air} or lb_{water} per lb_{air}). Because the volume of dry air changes with temperature whereas the mass of water does not, the units of absolute humidity are not strictly temperature independent.

Temperature-independent measures of moisture concentration are extremely important. Indoors and outdoors will tend to have the same moisture concentration (and vapor pressure and humidity ratio, and mixing ratio and dew point). Moisture generation adds some humidity; ventilation and infiltration reduce that addition. The net increment is rather small in most buildings. We will see in Chapter 9 that one measure of the likelihood of mold growth is increment in indoor vapor pressure over and above the outdoor vapor pressure. The indoors and outdoors will *not* have the same relative humidity.

Relative humidity, a dimensionless number expressed as a percent, represents the ratio of the actual vapor pressure to the saturation water vapor pressure. Go back to Figure 2-5 which represents saturation water vapor pressure, that is, the water vapor pressure that the air would reach once the free water surface donated to the adjoining airspace all the water molecules it possibly could. But suppose that the airspace contained only half the mass of water vapor molecules it possibly could—then the relative humidity of the air would be 50%. How can we create air at 50% relative humidity? We could isolate the free water surface from the air and manipulate the air humidity mechanically. Or perhaps open a window, depending on the outdoor conditions. Or mix the saturated air 50–50 with bone-dry air. Or insert a water collector (a dry sponge, salt) into the system.

Relative humidity is a means of characterizing the humidity in the air that is very temperature dependent. Study Figure 2-6. The saturation curve represents 100% relative humidity (RH). Any vertical line between the *x*-axis (representing zero humidity in the air, 0% RH) and intersecting the saturation curve (100% RH) is divided into increments of relative humidity. If the *y*-axis used units of vapor pressure, the increments would be exactly evenly divided. (Recall the little p_w in the denominator of the relation between humidity ratio and vapor pressure—it means that the increments using humidity ratio will not be exactly equal, but will be off by about 1%.) Now suppose that we could insert a small relative humidity sensor into our closed jar with only air inside. Heat up the jar, the relative humidity goes lower; cool the jar, the relative humidity rises. Keep cooling the jar, it reaches dew point, and at that instant the relative humidity is 100%. These rules represent principles that are well established and correct as long as they pertain to clean containers such as glass or metal jars.

Recall that the heat of vaporization permits an energy value to be assigned to a mass of material that changes phase. The more water in the system, the more energy might be necessary to turn it to vapor. Also, higher-temperature systems have higher energy. *Enthalpy* is the sum of these two energies. The energy measurable with a dry-bulb thermometer is called *sensible energy;* the energy "hidden" in vapor form, hidden as increased kinetic activity of water vapor molecules, is called *latent energy.*

Users of sling or aspirated psychrometers may be familiar with *wet-bulb temperature.* The traditional method for measuring humidity in a space involved first measuring air temperature, called *dry-bulb temperature;* at the same time, the bulb of another thermometer is covered with a fabric wick, and the wick is wetted with pure water. Air is made to move quickly across the wick, either by slinging the two mercury thermometers in the air, or blowing air mechanically across the wick (aspiration). As molecules active enough to leave the matrix of the wick do so, the molecules left behind in the wetted wick are less energetic, thus cooler. The wet-bulb thermometer will continue cooling until it reaches a stable temperature, which will be the measured wet-bulb temperature. At this point the air in immediate contact with the wick is saturated. At this point, the air that is in intimate contact with the materials of the wick has a lower temperature than the surrounding air, and it has a higher humidity ratio. This is unstable, and nature tends to correct it. There will be heat transfer through the air at a certain rate that depends on the thermal conductivity of the air. There will be moisture movement through the air to correct that imbalance as well, and the rate of flux depends on the water vapor permeability of the air. Both of these transport properties are known, and the ratio of the two, heat conduction to vapor diffusion, is termed the Lewis relation. It is that relation that determines the effective wet-bulb temperature. Wet-bulb temperature is also described using thermodynamics, and only a small correction is necessary to compare the two. Figure 2-7 shows the relationship between dry-bulb temperature, wet-bulb temperature, and dew point temperature. If the theory of wet-bulb temperature is tough, the practice is even tougher. It takes time for temperature equilibrium, contaminants in the water or on the wick will have their say, and the bonding of water to the wick may be a significant distorting factor. Besides, flailing mercury thermometers can be damaging to anything or anyone nearby.

The *specific volume* of an air sample is the ratio of the volume of the air–water mixture to the mass of dry air. If air is warmed, the volume increases, so the specific volume increases. If humidity is added to the air, then for the same volume, fewer molecules are molecules of dry air (since more

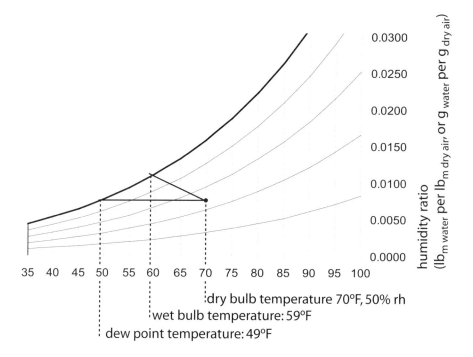

Figure 2-7
Relationship between dry-bulb, wet-bulb, and dew point temperatures.

of the molecules are water molecules), so the specific volume increases. The specific volume of room-conditioned air is typically around 13.5 ft³/lb of dry air. Notice that specific volume is not exactly the reciprocal of density of an air sample; *density* is the ratio of the total mass to the total volume of the sample.

Absolute humidity is the mass of water per volume of the air–water mixture ($M_w/V_{mixture}$). Absolute humidity can be calculated as the ratio of the humidity ratio (M_w/M_{da}) to the specific volume ($V_{mixture}/M_{da}$).

MEASURING TEMPERATURE AND HUMIDITY IN THE AIR

The traditional temperature-measuring device is a mercury thermometer. Electronic equipment may use thermocouples, thermistors, or resistance temperature detectors (RTDs). An RTD is typically a short length of platinum wire that will enlarge or contract with temperature changes, and the electrical resistance changes with dimension. Resistance must be read with a bridge measurement or other electronic means. The output is linear but weak. The thermistor also has a resistance output. Thermistors can be selected for range of application. They are much more sensitive to temperature than RTDs, but their output is nonlinear and requires electronic correction. Thermocouples are simple junctions of dissimilar metals. We know that any time that dissimilar metals are connected, a voltage potential is created. The potential is a function of temperature. If the circuit contains two junctions, one at the sensing point and another at a reference temperature point, the tiny voltage difference will reflect the temperature difference between the two. The temperature at the reference junction must be known.

For humidity measurements, traditional sling psychrometers served researchers well for many decades. Most reside now in desk drawers with slide rules and ruling pens. Aspirated psychrometers are still used widely.

The basic instrument for humidity measurement, though rather expensive, is a chilled mirror dew point sensor. This instrument places a tiny mirror in an airstream. The mirror is chilled thermoelectrically (using the exact reverse of the thermocouple temperature–voltage relation described above). Light from a laser or light-emitting diode is reflected off the mirror to a photocell. The change in light diffraction that occurs at the moment of condensation on the mirror is picked up by a photocell, and that signal is used to maneuver the mirror temperature to the right at the dew point temperature. These instruments require no calibration and little more care than occasional mirror cleaning.

Common humidity instruments use a polymer plate. The dielectric properties of polymers vary with humidity. Instruments with well-characterized polymers and sensitive output readings may cost several hundred dollars. But instruments in the $30 range can provide good readings. Instruments that promise quick readouts use very thin sensing elements, and these can readily be contaminated. Robust instruments may sacrifice quickness of response.

THE FOURTH PHASE: AN INTRODUCTION

Up to now we have dealt with ice, snow, pure water, dry air, water vapor, and the glass and metal receptacles that contain them. Thales of Miletus tells us that all things are made of water, and he was talking about everything: the soil, the sky, animals, plants, you, and me. He might have been talking about building materials—wood, brick, stone, concrete—all of which have measurable moisture contents. How should we describe the phase of this water? It's not vapor, certainly. It seems odd to consider it a solid like ice or snow. And it is not runny like liquid water. It is best to think of the water contained in hygroscopic and porous materials as being in another phase, that of *bound water*. Bound water may indeed be a whole range of phases, which seem to have a little bit of solid, liquid, and gas combined. The water in wood tends to stay put (solid), does slosh around to some extent (liquid), and remains somewhat permeable to vapor movement.

With bound water, the physics and chemistry of water relations get complex and interesting. We might begin with solutions such as table salt. Take once again our setup with a free surface of pure liquid water in equilibrium with air at saturation vapor pressure. Measure the humidity in the air, then add a few sprinkles of salt to the water. *Raoult's law* tells us that the vapor pressure of the solvent (water in this case) will be reduced from the vapor pressure of pure liquid by the mole fraction of the solvent. One mole of sodium chloride (the solute) will readily dissolve into 1 mole each of sodium and chlorine ions. The ratio of the number of moles of water to the number of moles of water and ions combined gives the mole fraction. If that fraction is, say, 8:10, the vapor pressure has been reduced to 80% of its previous value. It is easy to imagine what is happening. Before adding the salt, water molecules appeared at the surface at a certain rate, making full use of the available surface area. But nothing keeps the ions from the surface, so they stand in the way of water molecules trying to head out. Raoult's law is ideal, there are many exceptions. But in general, adding anything to pure water will reduce its vapor pressure.

Several factors besides dissolved salts can influence the vapor pressure over a free liquid surface. Principal among these is surface contamination, say from oils or floating materials. I was amazed once to find rather dry conditions inside a house that had a crawl space which I was assured remained continually flooded. I opened the crawl space hatch, saw my reflection, measured the wood moisture content, smelled the crawl space air, and everything indicated drier conditions than should have been. I looked at my reflection once again and saw the faint color effects of an oil film on the water. That explained very well the quite dry conditions above the water. (First aid for a flooded crawl space until it can be pumped dry: a quart of mineral oil poured on the surface.)

Table salt dissolves in water into ions of sodium and chlorine. Water molecules bind to these ions because of the electrical potential in the ions. The attachment of water to salt is very strong, so strong that table salt is considered deliquescent. It will suck as many molecules as it can from the air to transform itself out of the dry crystalline state into a saturated soup. Put two flasks inside a closed bell jar container, water in one flask and salt in the other. The water will jump from the original flask to the salt flask, slowly of course, by virtue of the evaporation from the water surface onto the preferred salt crystal and salt ion surface. The U-tube in Figure 2-8 shows two water volumes, one pure and one a salt solution, separated by a semipermeable membrane, one that readily transfers water molecules but not salt. The salt will pull the water far out of gravity equilibrium using osmotic pressure. Incidentally, a semipermeable membrane used in kidney dialysis is the Visking membrane. The Visking Company was founded in 1925 in Chicago to provide polymer sausage casings. That company gave rise not only to red sausage casings and the Visking membrane, but in the 1950s it also marketed polyethylene sheet material under their brand VisQueen, by which it is widely known today.

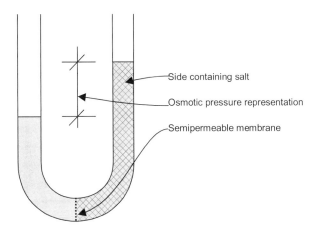

Figure 2-8
Osmotic pressure
(solute potential).
Water, which can pass
through the semi-
permeable membrane,
attaches itself to salt
ions, which cannot.
Osmotic potential can
overcome gravitational
potential.

Solutes in water produce a *solute potential*. A potential is any condition capable of driving work. Solutes in water are capable of driving water across a semipermeable membrane and making a solution climb in. Water tends to move from the "unsalted" to the "salted." Solutes form one type of material to which water molecules may bind.

Let's take another example of water bonding with nonwater molecules: the surfaces of water containers. See the meniscus in Figure 2-9, which shows a magnified view of water against a glass container. The water makes a *contact angle* with the glass. Water contained in a capillary tube may rise. The water is pulled up by the adhesive forces of the surface acting on the water molecules. Of course, we must idealize the water–container interface in order to assign a single number as the contact angle. Surfaces may be rough. Or a droplet of water may be running down an inclined glass surface; the downhill angle may not equal the uphill angle. Nevertheless, the contact angle is a good expression of the relative surface energies of the solid and liquid surfaces.

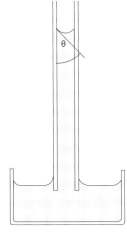

Figure 2-9
Water adheres to glass, forming a contact angle
between the surface and the meniscus of the liquid.
Contact angle is always measured within the liquid.

Water adheres to most surfaces. Surfaces have energy; they have non-neutralized electron fields about them, and the polarity of the water molecule can provide some satisfaction and resolution. The forces of adhesion—surface molecules to water molecules directly—can be quite strong. Once water gets onto a surface, it may be difficult to remove. Water on dishes can be removed by wiping with a surface of even higher energy—a dry dish towel. A monomolecular layer of water that adheres to a surface may be bonded very tightly, and there may be substantial remaining electrical potential not satisfied by a single layer of water molecules. Subsequent layers may be bonded to the layers below. In some chemical models, this bonding may take on a lattice shape, so use of the term *layer* may be justified. But at a macro level we can imagine a mass of water molecules that adheres to a surface, and the strength of adhesion is a function of the distance of the particular molecule from the surface. At a distance out from the surface, where the meniscus of the water surface lies flat, the remaining forces are only the forces of water-to-water cohesion (see Figure 2-10). Water bonded strongly to a surface is said to be *adsorbed*. It is adhered to the surface. Stamm (1964) says that the thickness of water adhered to the surfaces of wood (in the cells as well as at the surface) may be around the thickness of 10 water molecules. This becomes important in understanding how mold uses water to digest and grow, as we shall see in Chapter 9.

Water that is indirectly attached to surfaces, usually by virtue of the surface geometry, is called *absorbed water*. The surface geometry may be cellular (in organic material) or porous in aggregations of granular material. These cells or grains have interstitial pores, and the pores form a matrix. The potential that determines the amount of absorbed water in a material is termed its *matric potential*.

The amount of water attached to a surface is a function of the surface energy of the surface. It is also a function of the area of the surface, obviously. At a microscopic level, the surface may be rough, discontinuous, turned in upon itself, and porous. So the surfaces of these materials, from the water

Figure 2-10
Water molecules in immediate contact with surfaces are either adhered or adsorbed. Molecules more loosely attracted to surfaces are absorbed. There is no specific dimension distinguishing the two.

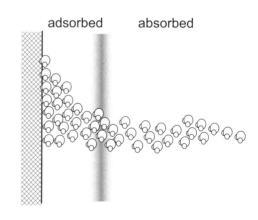

molecule's point of view, may be irregular. They may be mountainous and craterous terrain. The proximity of two surfaces within a complex pore can create conditions like those in the capillary tube shown in Figure 2-10. The matric potential may not be continuous in materials.

Matric potential operates much like capillary rise but at a more random level. We know that the smaller the capillary tube, the higher the rise of the liquid in the tube. That is because in small tubes, the adhesive surface is strong compared with the gravitational action on the smaller mass. Surface tension can be pictured as lifting the mass of water beneath the meniscus. When a liquid is attracted to a surface, it will move naturally from a larger pore to a smaller pore. It will not, by nature, move from a smaller pore to a larger, and certainly will not naturally move from a pore to the open air. This fact deserves a name: the *rule of capillarity*.

Temperature affects capillary movement. The colder the temperature, the higher the capillary rise. This makes sense. Surfaces that are warm allow the surface water molecules to evaporate more readily. Under warm conditions, the surfaces are drier and the tendency for water molecules to remain attached to the surface is reduced, so the capillary rise is lower. This becomes quite important as we inspect for moisture damage to exterior masonry during cold weather. If a masonry building benefits from waste heat from indoors, it may stay quite dry; if it is not heated (or if it is insulated, discussed in Chapter 4), the risk of water damage is increased. Among the stone buildings of Europe, it is quite easy to distinguish those that are heated from those that are not—the unheated buildings suffer greatly from the "rising damp" of moisture out of the soil into the stone.

Water and Building Materials

BACKGROUND

In the short period from 1937 to 1942, the building industry in the United States, prompted by insulation manufacturers, developed the practices of moisture control that have been in use, for better or worse, until the present day. We can summarize these 50-year-old practices as follows:

- Thermal insulation provides considerable benefits by reducing conductive heat transport through building envelope assemblies. But insulation can lead to moisture problems.
- Moisture moves by diffusion. That is, moisture moves from locations of high moisture concentration to locations of lower concentration via diffusion or the random kinetic activity of gas molecules.
- We can trace a steady-state thermal gradient through a building envelope assembly using the thermal resistances of materials. We can trace a vapor pressure gradient through a building envelope using values for the vapor permeance of materials.
- We can compare these two gradients given the fact that we know the saturation vapor pressure at any temperature. This comparison is called a *profile analysis*.
- If the calculated vapor pressure exceeds the calculated saturation vapor pressure at any location in the assembly, "condensation" is said to occur. If that is the case, two approaches are suggested: (1) the lazy person's approach—the assembly is disallowed, or (2) the official (ASHRAE) approach—the rate of accumulation is calculated and compared to the ability of materials and assemblies to withstand this accumulation.
- In any case, vapor barriers are recommended for wall assemblies, and attic ventilation is recommended for attic assemblies.

Although this has been considered by many to be the workhorse and the governing paradigm of moisture control for several decades, some serious flaws have appeared. Before discussing those flaws we should study, first, how this paradigm arose, and second, how it is done correctly and well. Afterward we can work toward better approaches to moisture control.

Wood Frame Construction

Standard U.S. residential single-family construction until the middle of the twentieth century has been light-frame wood construction, with wood clapboards and trim. The woods used were pine, cedar, or redwood, and the entire exterior was painted. The construction contains cavities which were rarely insulated. When they were, it was usually done as draft stopping and the materials were usually indigenous organic materials (sawdust, cotton) or Cabot's eel grass. But by the middle of the 1930s, other insulation materials came into use, including fiberboard panel products (e.g., Celotex, originally made of sugarcane), expanded mineral products (e.g., perlite and vermiculite), and mineral wool products (e.g., slag wool, rock wool, and glass fiber). Fiberglass was invented around the time of World War I in Germany as a replacement for asbestos, which had become scarce. In the 1930s, widespread exterior paint peeling began to be reported. Painters were complaining that insulation "draws water" (Rogers, in BRAB, 1952), and some objected to painting insulated houses. To deal with this problem, a coordinated effort got under way in which the insulation industry conducted research and developed recommendations, and in the 1950s, the paint industry marketed those recommendations.

U.S. Forest Products Laboratory

The U.S. Forest Products Laboratory (FPL) was the first organization to tackle the problem, because it reflected poorly on standard wood construction. In 1933, F. L. Browne, senior chemist at FPL, cited two types of circumstances that had been observed to cause abnormal conditions of exposure leading to paint peeling. The first type was rainwater seeping through leaky joints left by "poor carpenter work or faulty design." The second type was "moisture originating within the building and carried by air circulating within the hollow outside walls. When moisture laden air comes in contact with surfaces at sufficiently lower temperature, water condenses." This distinction between the two moisture sources or moisture loads has rarely been described so succinctly or clearly ever since.

Larry V. Teesdale, senior engineer at FPL (Figure 3-1), then published the technical report *Condensation in Walls and Attics* (Teesdale, 1937). Teesdale was a strong supporter of the use of insulation in light-frame con-

Figure 3-1
Larry V. Teesdale, senior researcher at the
U.S. Forest Products Laboratory. Photo
courtesy of USDA Forest Service Forest
Products Laboratory.

struction for comfort and energy saving, and he recognized that these practices introduce unanticipated moisture problems. For Teesdale, the insulation
itself, which warms materials at the interior and chills them at the exterior,
was a major factor in moisture accumulation in cavity walls during cold
weather. "Because of the lower sheathing temperatures, condensation will
occur on the sheathing" (p. 3). "Insulation, because of its efficiency in reducing heat loss, lowers the temperature within the wall and thus sets up
the condition that increases the amount of moisture that may accumulate"
(p. 4). "Moisture accumulation within a wall is affected by five factors:
(1) outside temperature and humidity, (2) efficiency of the insulation . . ."
(p. 5). What Teesdale was pointing out was that cold materials tend to be
wetter than warm materials, simply by virtue of their lower temperature.
This phenomenon is described and discussed at length later in this chapter.

Then on page 4 of the report, he states: ". . . [T]he potential buyer of insulation often hears that certain types 'draw water' and become wet. This is
not true." It appears that Teesdale was trying to have it both ways here: On
the one hand, he recognized exterior wetness as a consequence of insulation
use, but as a supporter of insulated structures he objected to pithy expressions such as this that could adversely affect public perceptions of insulation.

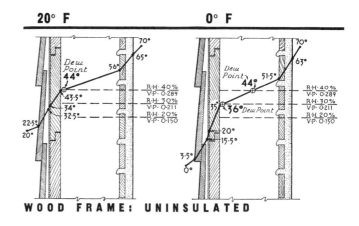

Figure 3-2
Early profile constructed by Teesdale. The vapor pressure is represented simply by horizontal lines penetrating the wall assembly, leading to the misapprehension that somewhere in the wall it "reaches dew point." [From anon. (Teesdale), 1938.]

Teesdale's report contained the first representations of wall sections with superimposed thermal gradients (see Figure 3-2). For certain indoor and outdoor temperatures, the gradient line represents a temperature profile through the assembly. Teesdale and later researchers were approaching a method to determine if "condensation" is occurring in the building assembly. Teesdale's method of representing humidity was crude. He simply calculated the dew point temperature of indoor air and drew that and its intersection with the thermal gradient. Such an approach leads directly to a common misunderstanding in which walls "reach dew point" somewhere in their thickness. They do not reach indoor dew point, but the physically correct representations of heat and moisture effects in wall assemblies did not appear until the following year.

As means to avoid condensation in walls, Teesdale recommended:

■ Vapor barriers for new construction
■ Attic ventilation
■ Elimination of intentional moisture sources should water damage appear

■ A wintertime allowable RH value of 30%
■ Attention to forthcoming test results

Note that *not* using insulation does *not* appear as a means of avoiding condensation, although he had shown three times in the paper that insulation itself leads to moisture accumulation and condensation. The report did not present research findings, although research was under way at the FPL; rather, it was an occasion to provide the recommendations in advance of the presentation of the research findings. That may seem out of sequence, but it is rather typical for the design and construction industries.

T. S. Rogers and the Architecture Press

The next step was taken by Tyler Stewart Rogers, trained as a landscape architect at Harvard and a writer on architectural technology subjects. He published his seminal article "Preventing Condensation in Insulated Structures" in the March 1938 *Architectural Record*. The article is important in several regards. It was the first such article in a major building industry magazine. It introduced many of the concepts, conventions, wordings, and diagrams that are used to the present day. It exhibited considerable graphic appeal, which is normal given the architecture background of its author. "Architects, owners and research technicians have observed, in recent years, a small but growing number of buildings in which dampness or frost has developed in walls, roofs or attic spaces. Most of these were insulated houses, a few were winter air-conditioned. The erroneous impression has spread that insulation 'draws' water into the walls and roofs" (Rogers, 1938, p. 109). Once again that pesky expression occurs—insulation "draws water"—and again it is countered strongly. Rogers described research that was under way under Teesdale at FPL and Rowley at the University of Minnesota (see below). Like Teesdale, Rogers was a supporter of insulation for buildings. In 1939 he became director of technical publications for Owens-Corning Fiberglas.

Rogers showed thermal gradients through wall sections, recopied from Teesdale (see Figure 3-3). He also showed (not on the same wall section) vapor pressure gradients with and without a vapor barrier. This is a step beyond Teesdale's representation. Rogers also added perspective depth to the wall sections, which made the phenomenon appear more real.

Rogers also recommended vapor barriers. He showed architects for the first time in this article how membranes of different materials could be added into wall systems. The membranes he described came from the roofing industry and from the packaging industry. The packaging industry, after all, needed to master the principles of moisture transport, to prevent the packaged goods from becoming overly wet or dry during storage and transit.

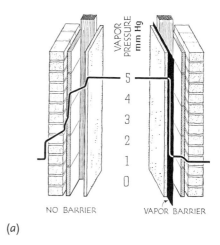

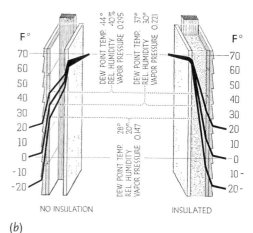

Figure 3-3
Temperature and vapor pressure profiles on two different scales, with no superposition. (From Rogers, 1938.)

(a)

(b)

Frank Rowley

The research Rogers described, funded through the National Mineral Wool Association, was conducted by Frank Rowley, professor of mechanical engineering at the University of Minnesota (Figure 3-4). Rowley had been measuring conductive heat flow through building materials during the 1930s, and this work led him to renown within ASHVE (American Society of Heating and Ventilating Engineers, now ASHRAE). He was president of the society in 1932. Most of the original R-values of building materials listed for ASHRAE's early heat-loss calculations came from Rowley's research.

Rowley developed both a theory and a testing campaign for moisture in insulated assemblies. The theory he proposed was the theory of vapor diffusion through solid materials (Rowley, 1938). Diffusion, you may recall, occurs by random kinetic activity of molecules. The reason Rowley selected this mode of moisture movement was expressed in the first paragraph of his paper:

Figure 3-4
Frank Rowley, University of Minnesota, 1934.
Rowley provided the theoretical and practical
basis for adoption of the diffusion principle
in building envelopes. ASHRAE Transactions
1934 frontispiece. © American Society of
Heating, Refrigerating, and Air-Conditioning
Engineers, Inc., www.ashrae.org.

For convenience it has often been assumed that the laws for vapor
transmission are similar in form to those governing the flow of heat
through the walls of a building, and that coefficients of vapor trans-
mittance may be developed for materials or combinations of materials which may be applied in the same manner as coefficients of heat
transmission. In making this analogy it is assumed that the difference in vapor pressures between two parts of a structure is the mo-
tive force which causes the flow of vapor. . . . (Rowley, 1938, p. 41)

In other words, the diffusion theory was proposed at the outset as the
explanatory mechanism not because it was validated or shown to explain
the observations, but because it was analogous to conductive heat flow,
with which Rowley was most familiar. Rowley went on:

Before accepting a complete analogy between the two problems an
analysis should be made to determine those elements which are
similar and those which may be conflicting. . . . Vapor may be
transmitted by molecular diffusion and convection, and the condensed vapors may be transmitted by capillarity or other means.

He concluded:

> . . . [D]ata available indicate that in many cases the flow of vapor through a material or combination of materials is proportional to the vapor pressure drop along the path of flow [and] there will be many different conditions under which the flow of vapor may not follow any simple law.

Although he aimed to be complete in his description of how water moves in buildings, the focus he applied to diffusion had the effect of drawing many others into this explanation for moisture transport.

In this 1938 paper, Rowley was the first to convert the thermal gradient to a saturation vapor pressure gradient and to superimpose saturation vapor pressure (temperature) and vapor pressure profiles on the same section diagram. The diagrams show great care in representing linear temperature gradients as curved saturation pressure gradients (see Figure 3-5).

Rowley also undertook a campaign to measure condensation on plates of aluminum placed in the cavities of wall and roof assemblies and subject to artificial cooling in a climate chamber (Rowley et al., 1939). This research was funded by the National Mineral Wool Association, as had much of his previous work on thermal conductivity. His test buildings appear to have been constructed with great care. His setup thus excludes (by intention) radiant and convective effects, so the effects of conductive heat flow and diffusion moisture transport stand out. It is therefore not surprising that his findings are consistent with his diffusion theory. He concluded with recommendations for vapor barriers as well as for attic ventilation.

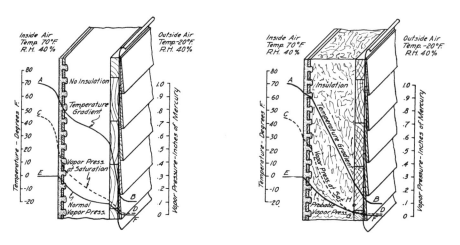

Figure 3-5

Saturation vapor pressure and vapor pressure curves on the same section. (From Rowley, 1938.)ASHRAE Transactions 1938. © American Society of Heating, Refrigerating, and Air-Conditioning Engineers, Inc., www.ashrae.org.

U.S. Federal Housing Authority

The material presented above—Teesdale's FPL research, Rogers's articles in the architecture press, and Rowley's ASHVE research, together with some vapor permeance measurements done at the National Bureau of Standards and Canadian Scientific Liaison Office—constitutes the entire research output from North America on the subject of moisture transfer in buildings prior to World War II. Prior to the war there were no "model" building codes, and the only regulatory documents were municipal building codes in larger cities and the Minimum Property Requirements of the Federal Housing Authority (FHA).

In January 1942, the *Property Standards and Minimum Construction Requirements for Dwellings* of FHA was revised significantly. It is a mimeographed document, very difficult to find, that contains prescriptive requirements for:

1. *Vapor barriers.* Provide a suitable membrane with a permeance no greater than 1.25 grains of moisture per square foot, hour, inch of mercury pressure difference.
2. *Basementless spaces.* Provide a sufficient number of foundation wall vents to assure a total ventilating area equivalent to 0.5% of the enclosed area plus $\frac{1}{2}$ ft^2 for each 25 lineal feet of wall enclosing that area.
3. *Attics* (includes airspace between ceiling and flat roofs). Provide effective fixed ventilation in all spaces between roofs and top-floor ceilings, with the net ventilation area for each separate space to be not less than 1/300 of the horizontally projected roof area.

It was here that the prescriptive recommendations of Teesdale, Rogers, and Rowley first appeared with threshold values and graduated from being rough recommendations to being precise enforceable requirements. All of the significant research that might have supported these prescriptive requirements has been described above, and the research lacks support for the numerical threshold values in this document (Rose, 2003). Thus the values in FHA (1942) must be seen as arbitrary. Nevertheless, they have become the basis for U.S. practice up to the present day.

As Trechsel and others point out, the United States had a lot on its mind through the economic depression of the 1930s and the war that followed. During this period, insulation was introduced and the groundwork was laid for the construction boom that followed. The amount and quality of work by just a handful of people under trying circumstances remains a remarkable achievement.

POST–WORLD WAR II

Following World War II, the Housing and Home Finance Agency (HHFA), which directed FHA, undertook research to confirm (or not) the regulations put forward in January 1942. The principal investigator for HHFA was Ralph Britton. He contracted with Pennsylvania State University to conduct a series of tests on walls and roofs with the purpose of assessing the condensation performance of various wall and roof assemblies (Britton, 1949a). The basis of his studies was the performance of wall and roof assemblies that were in compliance or not with the values put forward in FHA (1942). Before reaching conclusions, the work was interrupted for lack of funds. Nevertheless, the interim reports are valuable in that they illustrate many factors besides diffusion that influence moisture performance of assemblies. Despite the inconclusiveness of research results, Britton authored a booklet *Condensation Control in Modern Buildings* (HHFA, 1949) which was widely used in postwar housing construction and contained elaboration and refinement of the FHA (1942) recommendations.

The late 1940s saw the introduction of the first model building codes, and they borrowed the FHA 1942 recommendations practically intact (BOCA, 1948). Ramsey and Sleeper's *Architectural Graphic Standards* (1951), a standard reference work for architects, introduced a page of moisture control information using tables directly from *Condensation Control* and drawings directly from T. S. Rogers's 1938 *Architectural Record* article.

The National Paint and Varnish Association (NPVA) opened their "War Against Water" campaign around 1951. The NPVA produced two documents, "How to Win Your War Against Water" and "The Menace of Moisture" (see Figure 3-6), and slide shows based on these documents which were seen by over 50,000 viewers around the country. The aim of the documents was to market the new moisture control practices in an effort to curb paint peeling in insulated buildings. The language of the document was consistent with the paranoia of the McCarthy era:

> If you're to come out of the battle as conqueror, you need to know the exact nature of your enemy and the tactics he employs.

> The villain of the piece is "dat ol' debbil" Moisture. In his program of deviltry, he may be innocently aided and abetted by the insulation that add so much to the modern house.

> Your enemy, Moisture, knows where man-made structures are open to attack. At these points he can enter and cause costly damage. It's up to YOU to beat him at his dangerous game!

> They seem innocent enough, these three pools of moisture: the milk from the bottle, the steam from the shower, the vapor rising from

the whistling tea kettle. But are they? Oh, no . . . they're up to no good. Where do they go from here? Believe it or not, they have an engagement. At the "*dewpoint*"—if you please.

There are three important steps to take in beating your adversary— One is to improve your facilities for ventilation. A second is to guard against excess humidity in your household. The third is to install barriers to halt the attack of moisture before it gains real headway.

This campaign was probably the first of several campaigns in the U.S. construction history to induce fear in the users of buildings of the hidden dangers their buildings contain (see Chapter 9). Needless to say, the marketing of moisture control regulations using such tactics makes future review of those regulations quite difficult. As stated above, science is a poor tool to allay the fears of building users.

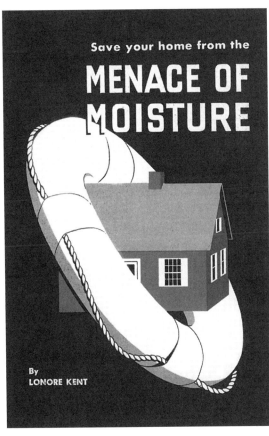
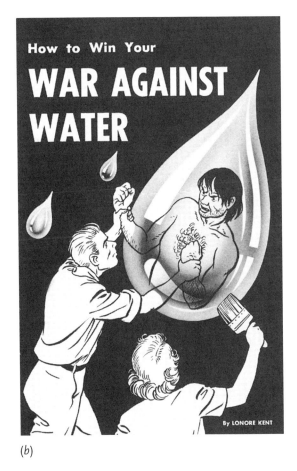

(a)   (b)

Figure 3-6
Covers of the National Paint and Varnish Association pamphlets "Menace of Moisture" and "How to Win Your War Against Water." The NPVA sought to market the new recommended practices of moisture control by creating fearsome images of the "villain" moisture.

1952 CONDENSATION CONFERENCE

In 1952, the conference *Condensation Control in Buildings As Related to Paints, Papers, and Insulating Materials* was convened by the Building Research Advisory Board. Conferees included Teesdale, Rowley, and Britton—all those who played a role in the new concern for "condensation" problems. Representatives from the paint, paper, and insulation material industries were in attendance. The conference proceedings show many challenges to the diffusion paradigm and the recommendations, but overall, it found general acceptance among the 120 participants.

By the time of the conference, Rogers had become the dean of thermal design of buildings. He opened the conference with a surprising revelation about the motives for the work on moisture control in the late 1930s:

> Condensation has occurred in buildings from the earliest days of man's shelter. I am sure the cave dwellers complained of it. In recent years it has come into prominence, not because of its newness, but for several other reasons: One of these is that we should no longer tolerate the annoyances and destructive action of unwanted moisture. We have advanced so far in building design that imperfections of this character simply must be eliminated. Another reason is that with new materials and techniques and design we have new things to blame for the faults in our buildings. It is never in fashion to blame ourselves, of course; it is always some other Joe who caused the trouble. So paint failures were at first blamed on insulation until the insulation industry, in self defense, had to undertake research to establish its innocence. (BRAB, 1952, p. 3)

This is frank talk from an industry spokesperson. He was stating that the industry's research efforts were conducted to protect the insulation industry in light of anticipated moisture damage that might occur in insulated buildings. Tyler Rogers continued:

> While this research and similar work by the paint industry was going on, there was a great deal of buck-passing. The insulation men blamed the paints or the wet lumber and some painters retaliated by refusing to paint an insulated house. Then the building paper manufacturers got caught in the middle; their new sheathing papers were blamed for causing condensation instead of shielding a building from dampness. The foils were soon in the ring with the papers, while architects, builders, building owners and the general public watched this battle royal and wondered if any of the fighters was worth betting on.

The efforts by which the practice recommendations were marketed were described. The success of the "War Against Water" campaign was applauded. W. B. Moore (Reynolds Aluminum) described the marketing thus:

> I think it is quite analogous [between aluminum foil and mechanisms for condensation control] to realize that in a period of less than twelve months, through national advertising, through local advertising and through point of purchase advertising, a product was created that it will take a great deal of promotional work to kill.

T. S. Rogers closed the conference with the following:

> My final recommendation is, let's dare stick out our collective necks and put down our best opinions, based upon technical background, as the thing to do. State it simply: This is what we believe you should do now. And then have the courage to go out a year hence, or six months hence if we need to, and say, "I have learned a little better, so now do it this way." I would rather see the lay-public, the building public, know what we know here today, in the best way we can express it, than to wait until tomorrow or the day after to find a few more gaps filled in.

In summary, hygrothermal studies began with the attempt to answer the question of why paint peels in insulated wall assemblies. The correct answer would be that paint peels for several reasons, including: (1) there are problems involving flashing and rainwater management; (2) exterior materials in insulated assemblies are cold, and cold materials are naturally wetter (more on this below); (3) water from humid indoors may load water onto exterior sheathing and siding materials; and (4) certainly not least, there are problems related to poor paint and substrate preparation. Teesdale, Rogers, and Rowley provided not so much answers as recommendations: vapor barriers and ventilation of attics and crawl spaces. Those recommendations stress indoor vapor pressure as a wetting agent, and that stress tends to mask the importance of the other means by which assemblies get wet—from poor flashing and from the coldness of exterior materials. The earliest writer, Brown the paint chemist, got it right by stressing the flashing.

THE DIFFUSION PARADIGM

The historical material above introduces the paradigm that has governed moisture control in buildings since its inception. We may call this the diffusion paradigm because its central tenet is that moisture moves through building envelopes by diffusion (i.e., by kinetic activity of vapor molecules).

Recall that molecules in the air travel at very high speeds and have billions of collisions every second. Their average travel path can be calculated: If the average speed is, say, 650 m/s and if a molecule experiences 13 billion collisions per second, the average path length is 50 billionths of a meter (50×10^{-9} m). This path length is tiny compared to the sizes of pores and holes in building materials. Gypsum wallboard, for example, is produced by a foaming process, leaving cavities that may appear downright cavernous under an electron microscope. Gas may move through such materials with relative ease. Although any gas, including water vapor, can make it through tiny pores, it does so very slowly.

The history rundown also has introduced the *profile method*, which traces the temperature and humidity profile through a building envelope assembly. For the remainder of this chapter we look closely and critically at heat and moisture analysis of building envelopes. Before proceeding with the method itself, we must address other issues, including:

- Conduction and diffusion
- Vapor permeance and its measurement
- Selection of design values for indoor and outdoor air conditions
- Air films

Conduction and Diffusion

There are three forms of heat transfer: conduction, convection, and radiation. For whole buildings, heat transfer by convection may be significant; infiltration and ventilation may amount to a large fraction of the heating and cooling load. In building envelopes, however, heat transfer by convection—air movement—may be quite minor because the heat capacity of air is so low and the assemblies are often designed to restrict airflow. Heat transfer by radiation may be quite significant, especially the heating of sunlight and the chilling of nighttime radiation. The profile method ignores the effects of sunlight, which can be quite major, especially for windows, roofs, and wall claddings that absorb water and are subsequently struck by sunlight. As we just saw, the focus that arose historically was on conduction. One reason is its obvious importance—it remains the largest determinant of heating loads in most U.S. buildings. Another compelling reason for a focus on conduction is that conduction lends itself nicely to engineering analysis. The equations are compact, theory mirrors experiment, and the thermal properties of materials remain rather constant for wide ranges of temperatures. Another argument may be that the insulation industry sponsored much of the research of the time, and the role of insulation is seen most clearly in conduction analysis.

In the same way that conduction is only part of the heat transfer picture, diffusion is only part of the moisture transport picture. We know that water flows through parts of buildings. It can enter and drain back out again, with gravity as the governing potential. Water can be adsorbed and absorbed into porous and hygroscopic building materials, with capillary suction as the governing potential. Water may move through a building assembly; the air current may carry moisture and it may encounter chilled surfaces. Air can deposit large amounts of water into building envelope assemblies. However, neither moisture movement along air paths, liquid flow by gravity, nor capillary transfer of moisture is taken into consideration in the profile method.

In one dimension, the flux for both conduction and diffusion is a simple product of the conductance or permeance and the difference in driving force—temperature or vapor pressure.

Fourier conductive heat transfer was named for the very prolific French mathematician and physicist of the early nineteenth century. His description of heat conduction is expressed as

$$\dot{q} = k\frac{dT}{dx} \qquad \text{or} \qquad q = -k\,\text{grad}(T) \qquad (3\text{-}1)$$

where q is the heat flux, k the thermal conductivity, and dT/dx the change in temperature for the change in dimension along the path of flow. These two expressions represent essentially the same physical facts. The expression on the left is the kind traditionally found in the United States, with the driving force or potential expressed as a slope (dT/dx) of change in temperature for a change in dimension. The expression on the right is typical of that found in Europe, with the potential expressed as a *gradient* (grad), which is a vector. They both express the fact that the flux of heat is proportional to the temperature difference across the component or assembly.

Diffusion flux is modeled in the same way as conductive heat transfer. In one dimension the transfer is said to follow *Fick's law,* expressing the proportionality of mass flow for difference in vapor pressure or concentration. Adolph Fick made contributions in both medicine and physics, and this statement of proportionality is from 1855.

$$\dot{m} = \mu\frac{dp}{dx} \qquad \text{or} \qquad m = -\mu\,\text{grad}(p) \qquad (3\text{-}2)$$

where m is the mass flux, μ the permeance, and dp/dx or grad *(p)* the change in vapor pressure across the thickness of the assembly. Like heat conduction, mass diffusion occurs in three dimensions. But for a uniform wall of wide extent, flow can be considered to be uniform, at least away from the edges of the wall, so one-dimensional modeling is not out of the question. Increased computing power permits modeling in two and three dimensions. The profile method uses one-dimensional analysis.

In Fourier and Fick analysis, the proportionality constant is presumed to be just that—a constant. Those familiar with building materials know, for one thing, that the thermal conductance of materials may be a function of their temperature. Part of the heat flow through materials such as fiberglass, for example, is radiative, from one fiber to another, and radiative heat transfer is a function of the temperature difference to the fourth power. So heat transfer is better approximated if we allow the proportionality to vary with temperature.

Values of Vapor Permeance

The unit for vapor permeance that was selected in the 1940s for use in the United States is the *perm*. One perm represents 1 grain of water per hour per square foot of material surface area per inch of mercury vapor pressure difference. A grain represents 1/7000 of a pound in avoirdupois measurement. Recall that pound is a unit of weight rather than mass. As long as we work terrestrially, we can assume a uniform gravitational constant and assume that someone using the term *pound* really means the mass of material that weighs 1 pound. It's sloppy, troublesome, in need of correction, but we can live with it. The term *grain* comes from the use of cereal grains. It is the smallest unit of weight in the I-P system. Frank Rowley of the University of Minnesota did some of the earliest U.S. work in vapor permeance. He reported his results in grams (not grains) per square foot per 24 hours per inch of mercury vapor pressure difference (in.Hg). There are approximately 453 grams in a pound (mass).

What is a vapor barrier? The research of the 1930s (Teesdale, Rowley, and Rogers) did not assign a permeance number to the term *vapor barrier*. In January 1942, the Federal Housing Authority produced the document *Property Standards and Minimum Construction Requirements for Dwellings* (FHA, 1942). It is now an obscure document, existing only in mimeographed form, with apparently only one remaining copy in the library of the U.S. Department of Housing and Urban Development. But it contains the original statements of the three principal moisture control requirements that persist in US building regulation and practice. It contains the *1/300 rule* for attic ventilation, the *1/150 rule* for crawl space ventilation, and the first specification for permeance in a vapor barrier membrane: "2.5 grains per hour per square foot per pound per square inch vapor pressure difference."

After the war, the disarray in permeance units got under way. Following is a sampling of nine statements of what constitutes a vapor barrier.

■ Britton, September 1947: "$1\frac{1}{2}$ grains under 1 psi. pressure."

■ *Condensation Control in Dwelling Construction*, HHFA, 1949: "A good vapor barrier should permit not more than 1 grain of water vapor to pass through an area 1 foot square in 1 hour when the vapor pressure difference is calculated on the basis of 1 inch of mercury when tested by a dry method. It should have sufficient mechanical strength to permit handling during erection without damage. It should also retain its vapor resistance qualities for the life of the building, or, if a paint film, until it is renewed. When the vapor barrier is installed it should not have an average vapor transmission rate greater than 1.25 grains per square foot per hour per inch of mercury differential including joints, fittings around outlet boxes, and the like. Damaged vapor barriers should be replaced or restored" (see Figure 3-7).

■ BOCA, 1950: "Cellular spaces shall be ventilated or shall be provided with interior non-corrodible vapor-type barriers complying with the approved rules."

■ Federal Specifications UU-P-147, May 1948, quoted in ASHAE Guide 1958: "Class A, where a high degree of water vapor resistance is required, 4 grams per (square meter) (24 hour) (i.e., 0.576 perm). Class B where a lower degree of water vapor resistance is required, 6 grams per (square meter) (24 hour) (i.e., 0.864 perm)."

■ Lund (a colleague of Frank Rowley from the University of Minnesota, from the conference *Condensation Control in Buildings*, 1952: "1.25 grains per square foot per hour per inch of mercury."

■ Minimum Property Standards, 1958: "Except for unfurred masonry walls, a vapor barrier having a vapor transmission rate not exceeding 1 perm shall be installed on the warm side of the walls when: (a) the "U" value of the wall is numerically less than 0.25, or (b) the wall has siding, sheathing, sheathing paper, or combinations of other materials on the cold side of the wall which materials, as applied, have a vapor transmission rate of less than 5 perms (ASTM dry cup) and the dwelling is located in an area having a design temperature of zero or colder."

■ ASHRAE Guide, 1958. "Unfortunately, there is no general agreement as yet to report results as coefficients of permeance, or of permeability where appropriate, as adopted in this chapter, or to use the same basic units."

■ ASHRAE Guide, 1961: "Water vapor barriers are those materials which retard the transmission of water vapor with reasonable effectiveness under specified conditions. The permissible rate of water vapor transmission (permeance) of a barrier material depends upon design criteria for the structure or system being insulated."[1]

As mentioned in the Introduction, in the 1970s a court case in Pennsylvania held to the ASHRAE 1961 definition and ruled that a membrane placed in the subject building was not a vapor barrier because it did not absolutely stop the transport of moisture. As a consequence, ASTM recommended adoption of the term *vapor retarder* rather than *vapor barrier,* and this position is found in ASTM Standard E755.

Permeance is water vapor conductance through materials. A material with a permeance of 1 perm allows 1 grain of water vapor to pass through each square foot of material per hour per inch of mercury vapor pressure difference. One perm = 1 grain/(hr-ft^2-in.Hg). Permeance is a unit of vapor transport regardless of the thickness of the material. If we imagined a thick material being sliced into layers, we can imagine each layer providing the same resistance to flow, and the total resistance to flow being the sum of the individual resistances. We might thus assume that the permeance will be a linear function of the thickness of the material. We have not proven this, and in practice it becomes quite incorrect if different parts of the material are at different moisture contents. Permeance is defined for a material of given thickness. *Permeability* is defined as conductance of moisture flow for a unit thickness. The units of permeability are grain-in./hr-ft^2-in.Hg or, canceling units of length, grain/hr-ft-in.Hg.

With the (attempted) introduction of metric system units into U.S. construction, equivalent metric units for permeance and permeability needed to be introduced. By conversion of units, 1 perm = 57.45 ng/(s·m^2·Pa). The unit ng is nanograms or 10^{-9} gram, a very tiny mass. A nanogram is to a gram as a byte is to a gigabyte. A gram of water is represented by a volume the size of a sugar cube. This reinforces the notion that control of diffusion is control over minuscule quantities of water.

The standard test for vapor permeance of materials involves use of the wet cup and the dry cup. The dry-cup or wet-cup test is selected depending on whether the material is expected to be dry or wet under critical service conditions. For the dry-cup test, a sorbent mineral such as silica gel is des-

---

[1]ASHRAE Guide, 1961 went on: "A water vapor barrier does not necessarily *stop* the flow of vapor, but serves as a medium of control to *reduce* the rate and volume of flow. . . . By retarding water vapor transmission, water vapor barriers help to (1) keep the insulation dry, and reduce the heat load requirements for the cooling system; (2) prevent structural damage by rot, corrosion, or the expansion effect of freezing water, and (3) reduce paint problems on exterior wall construction."

JUNCTION OF SECOND FLOOR AND WALL, BALLOON CONSTRUCTION

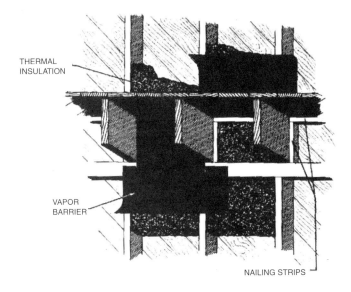

THERMAL
INSULATION

VAPOR
BARRIER

NAILING STRIPS

Figure 3-7
Vapor barrier installation. (From HHFA,1949.)

iccated then cooled to room temperature; a material specimen is attached to the top of the cup so that edge effects and air movement are minimized. Then the sample is placed in a chamber that maintains constant room temperature and 50% relative humidity. It is weighed at regular intervals and the weight gain by the sorbent is noted. The rate of gain, taken for the early part of the test when the cup humidity is still presumed to be very low, indicates the vapor permeance. For the wet-cup test, water is used in place of the sorbent. The interior of the cup is taken to be at 100%. The water is maintained up close to the underside of the test cell. It is very difficult to conduct this test well, and it is easy to wet the specimen in doing the wet-cup test. These procedures, and their interpretation, are described in ASTM E96, "Standard Test Methods for Water Vapor Transmission of Materials."

Unfortunately, results from ASTM E96 are not particularly dependable. Several round-robin tests of water vapor permeance have been conducted, resulting in a wide range of values (see Toas in Trechsel and Bomberg, 1989). Despite the difficulties in reproducibility of permeance values using conventional techniques, several researchers remain strong supporters of permeance measurement techniques and of building regulations that make use of these values. Other researchers recognize the wide error involved in measurement and see difficulties in applying numbers with high variability to uses that require definite determinist outcomes such as approval or disapproval.

The water vapor permeance of materials is a very strong function of moisture content. Look, for example, at the vapor permeability of oriented strand board (OSB) as a function of the sample moisture content (see Figure 3-8). Water vapor moves with great difficulty across a matrix that is filled

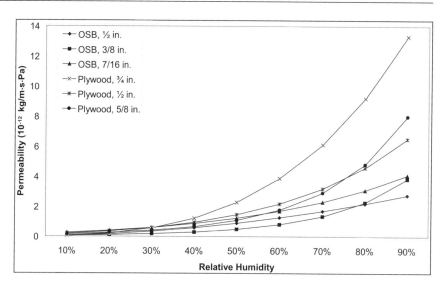

Figure 3-8
Permeance values of various samples of plywood and oriented strand board (OSB). Note the variance among samples as well as the variation from dry to wet materials. (From Kumaran, 2002.)

with air. But as the moisture content increases and as the layer of water that coats the cell walls increases from one to several molecular layers, transport through the material is facilitated as water travels along liquidlike pathways, and evaporation at the dry end can be expedited. This variability of vapor permeance with moisture content is found in ceramic materials (e.g., concrete, stone, brick, gypsum) as well as organic materials such as wood and paper.

Sources for permeance and permeability values, such as ASHRAE *Handbook—Fundamentals,* Chapter 25, often provide a range of values. If the material is wet, a higher permeability value would be selected. If the material is cold, such as exterior materials under cold design conditions, it tends to be wet, so wet-cup values would be selected. Indoor materials during winter tend to be dry, so dry-cup permeance values would be selected. Note from Figure 3-8 that the difference between wet and dry permeance values may vary by, say, 10:1. This book gives no table of permeance values. The values shown in ASHRAE *Handbook—Fundamentals,* Chapter 25, are the values that are relied on most often. An effort is under way at ASHRAE to review the values found in that table. In using the profile method, only one number can be used. The permeance value that is selected from a range can have a strong impact on the outcome.

Indoor and Outdoor Temperature and Humidity

Indoor conditions may have a strong impact on the outcome as well. The principal assumption in the profile method is that the water that will be used in the calculations is the humidity contained in the indoor air. Teesdale recognized this and concluded that control of indoor humidity was critical to good building envelope performance. Historically, the profile method has been used to estimate the effects of wintertime conditions. In residences, tradition indicates the use of 50% relative humidity indoors, although 35% RH is a recommended humidity level for northern climates. In buildings with engineered HVAC systems the indoor conditions selected are usually the set point conditions.

The profile method can be used to estimate the effect of summertime conditions as well, in which case the loading comes from outdoor air. However, during summer, the indoor and outdoor vapor pressure difference may be small compared to winter. Based on this, the early investigators dismissed concerns for summertime "condensation." Current investigators find many summertime moisture problems, but they appear to be due to airflow, leakage, and solar vapor drive (discussed below). These problems do not lend themselves to classical profile analysis.

The traditional application for the profile method was extreme cold weather. Cold weather temperatures were selected using tables available in ASHRAE *Handbook—Fundamentals* (up to 1993) that gave "99%" and "$97\frac{1}{2}$%" winter conditions. These are described as representing temperatures that have been equaled or exceeded by 99% or 97.5% of the total hours in the months of December, January, and February (a total of 2160 hours) from 15 years of data. In a normal winter there would be approximately 22 hours at or below the 99% value and 54 hours at or below the 97.5% value. The choice of relative humidity at cold design temperatures has little importance, as the saturation vapor pressure is low. Relative humidity values of 70% or 80% were commonly used.

Air Film

At either side of a building envelope assembly lies an air film. Air has rather high thermal resistance. As building materials go, air has the lowest thermal conductivity, thus the highest thermal resistivity, of all. Manufacturers of insulation materials will explain that it is not their aim to sell insulating *material* as such, but rather, to package air using the least amount of packaging material. These values pertain only to still air. Still air may be captured within the gaps of insulating material, but without such packaging, air is in rather constant motion. Wind pressures can wash air from a surface. So can temperatures at vertical surfaces of materials that may be slightly different from the air temperature, causing buoyant flow up or down. The actual thermal resistance of an air film may be unknowable. Nevertheless, some value for thermal resistance of an air film must be selected. ASHRAE *Handbook—Fundamentals* gives some guidance on this selection.

In uninsulated building envelopes, the indoor air film may play an important role in both surface conditions and overall heat transfer. The outdoor air film is usually so buffeted by wind that its effect is small. But it is not insignificant. Imagine an infrared thermograph taken outdoors of two similar buildings, one insulated and one not. We would expect to see a stronger glow from an uninsulated building, but this is only because the outdoor air film resistance is greater than zero. A still air film (i.e., an air film with a relatively high thermal resistance) allows the uninsulated building to keep the outdoor surfaces at a measurably higher temperature.

The vapor permeance of the air film, on the other hand, is very high. The vapor pressure across the air film may be expected to be almost constant. We will have occasion below to consider surface relative humidity in determining the potential for mold growth on a surface. This is the expected relative humidity exactly at the surface, determined from the vapor pressure measured at the air of the room and the surface temperature determined by surface measurement.

THE PROFILE METHOD

A bit of terminology at the outset: The method being described here has had several names. The term *dew point method* is widely used; however, dew point temperature never enters into the analysis or calculations. You may recall that Teesdale's presentation of the method used dew point temperature, but it was overridden by the subsequent researchers. The method is often called the *ASHRAE profile method* because its "official" description is found in the ASHRAE *Handbook—Fundamentals*. ASHRAE has no ownership of the method. In Europe it is called the *Glaser method*. In this book it is called the *profile method*.

The profile method arose from the work of two researchers, Teesdale and Rowley, and one architect/publicist, T. S. Rogers. Recall that Teesdale's profiles from 1937 show temperature plotted on a building section, with horizontal lines indicating different indoor dew point temperatures. In looking at these charts, one would think that the effect of the indoor air dew point, thus indoor air vapor pressure, penetrates undisturbed through the thickness of the assembly. Teesdale himself asks where the assembly reaches dew point. Many writers (e.g., Massari and Massari, 1985) have adopted this language and the picture of water accumulation that accompanies it. The language *reaching dew point* seems to indicate that one could plot a temperature profile through a wall, find the point where that profile intersects a horizontal line indicating indoor dew point temperature, and expect burgeoning water at that location. This impression is decidedly incorrect. If water accumulates, it does so on the surfaces of materials, not within the thickness of materials. But more important, the vapor pressure within a building assembly is affected by both the interior and exterior vapor pressures, and a gradient is established between those two. There is no single dew point to be reached, but a range of humidities, bounded by the vapor pressures indoors and out.

Rogers showed two charts, one showing temperature with a temperature scale and one showing vapor pressure. Rowley put the two measures together by converting temperature to saturation vapor pressure (see Figure 3-5). Note that when Rowley shows the lines of saturation vapor pressure as curved, indicating quite correctly that if the temperature drop between two points is linear, their vapor pressure representation is not. The saturation vapor pressure curve follows the same curve as the 100% line in a psychrometric chart.

A description and example of the profile method is maintained in ASHRAE *Handbook—Fundamentals*, Chapter 23. Figure 3-9 gives a template for calculating values using the profile method. The standard method proceeds as follows:

1. List the building assembly components in sequential order. For each component list thickness dimension, thermal resistance value, and vapor permeance or its reciprocal, permeance resistance. Determine the permeance resistance of each component. Thermal resistance values, permeances, and permeance resistances are given in ASHRAE *Handbook—Fundamentals*, Chapter 25.

2. From ASHRAE *Handbook—Fundamentals*, select thermal resistance values for the indoor and outdoor air films. The examples in ASHRAE *Handbook—Fundamentals* give good guidance here.

3. Select indoor and outdoor design conditions of temperature and relative humidity. ASHRAE *Handbook—Fundamentals* contains tables showing outdoor temperatures that represent 99% or

Component name	R-Value $(hr\text{-}ft^2\text{-}^\circ F/Btu)$	Permeance $(gr/hr\text{-}ft^2\text{-}in.Hg)$	r perm $(hr\text{-}ft^2\text{-}in.Hg/gr)$	Temperature $(^\circ F)$	Saturation vapor pressure $(in.Hg)$	RH	Vapor pressure $(in.Hg)$
				T_i (=input)	svp_i (=f(T_i))*	rh_i (=input)	vp_i (=svp_i * rh_i)
	R_1 (from reference)	p_1 (from reference)	rp_1 (= 1/p_1)	T_1			vp_1
				T_m =($T_1 R_2$ + $T_2 R_1$)/(R_1+R_2)	svp (=f(T_m))*		vp_m =($vp_1 rp_2$ + $vp_2 rp_1$)/(rp_1+rp_2)
	R_2 (from reference)	p_2 (from reference)	rp_2 (= 1/p_2)	T_2			vp_2
				T_o (=input)	svp_o (=f(T_o))*	rh_o (=input)	vp_o (=svp_o * rh_o)

*See Appendix B for the function converting temperature F to saturation vapor pressure.

Figure 3-9

Profile method template. Formulas shown may be entered in a spreadsheet.

97.5% of the annual hourly temperatures. Users of the method must decide about the criticality of this selection. It is usually quite subjective.

4. Calculate the temperature drop across each component.

5. One method often used involves calculating the sum of all the thermal resistances, then calculating the total temperature drop, then noting that the temperature drop (as a proportion of the total) equals the ratio of the R-value of that component to the total R-value of the assembly. This approach has a disadvantage that will be apparent in the second round of calculations.

6. A better method shown in Figure 3-9 is iterative, that is, it requires successive calculations that are almost always done by computer. The temperature at any interface is calculated using the formula shown in the figure. Spreadsheets with this formula value must be configured for iterative calculation.

7. From the indoor and outdoor temperature and relative humidity, determine the indoor and outdoor vapor pressure. See Figure 3-9 or the calculation tool in Appendix A to find the saturation vapor pressure. Multiply the saturation vapor pressure at the design temperature by the relative humidity to get the actual vapor pressure.

8. Calculate the saturation vapor pressure at each interface as a function of temperature. Use Figure 3-9 or Appendix A.

9. Calculate the vapor pressure drop across each component. This may be done in two ways as above. The preferred way is to use iterative calculation, as shown in Figure 3-9.

At this point some users of the method will stop and check if the lines cross. If the lines cross, they say, condensation is indicated, and condensation is unacceptable, so the assembly is considered unacceptable. That is *not* how the method works, however. Let's continue with the proper method as described in ASHRAE *Handbook—Fundamentals*, then come back to this point about condensation.

10. If at any point the vapor pressure value exceeds the saturation vapor pressure, reset the vapor pressure at that point to the value of the saturation vapor pressure. After all, having vapor pressure exceeding saturation is quite rare. If calculations are iterative, any vapor pressure value may simply be inserted and the resulting vapor pressure gradients recalculated.

11. Calculate the vapor flow from the high-vapor-pressure side to the point that was reset. This is done by summing the perm resistances of components between the high side and the reset point,

calculating the vapor pressure difference between those two points, and dividing the vapor pressure difference by the sum of the perm resistances.

12. Calculate the vapor flow from the point that was reset to the low-vapor-pressure side, as above.

13. Subtract those two values to determine a rate of moisture accumulation.

If at some other point in the assembly the vapor pressure exceeds the saturation vapor pressure, repeat the steps above.

14. Compare the rate of moisture accumulation to the storage capacity of the material. No instructions are given in ASHRAE *Handbook—Fundamentals* Chapter 23, on how best to do this.

Normally, an estimate is made of the upper and lower wetness limits, and the quantity of water necessary to go from one limit to another is used in an estimate of acceptability of the estimated rate of accumulation.

Condensation

What is "condensation"? Until now, the word has generally appeared in quotes, because the precise use of the term should be distinguished from the popular use. *Condensation* (no quotes) is a change in phase from the vapor to the liquid state (see Figure 3-10). Leonard Haeger of the National Association of Home Builders defined it this way at the BRAB (1952) Condensation Conference: "I suppose in the beginning we should have a definition of condensation, and to practical men condensation is what you find on a highball glass at 5:30 in the afternoon." He is correct that materials such as glass, metal, and plastic provide an appropriate surface for change to the liquid phase.

But recall from Chapter 2 that water of sorption in porous and hygroscopic materials should be considered another phase, different from the

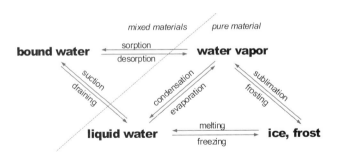

Figure 3-10
Change of phase for pure materials (gas, liquid, and solid) and for mixtures (bound water).

three phases of pure material. So the conversion of water from vapor to sorbed water is not condensation. *Sorption* is a better term, covering adsorption and absorption. Where the accumulation of water on a mirror or a highball glass occurs rarely and only at a discrete set of surface temperature and air humidity conditions, sorption (i.e., *adsorption* or *absorption,* meaning the takeup of water) occurs just about half the time. The other half of the time materials are *desorbing,* giving off moisture. The moisture content of sorptive materials is in constant flux, rising under conditions of higher relative humidity, lessening under conditions of lower relative humidity. But sorptive materials do not have a physical threshold of change in the way that nonsorptive surfaces do. Nonsorptive materials may require a coaster; sorptive materials often are coasters. Later we discuss what secondary conditions might be used as a threshold, distinguishing acceptable from unacceptable building envelope assemblies. For now, accumulation of moisture in sorptive materials should be considered half of the normal, unavoidable give and take of stored moisture.

Moisture accumulation occurs in sorptive materials in building envelopes under conditions other than the condition indicated as crossing of the lines on a profile chart. In fact, accumulation occurs any time the surrounding relative humidity rises above the relative humidity to which materials have adjusted, as that indicates a higher moisture content in sorptive materials. This is described below.

When someone says "You'll get condensation," referring to a building envelope assembly, usually the inside surface of the sheathing in cavity construction, we can quickly introduce some doubt if the surface at risk is wood or other sorptive material. The moisture content of the material may be on the uptake. But the appearance of droplets of water, as on the highball glass, cannot occur unless the accumulating porous surface is saturated.

Critical Summary of the Profile Method

For over 50 years the profile method has been the workhorse of moisture analysis in building envelopes. The principal assumptions, as stated above, are:

1. It assumes that water loads are from water vapor contained in the air, and it takes diffusion of that water vapor as the sole transport mechanism.
2. It uses steady-state analysis, which ignores heat storage and moisture storage effects.
3. It takes single values of permeance and thermal resistance, although these values vary widely from sample to sample and as a function of moisture content.

4. It is often interpreted as indicating condensation, when in fact it indicates one instance among others of moisture accumulation in materials.

Any analytic tool contains simplifications, and it has weaknesses as a predictive tool as a consequence of those simplifications. In building envelope assemblies that are unaffected by rainwater entry, where special care has been taken to preclude airflow through the assembly, where there are no cavities or the cavities have no internal convective airflows, and where the effects of sun and nighttime radiant cooling can be ignored, the rates of accumulation indicated by the method in theory are in line with measured values.

The profile method is blind to water problems that occur in building envelopes as a consequence of water accumulation (e.g., from poor flashing) and as a consequence of the flow of humid air through the assembly. Thus, the principal criticism of the profile method is this: It cannot detect types of moisture problems other than those related to diffusion. A very informal survey among building science colleagues seems to indicate that diffusion-related moisture problems account for less than 1% of the moisture problems found in buildings. We have been seriously sidetracked by the emphasis the profile method has received in the last 50 years.

The profile method has been widely misused. Many users have completed steps 1 through 7, discovered a crossing of the vapor pressure and saturation vapor pressure lines, and concluded that condensation and damage are imminent. Let us apply a term to this form of misuse: the *condensation shortcut*. The condensation shortcut has led to wildly exaggerated overpredictions of the likelihood of diffusion-related moisture problems. It has also led to advice on strategies to keep the lines from crossing—especially the requirement for a vapor retarder and for attic ventilation—that now deserve critical review and rethinking.

In summary, when the profile method is applied to building envelope assemblies, particularly those with insulated cavities, the results often show that a surface has a higher vapor pressure than the saturation vapor pressure, an untenable condition. Those users conclude there is "condensation," and they disapprove of that assembly. According to ASHRAE *Handbook— Fundamentals*, Chapter 25, the recognized authority in this area, if at any location the vapor pressure is greater than the saturation vapor pressure, the second stage of calculation must be done. That second stage involves setting the actual vapor pressure equal to the saturation vapor pressure and calculating the net accumulation of water on that surface. If the material is porous and hygroscopic, the user of the method must make a professional estimate of the risk posed by the calculated rate of accumulation. Usually, the rate of accumulation under diffusion is very small and is well within the safe storage capacity of the material. The actual risk can be calculated using transient modeling, which takes into account the storage of heat and moisture in building materials.

Storage of Heat and Moisture

Heat is required to change the temperature of materials. This is true particularly of dense materials [the Greek Letter rho (ρ) is generally used to indicate density]. The measure of thermal storage capacity of materials is specific heat. Specific heat (c) measures the amount of energy needed to raise the temperature of a material (see Table 3-1). The product of density and specific heat is the volumetric heat capacity ($J/m^3{\cdot}K$) or ($Btu/ft^3{\cdot}°F$). This represents the amount of heat needed to raise a certain volume of material to achieve a certain temperature change. Water and many solids have a high volumetric heat capacity; gases have a low volumetric heat capacity.

The profile method presumes that for a given indoor and outdoor temperature, enough time has passed with no change that the temperature gradient has settled in. At steady state, specific heat effects are not evident. The system has no credit for capacitance, it has only resistance. To account for thermal capacity of materials, the modeling must be transient (time dependent) rather than steady state (as discussed below).

Moisture may be stored in materials. We have seen how the moisture content of materials may be described using either a mass or a volume basis. How much water is there in, say, a 20-ft-long 2 × 6 frame wall with plywood and wood siding? The wood in the wall may weigh about 1000 lb,

Table 3-1 Heat transport properties of common materials

Component	Density, ρ		Thermal conductivity, k		Specific heat, c		Diffusivity, $\alpha = k/\rho c$	
	lb_m/ft^3	kg/m^3	$Btu/hr\text{-}ft\text{-}°F$	$W/m{\cdot}K$	$Btu/lbm°F$	$J/kg{\cdot}K$	ft^2/hr	$m^2/s \times 10^6$
Building brick	123.0	1970	0.40	0.7	0.20	800	0.016	0.444
Crown glass	154.0	2470	0.59	1	0.18	750	0.021	0.540
Ice (at 0°C)	57.5	921	1.30	2.24	0.49	2040	0.046	1.192
Sand	94.6	1520	0.19	0.33	0.19	800	0.011	0.271
Eastern white pine[a]	40.0	640	0.06	0.11	0.39	1700	0.004	0.101
Water	62.3	1000	0.348	0.613	1.000	4179	0.006	0.147
Air (50% RH)	0.074	1.1614	0.015	0.0263	0.241	1007	0.854	22.488

Source: ASHRAE HF (2001) except where noted.
[a]From FPL (2000).

half of which is framing lumber and half sheathing and siding. At 12% moisture content, the wall contains 120 lb of moisture. But a house may contain 10 such walls and an equivalent amount of lumber in floors and roof, which means that at equilibrium, the wood alone in a house may account for over a ton of moisture. Add to that the amount of water stored in other cellulosic material, such as drywall covering, books and cotton fabrics (assume 12% moisture content), and gypsum and other mineral materials, and the water stored in a building begins to appear considerable. Compare this to the amount of water stored in the air of a building. A 3000 ft^2 building with 8-ft ceilings contains 24,000 ft^3 of air. The specific volume of typical indoor air is 13.5 ft^3/lb. If the mass humidity ratio is 0.010, the mass of water in the air is 17 lb. It is obvious that the water stored in the building materials outweighs the water contained in the air by a factor of 100 or more. This is not to underestimate the amount of water that occupants may produce. From all uses (respiration, hygiene, cleaning, cooking) a person may produce a ton of moisture per year.

For further proof of the importance of the water stored in materials, imagine, or try, this experiment. Take two jars with tight lids and place a small sugar-cube-size piece of wood in one of the jars (Figure 3-11). Find a relative humidity sensor with a small probe, and place a probe in each of the two jars. Allow the two to come to equilibrium. What happens to the relative humidity if we slowly raise the temperature of the air in the jar? Those familiar with psychrometrics would quickly be able to state what would happen in the jar with air only: The relative humidity would go

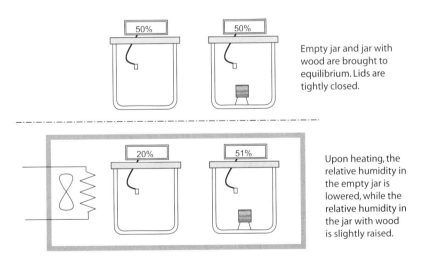

50% 50%

Empty jar and jar with wood are brought to equilibrium. Lids are tightly closed.

20% 51%

Upon heating, the relative humidity in the empty jar is lowered, while the relative humidity in the jar with wood is slightly raised.

Figure 3-11
Setup to study the effect of heating a jar containing air only and a jar containing a small block of wood. The two jars are allowed to come to equilibrium, as shown here. Upon heating in a warm-water bath (as shown), the RH in the air-only jar goes down, but the RH in the jar with wood rises slightly.

down. And in the other jar? In fact, the relative humidity may rise slightly. The amount of water in a small cube of wood that is driven out by warming up the cube will quickly overwhelm the effect that heat has in lowering the relative humidity of the air. To understand this effect, we must study sorption and suction isotherms.

Sorption and Suction Isotherms

Equilibrium is a condition where the net flux across a boundary is zero. Porous and hygroscopic materials may come to equilibrium with the surrounding air. If the air is dry, the materials tend to be dry. Wet materials tend toward equilibrium with wet air. The relationship between humidity conditions in air and the moisture content of materials is shown in the sorption isotherm (*Isotherm* indicates that the temperature is held constant). A sorption isotherm for wood is shown in Figure 3-12.

The chart shows a slight dependence on temperature. This temperature dependence is enough to explain why the relative humidity in a jar containing a small cube of wood goes up instead of down when heated. The amount of water in the wood so strongly overwhelms the humidity in the air of the jar that the system is, in effect, a system with a constant moisture content. Remember, the lid is tight on the jar. So at the same moisture content but a higher temperature, we move slightly to the right on the chart, in the direction of higher relative humidity. Mechanical engineers may be familiar with air in ductwork or metal containment, in which heated air shows lowered relative humidity. But heating a space surrounded by sorptive materials involves some transfer of water from the materials to the surround-

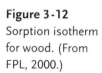

Figure 3-12
Sorption isotherm for wood. (From FPL, 2000.)

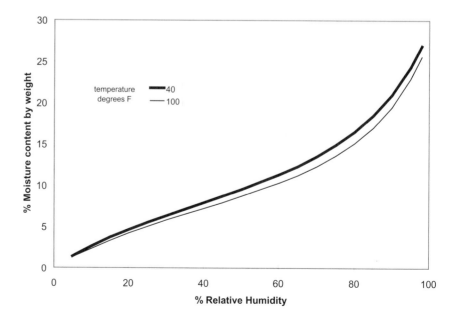

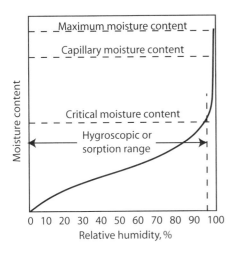

Figure 3-13

Generic curve showing the sorption isotherm range in the lower part of the chart and the suction range for higher material moisture content. The suction range includes moisture content values above the critical moisture content (fiber saturation for organic materials), including the capillary regime. From IEA, 1996.

ing air. It may lower or slightly raise the humidity in the air, depending on the availability of these buffering surfaces as well as the air-change rate in the space.

The slope of the curve relating moisture content to relative humidity is somewhat less steep in the midrange of relative humidity. Sorption isotherms for other materials show the same flattening effect. This means that for changes in relative himudity in this midrange, changes in the moisture content will be relatively small. This could be important for those responsible for historic artifacts and art—changes in moisture content may be small for relative humidity changes in that range.

Sorption refers to the exchange of moisture between the water vapor in the air and bound water in materials. The values in the sorption isotherm chart are approximate. The chart does not show the effects of hysteresis, nor does it show effects for relative humidity above 95%. Those effects are discussed in Chapter 5. As an introduction to this material, however, see Figure 3-13. This chart shows an extension of a sorption isotherm into the range where effects other than relative humidity govern the wetness of the material. Some of the other effects are drainage, capillarity, and osmosis. These effects are measured as the *suction potential*.

FUNDAMENTAL RULE OF MATERIAL WETNESS

Let us try to formulate a rule from previous discussions. Buildings are made primarily from materials that have a measurable moisture content. Materials such as wood, brick, stone, and gypsum are porous, and their chemical constituents provide binding sites for water molecules. The quantity of moisture they contain may vary as a function of surrounding conditions in the air or in adjacent materials. The sorption isotherm shows a close relation between moisture content and relative humidity, and relative humidity can vary with temperature: At the same vapor pressure, warm temperatures lead to low relative humidity, cold temperatures lead to high relative humidity. Cold materials tend to be wet, whereas warm materials tend to be dry. Larry Teesdale wrote quite forcefully that the wetness of material is a function of their temperature.

Let us add a few common, almost trivial observations. Bread kept in the refrigerator gets soggy, bread pulled from the oven is dry. We use heat in the dryer to dry our clothes. (Clothes may also dry outdoors during cold weather, partially and slowly, with sun and other weather conditions playing a part.)

At this point we may propose a general rule regarding the wetness of porous and hygroscopic materials: At the same vapor pressure, *cold materials tend to be wet and warm materials tend to be dry.* If we warm up a material, water molecules bound to the surfaces tend to escape; cool the material down and the water molecules that are whizzing and colliding in space tend to stay once they've landed. Sometimes when asking why a material is wet, we can simply inquire further whether it is warm or cold. I've heard it said that "moisture moves from the warm to the cold." Not exactly—if a warm material is close to a cold material, certainly some of the water molecules may go from one to the other, but there is no "pipeline" between the two materials.

RETHINKING MOISTURE CONTROL STRATEGIES: MOISTURE ENGINEERING

We wish to include the effects of moisture storage in our calculations of building envelope wetness. To achieve this we have to increase the complexity of our calculations. Engineers work with complex calculations regularly in making technical design decisions for buildings.

One example of analysis that is more complex than profile analysis but still rather simple might be the design of a floor system to resist gravity loads. The engineer determines, first, the design loads (live loads and dead loads) to be used as inputs; second, the analytic method (e.g., shear, moment, and deflection calculations, or span tables); and third, the acceptance criteria (e.g., 1/360 deflection). If the engineer works more prescriptively— judging from experience that a certain depth of floor member is correct, for example—that judgment is supported by the experience that comes from repeated uses of the calculation methods. If challenged, the engineer can always "run the numbers." Running the numbers is a way of ensuring proper performance. It is simpler to follow a prescriptive requirement than to ensure performance through calculation. Those who write prescriptive requirements are expected to have performance support for those prescriptions.

But prescriptions are based on assumptions, and often the assumptions that underlie prescriptions are not maintained with the same care as the wording of the prescription itself. So prescriptions may go out of date. Requirements for vapor retarders are predicated on the condensation shortcut of the profile method, and that is certainly out of date. The construction industry should be skeptical of these requirements and undertake a review. In this book we outline how that review process might proceed.

The purpose of a design tool is to create safeguards against future problems with guidance on material selection and composition of building assemblies. No two buildings are subject to exactly the same input conditions: material properties, climate, use, and so on. Design tools are necessary to interpolate from known conditions into individual cases that never quite match precedents from past experience. It is time to retire the use of the profile method as a principal design tool. Another design tool must take its place.

The approach presented here may be termed *moisture engineering*. It uses a definition, or at least a discussion, of loads, analysis, and criteria that can lead to design decisions. This is the approach that is being adopted by a proposed ASHRAE Standard 160P, "Design Criteria for the Prevention of Moisture Problems in Buildings."

Loads

Where does the water that affects building envelope assemblies come from? The greatest quantity of water comes as liquid water that splashes on the roof and walls. Roof leaks should never be considered acceptable. Some argue that roof systems should be designed to admit a small amount of leakage. Indeed, old roofing systems, with tiles or slates on spaced lath, with an open unconditioned attic below, probably underwent a fair amount of water entry and did not suffer. Modern roofing materials are not designed to permit drying, so they should not leak, and building assemblies should not be expected to forgive roof leaks.

Wind-driven rain can move water through facade elements. The amount of rain hitting a facade is discussed below, but it is a function of (1) the design rainfall, (2) the coincident wind speed, (3) the part of the building (edges are hardest hit), and (4) the amount of overhang protection for the wall. Wall surfaces contain cracks. The cracks may be well designed and necessary, such as the overlaps in clapboards or control and expansion joints; or they may be unintentional and deleterious, such as leaks at windows or openings created by movements of materials. If the facade treatment involves several layers of weather protection, such as underlayment beneath cladding, risk to the interior of the wall is greatly reduced.

How much water gets past a weather barrier for design purposes? The question is quite difficult to answer given the variations in buildings, how they change over time, and the conditions to which they are subject. Moreover, water penetration is never uniform but is concentrated at the sites of leakage. For starters, we might say that the question has two answers: either zero or some nonzero value. To date, the presumed design value has been zero; that is, we have not designed building envelopes so that they are capable of drying water that enters accidentally. ASHRAE Standard 160 asserts the need to use a nonzero value for bulk water load. Just what that value is can be debatable, but it is likely to be between 1 and 4% of the amount of water that is applied to a vertical wall. This represents a shift in concern from the wetting potential of a wall system to the drying potential.

Consider a basic risk analysis of a wall system in which we estimate the likelihood of a water problem, and compare that to the severity of the problem. From a long-term-durability point of view, it may be preferable to increase the likelihood of occasional wetting slightly if we achieve a significant reduction in severity, that is, an increase in the ability of a wetted wall to dry out. (This is not intended as a legal opinion, which would probably differ.) Including a vapor retarder reduces the wetting potential associated with vapor pressure difference and reduces the drying potential. As long as the design emphasis remains on wetting, vapor retarders will continue to be recommended. When design emphasis shifts to improved drying potential, vapor retarders will not be recommended. Which is better? Given the fact that a very small percentage of building problems (1 to 5% at most in the author's experience) are associated with wetting by water vapor diffusion, the argument for enhanced drying potential becomes much stronger. I would recommend that for design purposes we assume that 2% of the water that impinges on a wall traverses a weather barrier: brick, wood cladding, vinyl siding, stucco finish. Our models are not sophisticated enough at this point to do much more than model that water being distributed evenly at the back side of the weather barrier. Future computer work may allow more realistic models, with local wet spots.

Profile analysis is predicated on the assumption that the water that will damage building envelopes is found in indoor humidity, which is to be excluded from building cavities. In fact, the most damaging water may be accidental water entry, which must be able to evaporate from building cavities. These two understandings of loads lead to widely different advice governing the use of vapor retarders, as we shall see below.

Analysis

Most models of hygrothermal performance of building envelopes use computers to calculate the temperature and water distribution using finite-difference modeling. With these models, the assembly is discretized into individual nodes. Heat and moisture are transferred from one node to adjacent nodes, depending on the potential (temperature or vapor pressure) and the transfer value (conductivity or vapor permeance). For the computer model, each node "knows" only the material transfer properties that surround it and the potentials of the neighboring nodes. One example of the use of nodes is shown in Figure 3-9. When nature and the wall itself are calculating the thermal gradient, one particle within the wall does not refer to the sum of the R-value. Iterative calculations make it possible to calculate the gradient, as nature does, simply from the conditions of neighboring nodes.

For two-dimensional modeling, in the case of uniform conductivity, the midvalue is the average of the four surrounding values. To model transfer with both resistance and storage requires modeling over time. This is *transient modeling*, as opposed to steady-state modeling. The time scale must be discretized as well as the dimension scale. We can solve for any node m (or node m,n in two dimensions) at time $p + 1$ if we know the conditions at time p.

Additional complexity can be added to the analysis, but each additional complexity not only adds computational time but may affect the stability of the calculation. Unstable solutions cause the program to crash, with out-of-range values. A basic hygrothermal model would allow one-dimensional calculation of temperature and vapor pressure, given changing conditions of indoor and outdoor temperature, with constant values for thermal conductivity, heat storage, vapor permeance, and moisture storage. A more complex model might add:

- Heat transfer properties as a function of moisture content
- Sorption coefficients as a function of temperature and moisture content
- Liquid transport coefficients as a function of temperature and moisture content
- Latent effects, that is, the change in temperature associated with sorption and desorption of vapor
- The ability of the model to permit indoor vapor pressure to vary with outdoor vapor pressure, as occurs in dwellings
- Easy input
- Eye-catching output

The U.S. National Institute for Standards and Technology (Doug Burch) in the 1990s developed the transient hygrothermal computer model MOIST.[2] NIST conducted studies that provided:

- Sorption isotherm values for moisture content as a function of relative humidity (but not temperature)

---

[2] Download public domain http://www.nist.gov.

- Capillary transfer or liquid diffusivity as a function of moisture content
- Thermal conductivity as a function of temperature and moisture content
- Vapor permeability as a function of relative humidity

These were incorporated into MOIST. The model was made capable of calculating latent heat effects, and the indoor vapor pressure was allowed to vary. The assembly could be a vertical wall or an inclined roof assembly. It addressed solar effects, and the assembly could be assigned any compass direction facing. The resulting model was quite useful. Validations of the model against measured data demonstrated its utility. The model had limitations. It was not able to accommodate air movement (unintentional leakage or intentional ventilation) through the assembly. Once liquid condensation would form on a low-porosity surface such as polyethylene, the results were not dependable. It could not accommodate the addition of liquid water into assemblies. It was one-dimensional, so it could not capture corner effects.

Contributions of hygrothermal models by other countries were collected and compared by the International Energy Agency (IEA), Annex 24 (1996). Models with greater sophistication will appear soon. One hygrothermal model that has, through its development, sought to include effects identified as significant is WUFI by the Fraunhofer Institute for Building Physics in Germany (Künzel, 1995). It includes capabilities in applying wetting in two dimensions. We may compare the profile method to transient hygrothermal modeling. The results from transient modeling do a much better job of replicating physical processes. They have entirely supplanted the profile method as a design tool. This comes at the expense, however, of tinkering. A user of the profile method sees all the working parts of the calculation, whereas the parts of transient models are contained in computer code and thus are not transparent. The profile method can be compared to a bicycle, hygrothermal computer modeling to a car. But thanks to computer modeling, moisture engineering can provide performance predictions to any reasonable degree of consistency with measured values.

Criteria

What should be used to distinguish acceptable from unacceptable hygrothermal design of building envelopes? As we discussed before, "condensation" cannot be used because condensation—the phenomenological formation of water droplets—does not occur on the surfaces of porous and hygroscopic materials. In general, dry is better than wet. Excessively dry components of building assemblies may crack. But the general threshold is a wetness threshold. Building materials should retain their structural properties. Fasteners and other metal elements should not corrode. The surfaces should not exhibit mold growth. These are the common criteria that are in use. (At times, maintenance of surface coatings has been mentioned as a hygrothermal criterion, but coatings depend so strongly on surface conditions other than temperature and humidity that it is not included here.) Can these conditions be quantified?

The structural properties of most materials are well known. Most materials exhibit thermal expansion and contraction. Vinyl, aluminum, and steel show dimensional changes as a result of temperature change; these three materials are shown in order of decreasing thermal coefficient. Porous materials show dimensional change as a result of moisture content as well. Wood has significant dimensional change radially and tangentially but has little dimensional change longitudinally. Thermal expansion and contraction are considered fully elastic; that is, the material recovers fully from any excursion into a high- or low-temperature range. Materials such as vinyl siding must be detailed to accommodate this movement, of course. Wood is considered to be elastic within a range. Wood can be oven-dried such that its properties are different from commercial air- or kiln-dried lumber, but this does not occur in commodity wood. Solid wood can always recover from even the most extreme wetness. Wood products that are composites of wood and resin binders may have a moisture content beyond which there may not be elastic recovery. This would occur any time expansion of the wood ruptures adhesive bonds, as in the delamination of plywood. Many composite wood panel products are available. Elastic moisture content threshold values for these products deserve to be better researched and presented. If wood products show unrecoverable dimension swelling, this may be considered a limit of unacceptability. Composite wood products appear to be more vulnerable to saturation wetting than to wetting as a consequence of equilibrium with a humid atmosphere.

Steel rusts from water contact, of course. Many fasteners are designed to resist rusting through coatings, galvanizing, or by steel alloy selection. The measure of wetness of a surface is the water activity. Water activity measures the vapor pressure at the surface compared to the vapor pressure of saturated material. It corresponds exactly to the relative humidity at the surface. Water activity has been plotted against the corrosive potential. A rough threshold begins to appear in the range of 0.8 water activity (80% surface relative humidity) over a period of time such as a month. Harriman has an excellent discussion of corrosion effects, which may peak for different metals at different relative humidities between 70 and 99%. At too high humidity, oxygen cannot get to the surface (see Figure 3-14).

Mold detracts from physical appearance and in large quantities may give off an odor. Mold growth has traditionally been taken as a sign of bad

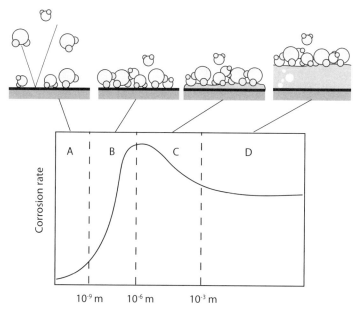

Figure 3-14

Lower rates of corrosion occur under dry conditions and at high humidities, as the film of water may block oxygen from the surface. (From Harriman et al., 2001.)

design and construction. IEA Annex 14 (1994) sought to develop a critical threshold value for wetness in building envelope assemblies. A threshold based on the threshold of mold growth was adopted which they took to be *average water activity greater than 0.8 for one month*. Subsequent studies seem to line up in general support of this value. Note that this Annex 14 finding is expressed in physical, not biological terms. Any model that has surface relative humidity as its output can be used to determine whether or not this criterion is being met. This threshold value is in the process of adoption by ASHRAE 160P.

A humidity threshold that describes excessive humidity for an allowable duration is of primary importance here. Other effects play a role, of course. Building contents that are subject to abrupt changes in humidity may crack.

In summary, moisture engineering is a reality. Selection of design loads must go beyond the traditional selection of indoor vapor pressure toward using liquid water loading as a real and unavoidable occurrence, requiring drying. Computer tools for transient modeling have brought calculated estimates much more in line with measured values. Holding to a criterion of 0.8 water activity average for one month seems to serve as a critical limit value against various forms of damage: swelling, corrosion, and biological growth. With this we bring hygrothermal calculations to the state of sophistication that has been commonplace in structural design and planning for over 100 years.

Roofs and Facades

INTRODUCTION

A roof protects and shelters the space, contents, and occupants beneath. It does this by shading sun and by moving precipitation out of the way. A roof is an exercise in practical geometry. Moving rain and snow is far and away the principal element in ensuring dry, healthful buildings. The guiding principle in the following chapters is this: Determine the quantity of water that must be managed, determine where it goes, and design how to get it there. Moisture problems in buildings begin as water problems, which begin as rain problems. By managing rainwater, we get most of the way toward the goal of delivering dry, healthful buildings.

Building codes provide little regulation of roofing practice. (Attic ventilation is one aspect of roof assemblies that is regulated by building code. It is addressed in Chapter 7.) Instead, roofing is placed in the hands of roofing professionals and providers of roofing products. If a roof leaks, building owners turn to roofing professionals, not to building code officials. Roofs must perform. A garage roof or a barn roof may be forgiven an occasional leak, whereas a chip manufacturing facility, for example, should have no leeway. A roof that fails is very easy to spot, by watermarks on a ceiling or buckets on a floor. A leak that has not yet appeared on the inside of the building, on the other hand, may require an infrared survey to disclose.

RAINFALL INTENSITY, SLOPE, AND WATERTIGHTNESS

Designers must have a design rainfall in mind for any building project. Rates of rainfall are available from local airports or from the National Oceanic and Atmospheric Administration (NOAA), and most data are downloadable. Desingers must know the snow load, of course, for structural code compliance. In addition to the design rainfall amount, designers should keep in mind a value for design rain-carrying wind speed, the horizontal component of rainfall. This will be helpful in estimating the benefits of over-hangs for buildings and for openings. The U.S. location that is known for water damage to sheathing during an EIFS (external insulation and finish system) crisis (more on that later) is Wilmington, North Carolina, located at the far eastern point of the state, where hurricane winds are able to project rain into cracks that would otherwise stay quite dry.

In addition to rain amounts and concurrent wind, designers should be familiar with the types of rainfall for their area. Hurricane, gully washer, heavy dew—all have impacts on design approaches common in water protection. Estimating the vertical speed of rainfall may help with estimates of how much wind will be thrown against a building for a given wind speed. How can the downward speed of a raindrop be measured? The way I found was to place a 45°-angle line on a car window, then drive through a rainstorm, asking a passenger in the car to say when the streaks of rain seemed to follow the line on the window. The car speed is the falling speed of the raindrops. The rain I measured seemed to fall at 20 or 25 mph, but these were for rather large droplets.

For any design rainfall, the density of flow may vary depending on the roof geometry. Rain should flow off the roof, of course. Rain that does not forms *ponding,* and ponding, as we shall see, is the condition most strongly associated with roof failure in low-slope systems (see Figure 4-1). For vertical rainfall we can imagine a projected roof in plan. High points and ridges will encounter only incident rainfall. Farther down the slope the density of flow represents the sum of the incident rainfall plus the contribution

Figure 4-1

Ponding on a ballasted low-slope roof.

from upstream. If the downhill run is 20 ft, a square foot at the eaves will experience a quantity of water that is 20 times that encountered by a square foot of roof at the ridge.

Valleys are quite special water-conducting surfaces. The quantity of water in a valley may be much greater than elsewhere on a roof (see Figure 4-2). The lower figure shows the geometry of the roof system, which includes a valley. The second figure represents a calculation of the rainfall density. The valley sees much more rainfall than any other part of the roof. In particular, the low end of the valley sees the most. This is *funneling*, the concentration of an area into a line and the concentration of a line into a discharge point. The point at the bottom of a valley receives rainwater from two entire triangular roof sections uphill on either side of the valley. It should be no wonder that the likelihood of damage is greatest in valleys or wherever the concentration is greatest. The same is true for low-slope roof assemblies (see Figure 4-3). The roof is a low-slope roof with two valleys that lead to a scupper. Note how much water is shoveled through the scupper at the discharge point. High-volume discharge points such as these should be detailed much for concentration, like the spouts of pitchers perhaps.

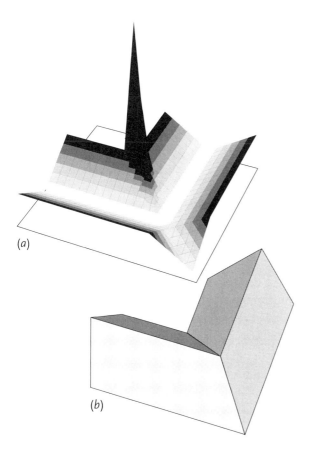

(a)

(b)

Figure 4-2
Water concentration (*a*) on a steep-slope roof (*b*) will be a strong function of the roof geometry. Note the funneling effect of a roof valley and the resulting concentration.

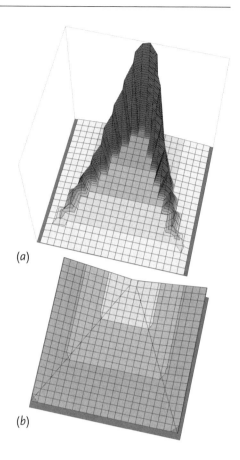

(a)

(b)

Figure 4-3
Low-slope roof assembly (b) that discharges to a scupper at the edge of the roof, and concentrations of water at each location on the roof (a).

One way of dealing with increased concentration is by increased slope. If water is channeled to a location of high concentration, increased slope can relieve the *dwell time* of water on the surface. The slope of a valley at the intersection of two sloped sections is less than the downward slope of the roof. This is evident by noting that for the same rise, the run of a valley is equal to the run of the slope times 1.414. Anyone who has walked a steep roof knows the relative ease of walking a valley. (Careless investigators may also know the ease of stepping through roofing materials in the valley.)

Figure 4-4 shows a condition called a *horizontal* or *dead valley*. Here two planes intersect to form a horizontal line that cannot drain. Ponding is practically assured. Complex picturesque roofscapes were popular during late Victorian and Edwardian times in England. The technology of the day involved soldering the flat seams that joined small sheets of lead or copper. They required frequent maintenance.

A second detail that seems to have arisen in that period is the *plugged valley*. Valleys are hard enough to flash correctly without imposing a giant impediment squarely in the pathway of the evacuating water (see Figure 4-5). The roofscape shown in Figure 4-6, combining a horizontal valley and a plugged valley, performs as poorly as it looks.

Figure 4-7
Drop of water on the granule-coated top side of an asphalt shingle. Note the slightly acute contact angle (measured within the water droplet).

If we made a capillary tube of asphalt shingle material, the water might rise slightly or descend slightly, but we would not expect surface attraction to cause the mating surfaces of shingles to fill with water by capillary attraction. The surfaces are not sorptive, at least as manufactured. But the nature of the surface may change over time. As dirt accumulates, the surface becomes more sorptive. Granules tend to dislodge, leaving crevices that can become residence sites for water. This can be more pronounced as ultraviolet radiation embrittles and water erodes the exposed bitumen.

Can water climb up the space between the shingles, shown in Figure 4-9? Neither the lower granule surface nor the overhead bitumen surface are strongly sorptive, and they have an nearly right-angle contact angle. So, no, water will not rise in the capillary space by surface attraction. Plus, gravity

Figure 4-8
Drop of water on the back side of an asphalt shingle. Note the nearly slightly acute contact angle.

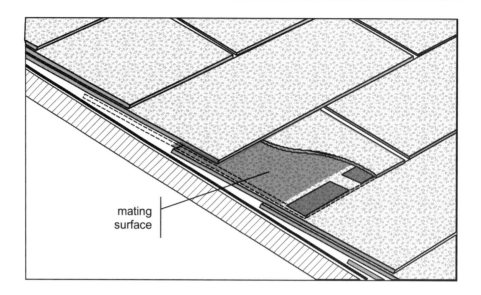

Figure 4-9
Mating surface between upper and lower shingles of an asphalt shingle surface. Water is unlikely to enter into the mating surface, but once in it is difficult to remove.

mating surface

keeps water out and the spots of sealant, shown in the figure, block water entry. Wind, however, can drive water up between the shingles, and once it is in it could be quite a chore to get it back out. Heat of the sun will turn much of the water to vapor; some of that may escape to the outdoors, and some may push through sheathing paper and sheathing toward the inside. The effect may be small, but solar-driven vapor from shingle roof systems may be an effect deserving attention. The problem of solar-driven moisture is described later.

Low-slope roof systems may employ several materials as the waterproofing surface. Built-up roofs (BURs) are traditional. They are composed of successive overlapping layers of reinforcing, usually fiberglass, laid in successive coatings of asphalt or coal-tar pitch. Asphalt cures to a mass that remains solid; coal-tar pitch may "float" in hot weather, possibly welding any cracks or discontinuities that occurred. Single-ply roofs rely on excellent waterproofing of joints. Single-ply roofs may be of rubber [ethylene-propylenediene monomer (EPDM)] bitumen modified with APP (atactic polypropylene) or SBS (styrene–butadiene–styrene), various thermoplastics such as PVC, or several other systems. Standing-seam metal roofs are a very popular form of low-slope roof; they are particularly suited to simple roofs because of the need to accommodate thermal expansion and contraction of the metal panels.

Let's look at a leak in a somewhat idealized low-slope roof system, composed of EPDM rubber membrane over a wood-based medium-density fiberboard recover board over a metal deck (see Figure 4-10). Assume, for starters, that there are air gaps at A and B. The first task that water has is to make it through the gap in the EPDM. The surface energy of EPDM is slightly lower that the surface energy of water, so it is slightly hydrophobic, and the contact angle is slightly greater than 90°. If we made a capillary tube of EPDM, the water would descend slightly. In fact, calculating how far the water would descend though the experiment might be quite difficult to pull off in practice. We use the relation from Chapter 2:

$$h = \frac{2\gamma \cos \theta}{r\rho_e g} \tag{4-1}$$

- The surface tension of water $\gamma = 0.0728$ J/m^2.
- The contact angle $\theta = 110°$ (say), so $\cos \theta = -0.342$.
- The radius $r = 1$ mm (say).
- The density of water $\rho_e = 1$ g/cm^3.
- The acceleration of gravity $g = 9.8$ m/s^2.

We calculate from this $h = -2.54$ mm. In other words, it would take a hydraulic head of -2.54 mm of water to push water through a hole of 1 mm radius (airgap A). The quantity 2.54 mm is 0.1 in. of water. If the water film is no deeper than $\frac{1}{10}$ in., the EPDM could be full of holes (of this radius) and the water would simply bridge over the holes. If the ponding were deeper, the hydraulic head could accomplish the task of pushing water through the opening. The ponding would have to be slightly deeper to overcome the surface tension, as the water would begin to escape from the opening.

The fiberboard beneath the EPDM is very sorptive. Water that gets to the fiberboard is adsorbed to the fiber surface and absorbed into the spaces between the fibers. When loaded with liquid water, most fiberboard can easily double in weight. The material was not designed for wetting. Wetting can swell the fibers and dissolve the adhesive bonds holding the fibers to-

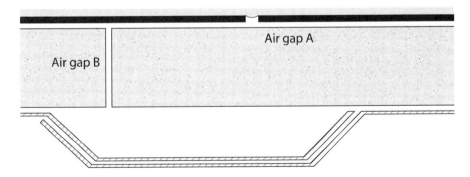

Figure 4-10
Roof composed of three layers: a top waterproofing layer of EPDM, an insulation layer of fiberboard, and a metal structural deck. Because of surface tension, water above the black membrane cannot penetrate a 1-mm-diameter hole in the membrane without the pressure of 2 to 3 mm of water thickness above the hole.

gether. But any water sorbed into the fiberboard is still in the assembly and still might not be considered a leak into the building.

Water may flow or it may diffuse through any medium, including air and liquid-permeable materials. When water drips onto a porous, hygroscopic material such as wood pulp fiberboard, it is first adsorbed onto the exposed chemical radicals of the cellulose (and to a lesser extent, lignin) molecules. Then it is absorbed into the matrix of fibers, filling first the interstices at branches and intersections of fibers. Third, it fills the available pores. Fourth, once the matrix is saturated, water may run across the surface, and with sufficient head, gravity may move water downward. Water may move through material or it may choose to reside in the material; it has liquid conductivity and moisture storage; and it has resistance and capacitance. The ratio of conductivity to storage is diffusivity. Diffusion mass transfer is omnidirectional as opposed to surface flow and gravity drainage, which are directional. Diffusion moves material from wet to dry regardless of direction. With a point source of water we may imagine a hemisphere of water that increases in size over time and that has a gradient measured radially outward from the point of impact. Assume that the rate of water contribution is uniform and constant. We can imagine a hemisphere at which the water concentration is a constant. The radius from impact out to that hemisphere increases over time, but the rate of increase diminishes over time. What does increase linearly is the surface area of this constant-concentration hemisphere. To picture diffusion, we might picture a hemisphere or a sphere enlarging linearly in area. The units of diffusion flux are m^2/s or ft^2/sec—area over time. You may see diffusion flux represented as length over the square root of time as well.

This "bubble" image works up to the limits of the sorption and matric potentials, but once those are satisfied, gravity takes over. And once again a water head overcomes the cohesive surface tension of the water that we see in incipient droplets on the underside of a leak. The head of water at a joint in the panel or within the thickness of the material is needed to push the reluctant droplets off from the porous but saturated surface.

Then it drops to the metal. Galvanized steel has a surface activity close to that of water. The contact angle is close to a right angle. At a hole it may bridge over smooth openings. But it is likely to be affected by roughness, by exposed steel, which, when oxidized, is very hydrophilic. Steel may have coatings or oils that will affect its properties, usually rendering it more hydrophobic. Dirt, too, can turn low-energy surfaces that bead water into high-energy surfaces that bind water—to the dirt, at least. Once on the underside it may attach itself to the metal and begin to drop down only after a small accumulation.

The upshot of this is that for a leak to send water actively through an assembly to the inside of the building, a hydraulic head or similar driving force must be provided. A hole, by itself, doesn't lead to leakage. So avoiding a hydraulic head in a roof design is generally more effective than trying to ensure lifelong watertightness of the upper membrane.

Two conditions provide hydraulic head: ponding and funneling. To avoid ponding on large roofs, ensure a minimum slope, usually $\frac{1}{4}$ in. to the foot, and avoid dead valleys. On large buildings it is best to provide the slope with inclination of the structure. On other roofs and complex roofs, the slope can be assured using tapered insulation. For funneling, design the discharge end so that water is effectively placed where it is supposed to go. Imagine a spout on a pitcher: The low ends of the flashing should be that effective.

Design for future repairs. Repairs need to be done at the sites of greatest concentration. Repairs will need to be done in those places that see the greatest concentration. Shingle roof systems allow several types of valley designs: open, cut, and laced (or woven). Of the three, only the open valley lends itself to handsome repair. Anyone who has seen mismatched valley shingles in a cut or laced valley would agree.

Another effective way to design for repair is to use a *sump*, a depression lower than the contributing roof surface (see Figure 4-11). A sump provides several advantages. For one thing, the thermal insulation at a sump is likely to be less than for the remainder of the roof. Strategic heat loss may be the perfect solution to drains and scuppers that ice up. For another, it provides a good distinction for maintenance, where cleaning the sump becomes a

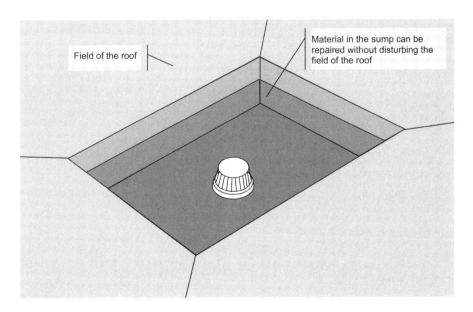

Figure 4-11
Sump in at a low-slope roof drain. Creating a sump allows for repairs to be limited to the sump area, not to the entire field area of the roof.

shorter chore (although perhaps more frequent) than cleaning leaves and debris from an entire roof. But the principal advantage in a sump is reparability. Imagine repairing a drain or scupper that requires adding new roof surface material. That can certainly be added, but the uphill edge of the new material is reverse-shingled; so more material can be added to counterflash, but the new material is still reverse-shingled at the uphill side; and so on. A sump, however, allows a repair to be effective and local, leaving the bulk of the roof intact.

What we've learned about a contact angle can help us design a *drip edge*. The purpose of any drip edge is to cause drips from the edges of materials. It is also to interrupt flow along the underside of materials. See Figure 4-12a, which shows water in contact with a surface making contact angle θ. As the surface is rotated, the water surface will, at one point, appear flat (Figure 14-12b). The optical appearance of a flat surface can help in making an estimate of this otherwise difficult angle measurement. The angle of the water against a vertical wall is the condition found in a capillary tube. If we continue the rotation (Figure 14-12d), we find the ideal angle for a drip edge surface—the angle at which water cannot climb back upward.

A practical application of this is in the proper installation of a drip edge (Figure 4-13). Metal drip edge comes in several styles; style D is shown. Installed properly, as in Figure 4-13a, the angle of the underside of the drip

Figure 4-12
If water makes a contact angle of q with a surface (*a*), then inclining the surface (*b*) can help measure the contact angle. (Use the reflection in the water surface.) Knowing the contact angle may help in design of a drip edge (*d*).

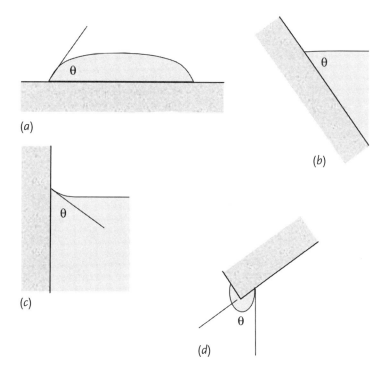

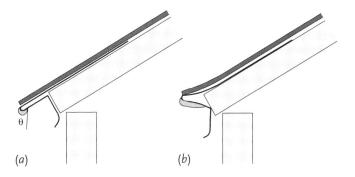

(a)   *(b)*

Figure 4-13
Contact angle of water with coated metal may be used to demonstrate a form of damage from a common construction defect—forcing the drip edge.

edge is less than the contact angle. If squashed into place (Figure 14-13*b*), water will not drip from the edge without a boost from momentum. The contact angle is also used to prevent dripping in some gutter leaf guards. These use a flow surface above the gutter that curves down and in, keeping contact with most of the water while letting leaves and debris fly past. These designs need special treatment at valleys, due, of course, to the much higher water concentration in those locations.

A roof system is composed of fields and flashings. Flashing occurs at the edges of fields. Fields are easy—they are intended to be waterproofed. Flashings are difficult—they are, by definition, interruptions in the field. Let's look at four flashing conditions: curb, wall, valley, and chimney. An excellent source for flashing information is the SMACNA (2004) *Architectural Sheet Metal Manual,* a handbook famous for the clarity and beauty of the drawings. See also the NRCA (2001) *Roofing and Waterproofing Manual* and the Canada Mortgage and Housing Corporation's *Best Practice Guide: Flashing* (CMHC, 2001).

A *curb* is an upright termination of a field (see Figure 4-14). The easiest curb is typically a simple turn-up of the field membrane. It is usually

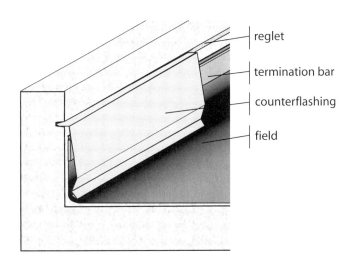

reglet

termination bar

counterflashing

field

Figure 4-14
A curb contains flashing—in this case an upturned edge of roofing membrane and counterflashing inserted into a reglet.

covered with counterflashing or is taken up a parapet to the underside of the coping. The counterflashing shown is let into a reglet or groove in the substrate. The height of a curb flashing is usually dictated by the snowload. The bottom 10% or so of a snowmass may be slush. Slush may behave as a liquid and may provide a hydraulic head for water entry well above the plane of the roof. Design curb heights have been marching steadily upward, from 6 in. to 8 in. and 12 in. Special care needs to be taken at the triple point where the roof plane meets the intersection of two curbs. The resulting conditions are usually addressed using materials such as uncured neoprene, which can conform to the shape of the triple intersection.

Wall flashing can take several forms, but a particularly interesting one is shown in Figure 4-15. How should water on the roof be drawn effectively into the gutter? Step flashing is usually applied at each shingle and applied against the sheathing of the wall. The siding material then serves as the counterflashing. Any water that happens to be running down the flashing finds itself deposited between the cladding and sheathing at the lower end. Up until 1992, the National Roofing Contractors Association *Roofing and*

Figure 4-15
Example of a roof that runs along the wall. The cladding (stucco in this case) acts as counterflashing. Water running down the flashing cannot enter the gutter but goes into the wall instead.

Waterproofing Manual showed details of exactly that. This changed, however, as problems with EIFS cladding became apparent in the 1990s (more on that below). Then it became clear that the water that runs down the angle of the step flashing (worse when wind blows toward the siding) falls into the space between the siding and the sheathing at the discharge end of the flashing. This water needs to be diverted to the outdoors and into the gutter. When this is not done, the resulting condition is seen as some form of water damage—paint peeling in the case shown in Figure 4-15. To get the water out into the gutter, NRCA and others now recommend a *kickout flashing* that turns the water back out toward the gutter at the bottom of the flashing run. I would prefer making that flashing out of neoprene or other rubber materials, which is much easier to contort past the many intersecting planes. Another approach, best used with EIFS or other cladding with a fixed thickness out from the sheathing, involves placing a board of treated material at least the thickness of the cladding against the sheathing, as shown in Figure 4-16. At the bottom of the flashing run, the flashing material is outboard of the cladding.

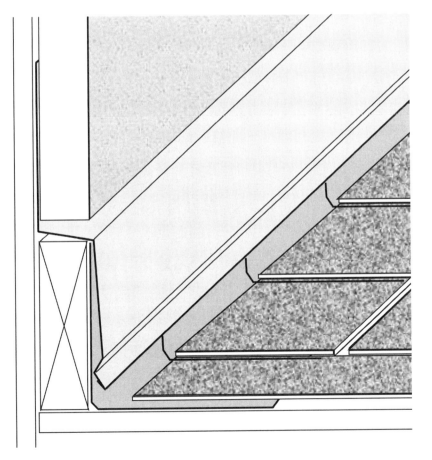

Figure 4-16
Use of a wood spacer at the step flashing to ensure that water at the flashing is deposited outboard of the finish material, not behind. The finish shown is EIFS.

Three types of valley flashing are common with asphalt shingle roofs. The best performer uses the inverted-V style of flashing shown in Figure 4-17, which helps ensure that water that is zooming down one plane of the roof is not inclined to be carried up the flashing on the other side. There are at least two other methods for flashing a valley. In a cut valley, one face is shingled at a time. Shingles from the first face are brought across the valley to the other side. Then the second face is shingled, allowing the valley to be overlapped, and the shingles on the second face are carefully cut along a line snapped up the valley. The cut shingle edges are held in place with roof cement. In a woven or laced valley, the two faces are shingled at the same time and the shingles that cross the valley are simply laced neatly.

Snow will sit in a valley, and the waterproofing behind the valley should extend sufficiently high in the valley to overcome the hydraulic head of slush. To get a sense of the design snow height, I know of no better way than cruising a project region after a large snowfall. The waterproofing material commonly used is self-adhering modified bitumen underlayment.

Chimney flashing is usually considered the classic difficult flashing condition requiring the best workmanship and detailing. A chimney protruding from a point high in the roof, up near the ridge, is very forgiving. A chimney installed in a sloped plane of a roof is a standard condition. It has four triple points. The flashing elements are shown in Figure 4-18. A cricket at the uphill side diverts water to the two sides of the chimney. The triple points at each corner of the cricket require solder or sealant. The flashing

Figure 4-17

Open valley with V-crimped metal valley flashing. This type of valley has the best performance and lends itself to repairs.

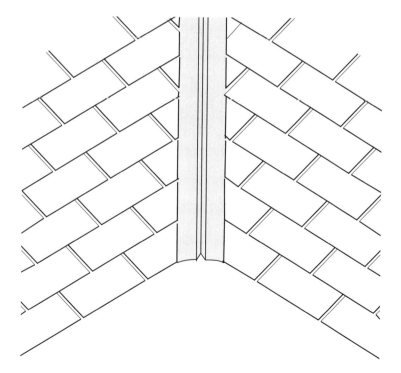

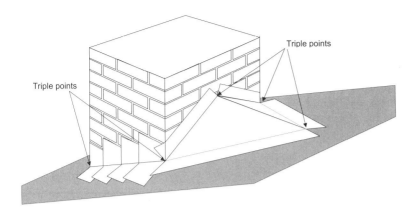

Triple points

Triple points

Figure 4-18
Flashing at the side of a chimney and cricket behind the chimney. The upturned edges must then be covered with counterflashing (not shown in this drawing). Shingles cover the flat part uphill of the cricket and are interlaced with the step flashing.

at each side is standard wall flashing, with another triple point at the downhill corner. The flashing across the bottom edge is standard curb flashing. This flashing requires counterflashing to cover the upper edges of the flashing material and is let into a reglet in the masonry. The counterflashing is not shown in the figure.

Canada Mortgage and Housing Corporation's *Best Practice Guide: Flashing* (CMHC, 2001) shows an interesting variation. If the triple point is so troublesome, why not design the flashing so that triple points are avoided? See Figure 4-19. On the uphill side, a simple curb flashing of a single length of material is applied. It has a smooth transition from the flat of the roof to the vertical part. Snow can sit here, so the shingles are held up-

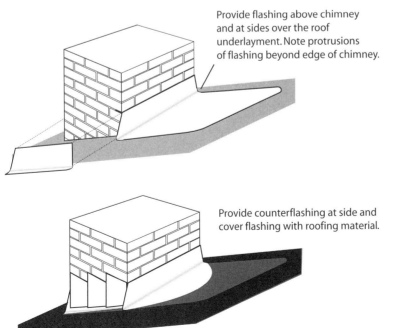

Provide flashing above chimney and at sides over the roof underlayment. Note protrusions of flashing beyond edge of chimney.

Provide counterflashing at side and cover flashing with roofing material.

Figure 4-19
Chimney flashing designed to avoid the triple point. (From CMHC, 2001.)

hill from this flashing. There is no cricket. The important detail is this: The flashing material extends out on either side beyond the box of the chimney by several inches. Water that drains from the end of the flashing begins its downward path well away from the side flashing. There is a triple point where the side flashing meets the back of the uphill flashing, but there is practically no water at that point. The wall flashing, too, extends beyond the triple point. In the drawing that flashing is shown as continuous rather than step flashing. All of the flashing materials shown in the drawing require counterflashing, which is not shown. A sloped piece of continuous flashing can be counterflashed with step counterflashing let into a reglet at the top. This Canadian approach shows much better rainwater management than its classical predecessor. Some, however, may find the obviousness of the water management projections objectionable. I don't; rather, I would recommend to designers that water management details no longer be kept out of the public view.

We cannot leave a discussion of roof systems without mention of the airfoil roof (Figure 4-20). You've seen this roof shape—it seems emblematic of architecture of the 1990s. I find it curious that literature on building design seems to ignore its own brainchild: Why this form, and why now? That may be a topic for another book; here we look at the performance. The roofing material typically used is standing-seam metal. (Flat-seam

Figure 4-20
Airfoil roof, the roof shape emblematic of 1990s architecture. All roof shapes have performance implications.

metal roofs went out with the soldering pot using molten lead.) The ribs, of course, follow the line of the curve; otherwise, the system would not drain. Standing-seam metal roofs are composed of a flat section with upturned edges, and those edges are sheltered from rain in a wide variety of ways, making a standing-seam rib. The higher the rib, the more protection the roof has against slush load and wind-driven rain. The panels are usually cold-rolled from flat stock to produce the ribs. The higher the ribs, the greater the weather protection. To make the panels conform to the curve, either they must be rolled to the curved shape (quite expensive and difficult, especially if the curve changes radius) or the rib height must be reduced (compromising the water integrity.) Kerfing the ribs is of course out of the question. If the rib height is sacrificed, additional clips must be used to fasten the panels to the roof, given the tendency for straight panels to regain their straightness. The most common form of roof failure is from wind uplift (i.e., the wind tends to pick up the panels), and bending the panels seems to encourage this form of failure. Not only that, but the shape of the roof itself—an airfoil roof!—seems to compound the problem. It seems odd or typical, depending on one's point of view, that a form so troublesome could become so emblematic.

ICE DAMS

In northern climates, overhangs can lead to ice damming. The causes and cures of ice damming are the subject of much building mythology, so a building science approach might help a bit. Snow provides thermal insulation; its insulating value depends on many factors, but it may lead directly to heat buildup in the attic. This heat buildup can cause melting. Ice dams occur when the snow on a roof melts at the underside of the snowmass, then refreezes. Old images of a mass of ice at the low end of a roof have been corrected by Canadian researchers, who provided Figure 4-21. What was absent from earlier ice dam sections was the lens of ice that extends uphill. It is this lens that allows the buildup of water, providing a water head sometimes several feet in height. This head provides the driving force that is moving water indoors.

Ice dams usually occur at isolated locations on a roof. Ice dams that occur all along a roof edge are the exception, not the rule, and they occur primarily in frigid climates. The isolated locations are found (1) at discrete heat sources inside the attic and (2) at valleys. The stovepipe chimney shown in Figure 4-22 is an obvious heat source. We would expect snow near the heat pipe to be melted much more quickly than snow elsewhere on the roof. Then notice the valley. Ice dams form much more readily in valleys than elsewhere on a roof. For one thing, water concentrates in a valley, so ice dams and icicles are much more prevalent there. Also, the snow pack is

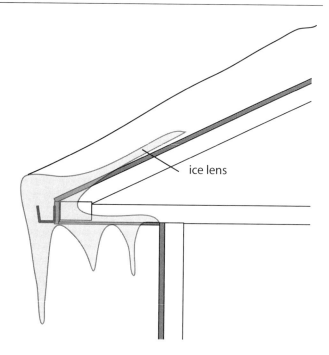

Figure 4-21
Actual profile of the ice in an ice dam event. Ice form within the snow mass, not just at the eaves, and snowmelt from above is directed into the attic. (From CMHC, 1999a.)

higher in a valley than elsewhere on the roof. This means that the roof temperature there is closer to the interior temperature than is the temperature on the rest of the roof.

So what to do about an ice dam on the roof? Look where it is located and judge what to do from there. Near a chimney? Check that the chimney is safe and lot leaking, or shift to heating equipment that does not make use of a chimney. Near ductwork? Look for leaks in the ductwork and "holidays" in the completeness of insulation surrounding the ductwork. Near openings in the ceiling? Block them closed; the wide variety of accessories used for firestopping would do nicely.

What about venting? In Chapter 7 we discuss attic venting in detail. For now, let's investigate its potential for solving the ice dam problem. In extremely cold climates such as northern Canada, venting is a must. The same is true for roofs that show ice damming around the entire eaves area. But in general, no, venting does not solve an ice damming problem. Wayne Tobiasson and his colleagues at the U.S. Army Cold Regions Research and Engineering Laboratory determined that an ice dam problem is worst when the outdoor air temperature is 20 to 22°F. If the underside of the roof can be kept at a temperature below freezing, ice dams do not pose a problem. Tobiasson et al. (1994) showed that *if* we assume that the only heat to the attic is the heat transferred by conduction through the ceiling insulation, *then* the heat carried out by the air (in at 22°F, out at 32°F) is consistent with the airflow rates we find in vented assemblies. We need to assume as well that the vents are not blocked by snow. Given his assumption that the sole

Figure 4-22
Ice dam. Two causes of the ice damming in this location—the heating stovepipe and the valley—are obvious. (From Rogers, 1964.)

heat source is ceiling conduction, he concludes that venting can work. Suppose we take his findings further; suppose that under the conditions he describes, we choose to block the vents. Then some snow melts to liquid water. The critical constant here is the heat of fusion (or enthalpy of fusion): 143.5 Btu/lb$_{m\ water}$. This is the amount of heat necessary to covert water held as ice or snow into liquid water. For a set of conditions such as those shown in Table 4-1, the attic air temperature can easily be calculated. If the temperature is above freezing, it is easy to calculate the rate of melting, using the excess heat to melt the snow on the roof. For the example given in the table, we find that a total of 2 ft^3/day will be formed. If that were spread evenly across a 2-ft overhang of a house with a 2000-ft^2 footprint, the thickness of the ice/water would be less than $\frac{1}{8}$ in. thick. Any building that has an ice dam representing greater than this daily melting rate would not match some of the assumptions made for the sake of calculation. The first assumption to go, especially where melting is nonuniform around the attic, is the assumption of conductive heat loss only. Chances are that most ice dams one is likely to find in the United States will be due to a heat source other than ceiling conduction.

The upshot of this should be clear: To correct existing ice dams, identify the vagrant heat source and correct it. For new building design there are two approaches. Construct the attic so that a continuous sandwich of insulation is at the roof plane, thus keeping the equipment in the conditioned space. Or, in an unconditioned attic space, avoid locating equipment there, make sure that any ducts are airtight and well insulated, pipes should be well insulated, and the ceiling should be made airtight. Venting is limited in its ability to dilute excess heat—limited by low quantities of flow through

Table 4-1 Calculation of the mass of snowmelt, assuming heat loss is by conduction only[a, b]

Constants

Density of water	D_{water}	62	lb/ft^3
Heat of fusion-water	H_f	143.5	Btu/lb_m
Specific heat of air	C_{air}	0.24	$Btu/lb_m\text{-}°F$
Specific volume of air	V_{air}	12.5	ft^3/lb
Snow R-value	r_{snow1}	1	hr-ft^2-°F/Btu-in.

Inputs

Attic insulation area	A_{attic}	2000	ft^2	
Roof area	A_{roof}	3000	ft^2	
Snow depth	D_{snow}	24	in.	
Indoor air temperature	T_i	70	°F	
Outdoor air temperature	T_o	22	°F	
Critical attic temperature	T_a	32	°F	
Attic insulation R-value	R_{attic}	38	hr-ft^2-°F/Btu	Represents 1/2 of 1/300
Vent section area	A_{vent}	3.33	ft^2	

Calculations

Total snow R-value	R_{snow}	24	hr-ft^2-°F/Btu	$=r_{snow1}*D_{snow}$
Temperature difference across insulation	dT_{insul}	38	°F	$=T_i\text{-}T_a$
Temperature difference across snow	dT_{snow}	10	°F	$=T_a\text{-}T_o$
Heat loss across insulation	Q_{insul}	2000	Btu/hr	$=A_{attic}*dT_{insul}/R_{attic}$
Heat loss across snow	Q_{snow}	1250	Btu/hr	$=A_{roof}*dT_{snow}/R_{snow}$
Heat for melting	Q_{melt}	750	Btu/hr	$=Q_{insul}\text{-}Q_{snow}$
Rate of melting	V_{melt}	0.084	ft^3/hr	$=Q_{snow}/h_f/D_{water}$

Outputs

Daily rate of ice/water formation	D_{melt}	2.0	ft^3/day	$=V_{melt}*24$
Air flow to prevent melting	M_{air}	3906	ft^3/hr	$=Q_{melt}*V_{air}/C_{air}/dT_{snow}$
Length of air column	L_{air}	1172	ft/hr	$=M_{air}/A_{vent}$
Air flow to prevent melting	M_{airmin}	65	ft^3m	

[a] The resulting mass is small (2 ft^3/day), indicating that most ice damming is due to heat contributions greater than conduction only.

[b] Principal assumption: the sole source of heat is conduction across attic insulation.

vents and a low heat capacity in air. Unfortunately, heat losses to unconditioned attics, especially stupidly wasteful losses, have no such physical limitations. Waterproofing underlayment should be used under any roofed areas where snow is likely to collect.

Roof overhangs should be designed to permit a full thickness of ceiling insulation up above the plate. Where the wall–ceiling junction is allowed to get cold, it will get wet. Wet spots collect dirt and carbon particles and permit mold to grow. Corners must be designed with a continuous pillow of insulation.

Suppose that the insulation at the corner of the building is insufficient; or imagine that wind from a soffit vent blows through the insulation, reducing its thermal resistance. Can we fix this problem from inside using an insulated crown molding? Perhaps—research that is under way should offer a practical answer to this question. But interior insulation is often not a good idea. I was asked to investigate condensation problems at the National Gallery of Australia, a lovely structure with 30-cm walls of dense, pure, white concrete. The concrete had high thermal conductivity, so the air films on the inside and outside offered about half the overall thermal resistance. Where the diffusers threw warm air across the walls, there was no problem. In locations where diffusers were closed or not installed, the surface was particularly cold and subject to condensation in their humidified building. The first stab at fixing the problem was to put rigid insulation on the inside walls. Unfortunately, that made the problem worse. To see why note the isotherms in Figure 4-23. We can see that the surface of the concrete is at 18°C without insulation, whereas the interface temperature between the concrete and insulation is 6°C at the center of the insulating panel. We know that temperature gradients are continuous and smooth along a surface. At

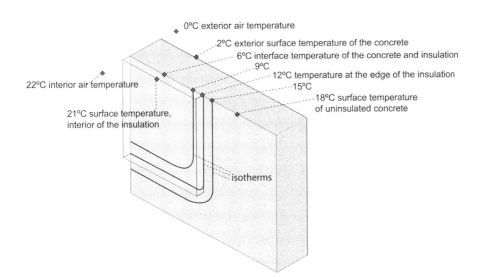

Figure 4-23
Cold edge effect, due to adding insulation onto a thermally conductive wall.

the edge of the insulation panel, the surface temperature is halfway between these two, or 12°C. So the impact of adding a panel of thermal insulation at the inside is to create an edge effect that is drastically chilled. I recommended correcting the diffusers rather than adding insulation.

PARAPETS

My colleague Joseph Lstiburek calls it "parapetitis," the disease affecting parapets, causing them to be common and recurrent sources of moisture problems. Originally, parapets provided protection against fire transmission in crowded urban settings. Now they are common edge terminations of low-slope roof systems. In older buildings, the parapet was an upward extension of the solid multiwythe brick or masonry wall, and the mass of the parapet provided a counterweight for the housing of the wood low-

Figure 4-24
Parapet construction is a steel frame building. It is very difficult to make the joint airtight where the wall meets the low-slope roof system. Fireproofing on the steel and fiberglass insulation (not shown here) do not provide adequate seals against airflow.

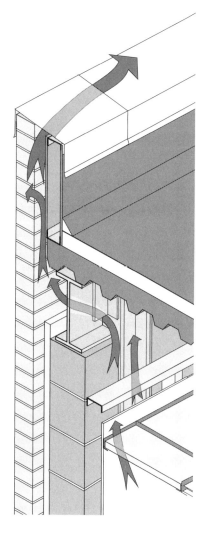

slope rafter system. It helped to prevent the low-slope roof system (a built-up roof in older buildings) from peeling at the edge in high winds. In addition, it provided protection against falling for workers on the roof. Most parapets since World War II have been of cavity construction. Since most cladding systems are thin, the structure of the parapet supports upward extension of the cladding system as well as itself, but it does not require weighty construction. It is often designed as an add-on.

Parapets are at the tops of buildings. Thermal buoyancy during cold weather causes the strongest air pressures to act outward at the very top of the building. If the joint between the wall system and the roof system is not airtight, air is likely to move through any openings and fill the cavity of the parapet as it moves outward (see Figure 4-24).

It is critical to achieve airtightness at this top corner of the building. Details of how to achieve continuity of an air barrier as well as insulation have been developed and presented in the Canada Mortgage and Housing Corporation's *Best Practice Guides* for many types of construction (CMHC, 1996, 1997, 1999, 2001). The most difficult condition for achieving airtightness is the one shown here, with a steel frame and infill [concrete masonry unit (CMU) in this case] in the same plane as the steel columns and beams, and with corrugated metal decking.

GUTTERS

To my knowledge, Eugène-Emmanuel Viollet-le-Duc is the only architect to have written of the importance of gutters and the only one to have highlighted gutters and downspouts in his drawings.

> The extent to which the absence of forethought on the part of architects is carried is incredible to those who have not observed it. For instance, in a public building erected not long ago, the gutters pass through the attics, and form in each room, under the windows, a little trough covered with a board, and where water may be drawn any rainy day; and the down-pipes carried through the thickness of the walls, pour torrents of water into the rooms during a thaw; and all this for the sake of not interfering with the lines of a certain classical form of architecture. Viollet-le-Duc, 1872

However, as Figure 4-25 shows, Viollet-le-Duc himself did not always keep his word, in this case sending a downspout through the thickness of the wall. From the rising damp pattern around the outlet, his warning to himself should have been better heeded.

Gutters are important for rainwater management. It is usually easier and safer to manage rainwater at the roof edge than at the ground level or

Figure 4-25
Downspout outlet at Pierrefonds. The architect advised in his writings against embedding downspouts in walls. Had he followed his own advice, the rising damp apparent here might not have occurred. (From Viollet-le-Duc, 1872.)

below. Recall from Chapter 3 that energy can be potential ($E = \rho g h$) or kinetic ($E = 1/2mv^2$). Potential energy is a function of height. The more potential energy, the more kinetic options are available. The higher the water, the more can be done with it.

Following are a few guidance principles related to gutters and downspouts.

- Make sure that water from the roof goes into the gutter. Ensure that any roof edge drips well into the gutter. Often, the gutter is installed after the roof edge material, so it lies atop the edge metal rather than behind.
- On sloped sites, locate downspouts strategically so that they discharge onto the surface of soil with good slope. Avoid dumping water on the uphill side of a building. Buildings with hip roofs have much discretion in this regard; gable roofs do not.

- Design the gutters, downspouts, and accessories. Architects such as H. H. Richardson and Frank Lloyd Wright had exquisite gutter and downspout design. Do not leave gutters and downspouts as an afterthought.
- Gutters should not allow standing water. Short runs can be set dead level. Longer runs should be designed with pitch to the downspout.

BUILDING FACADES

A facade is a roof. It is not just a roof, of course, but is like a roof in that it has the job of excluding rainwater. As we will see in Chapter 6, decisions about vapor retarders begin with an estimate of the quality of the rainwater exclusion on the outside of the building. The long-term durability of a building may depend in large part on how well the building facades manage water. The main elements of a facade are the walls and windows.

Water Loads to Building Facades

Let's begin with what Steven Vogel (1994) calls the *no-slip rule*. This rule says that any fluid moving past a surface shows a velocity gradient that is a function of the distance away from the surface. The gradient begins at zero right at the surface and reaches the wind speed some distance away (see Figure 4-26). That is, regardless of how hard the wind is blowing, the wind *right* at the surface does not move at all. So knowing what happens on the building site or within a few feet of the building is not a valid indicator of what is happening right at the surface. Wind does not wash our building walls clean. When wind heads toward a building, it is the edges of the building that feel the velocity (see Figure 4-27). Most of the surfaces may be affected by wind pressures: positive on the windward side, negative on the others. But wind flow will affect primarily the edges and corners of the building.

Facades stay quite dry as long as the overhangs are wide and as long as there is little wind. The facades of most buildings in most climate conditions see a fair amount of rain. Local weather stations publish data showing rain amounts with coincident wind conditions. Designers should keep these values in mind. Hurricane-prone buildings should, in theory, have greater attention paid to water management detailing than one, say, in Tucson.

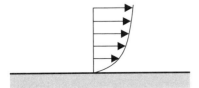

Figure 4-26
Velocity gradient. The velocity at a surface is essentially zero.

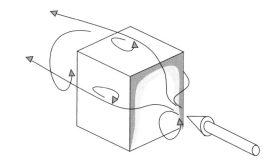

Figure 4-27
How wind moves around buildings. Building edges experience the highest wind speeds and the greatest water loading.

Raindrops may have a horizontal momentum imparted by winds. Rain often travels laterally with wind, but right next to buildings the momentum of the raindrop and the direction of the wind may part ways. If the raindrops are large, even the turning of the wind as it approaches a building may not deflect an oncoming raindrop away from the building. By the same token, a drip from a roof edge may fall almost directly downward even in a heavy wind if the head-on wind is deflected around the building. But wind and raindrop momentum will combine to create a strong loading of water at the edges and corners of buildings. Drizzle and snow are not likely to have much momentum (momentum is the product of mass and velocity), so they will be carried with the wind.

In short, rainwater loading on facades depends on (1) the magnitude of a design rainfall, (2) the coincident wind speed and direction, (3) overhangs, and (4) proximity to building edges. The facade rain load might be seen as a difficult amount to quantify; nevertheless, it is the design value that may be most closely tied to the effective service life of a building.

The water that loads the exteriors of buildings must be removed. The two ways that is typically done is by desorption/evaporation and drainage. Brick, stone, and other materials that are sorptive have water that clings in pores and cavities. This water cannot be drained away (recall the rule of capillarity—bound water cannot go to larger pores, and the outdoors is the largest pore of all). This water must be evaporated from surfaces of these materials. Assemblies made of non-sorptive materials must be drained. Such materials are normally discontinuous so are typically installed shingle-fashion. Such assemblies are usually comprised of layers so that any incidental water entry gets captured by material beneath and is shunted back out to the surface. Such layers are considered weather barriers or weather-resistant barriers (WRBs). To investigate the rainwater management in wall systems, let's investigate several examples of walls.

Stone Masonry

Consider a wall of dressed granite with a rubble stone backup (Figure 4-28). Granite surfaces are slightly hydrophilic. The stone is dense and not very porous. Water has essentially no pores to enter, so it runs across the

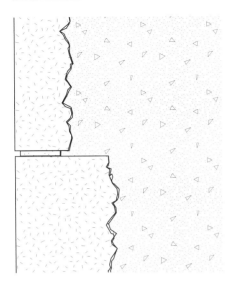

Figure 4-28
Wall with granite facing and concrete backup. The appearance of efflorescence and water on the granite surface can occur only due to a hydraulic head of water that enters at the roof.

surface until it strikes a mortar joint. Soft mortars, usually containing lime, may give and take with movement. Harder cement-based mortars have little or no elasticity. With the introduction of cement-based mortars and with engineering specifications for their use, lime mortars tended to die out. They required slaking, and slaking required handiwork and planning. Slaked lime is returning to the marketplace. It bears investigation not only by preservationists but also by designers of new buildings.

There are two types of mortar joints: head joints, which run vertically, and bed joints, which are horizontal. It is quite rare to find cracks in bed joints, as gravity imposes itself to close them once opened. Head joints, on the other hand, may see quite a bit of cracking because of the lack of closing force. If something tends to happen, and nothing tends to prevent it from happening, it will happen eventually, and only the rate is open to discussion. That is why head joints open incrementally over time and bed joints do not. Can water enter a head joint crack? Yes, if it is carried directly into the crack. Also, if a glancing wind is quite strong, it can carry surface water to there. Once there, water tends to enter by capillary attraction. The contact angle of water with mortar is quite acute.

I was asked to investigate water leaking out of the mortar joints at a granite-faced memorial arch. This triumphal arch had a granite skin and a concrete backing. Throughout its history, money was spent trying to prevent water leaking out of the joints with consequent salt staining of the granite surface. When I was called, the design team was under the impression that the water was being lifted up from groundwater by capillary action, then finding the joint and leaking out. I pointed out how that could lead to a lapse in the law of conservation of energy—we could put a little turbine under the drips and generate electricity for free. No, the rule of capillarity applies: Water moves from large pores to small pores. It never moves from small pores to larger pores without assistance. I asked for information on the roof, which was not visible from below. The original design had simply horizontal granite slabs on top. A metal roof was added in the 1970s, but the roof edge was held back a foot or so, and it deposited its water onto the horizontal surface of the lowest roof slab. What was happening was unmistakable—rainwater entered the inside of the structure, creating a head of water in the rubble, and water poured out the joints, pushed from above. The rule of capillarity held once again.

Is water repellent desirable on masonry surfaces? The most common chemicals applied to masonry surfaces are silanes and siloxanes. They reduce the surface activity, increase the water contact angle, and in general, reduce the overall water absorption. Applying any coating to masonry retards some drying through the coating. Masonry preservationists tend to shy away from such products, relying instead on good materials, detailing, and mortar work. Others find that the benefits are worth the reduced vapor permeability in the brick. In any case, one might consider a strategic application of water-repellent chemicals: for example, on windowsills or other inclined surfaces that otherwise could suffer damage from water or subsequent biological growth, and protect the remainder of the wall using good design, detailing, and execution. Figure 4-29 shows lichen growth on a facade of Indiana limestone. What is evident in this photograph is the way that growth on the vertical surface is sponsored or incubated by growth on the sill. Treatments with metals such as zinc and copper are more commonly used than organic treatments.

Figure 4-29
Biological growth and dirt on limestone sill and beneath.

Triple-Wythe Brick Wall

Consider the triple-wythe brick wall, typical of loft buildings in our cities from a century ago, shown in Figure 4-30. The outer brick may be water-struck or have a hard surface from firing. The backup bricks were softer. The buildings had handsome overhanging cornices, often of terra-cotta. The windows were wood units. The interior plaster was on metal lath held out from the interior brick. There was a radiator under the window. The overhang offered considerable protection—up to the time they were removed because the fasteners were corroding and threatening the public on the sidewalks below. What water did hit the brick was largely absorbed into the brick and the mortar joints. At structural defects, the cracking might go through all the wythes, but rarely would it make it through to the cavity behind the plaster. However, at the window, the water was not absorbed. Windows act as funnels, collecting the rainwater that hits them and funneling down to the sill. Depending on the quality of the sill and its conditions, the wall panel beneath the window tended to be the wettest part of the wall. That was fine, because the radiator at this location together with the lack of insulation tended to keep this panel hot and thereby dry. Recall the *wetness rule:* For the same vapor pressure, hot things are dry and cold things are wet. I have seen loft conversions where the insulation and heating strategy removed the overheating of the panel beneath the window—and it shows as extra wetting and occasional efflorescence. A triple-wythe brick or masonry wall usually had excellent water performance, at least up to the moment when structural cracks became large enough to let through quantities of water in excess of the sorptive capacity of the materials around those cracks.

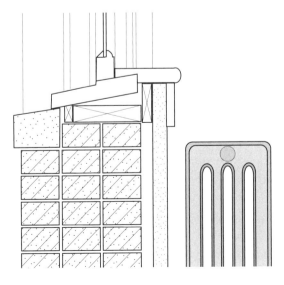

Figure 4-30
Triple-wythe brick wall. The brick beneath the window can be wetted from rainwater concentration at the sill. Drying is enhanced by the radiator and by air leaks around the window frame.

Single-Wythe Brick Wall

Consider a single-wythe brick wall with an air gap behind (Figure 4-31) For the last several decades, the mortar is typically hard, leaving hairline cracking at head joints. The brick may be suspended on a flashed shelf angle and will typically have weep holes; every third head joint left open is a common weep hole strategy. A wide variety of sheathing materials and sheathing papers are in use. Metal ties of many kinds tie the brick to the structural wall across the airspace. The airspace has mortar droppings, a very random variable in performance. Suppose now that water strikes the brick and finds the cracked head joints. Capillarity carries the water through the crack but stops as the crack begins to widen at the back side (recall the rule of capillarity). If air pressure adds to capillarity effects, water can be sucked through the opening in into the cavity. Air pressures might be created by wind pressures, particularly on the windward side; by mechanical pressures in the building; or by buoyancy pressures in the brick cavity, although that would be a minor effect if the shelf occurs every story. Negative air pressure can suck water right into the air gap. How much water that strikes the brick makes it to the back side of the brick? Some investigators say as much as 4%. Others are more conservative at around 1%. More work must be done in this area.

What happens with the water in the cavity? One thing that almost never happens is weeping through weep holes. There is simply too much sorptive mortar material for the water to course cleanly down to the weeps. Instead, the only way out appears to be for liquid water to evaporate and to leave through the air. Put your finger near a weep hole and feel for air movement. You may feel none. In that case, all of the vapor has to leave by diffusion, that is, by the likelihood that kinetically colliding vapor mole-

Figure 4-31
Single-wythe brick veneer. Rain that strikes the brick may be absorbed into the brick and mortar and may be driven into the cavity by air pressure. That water can be dried by air movement in the cavity, and more slowly by diffusion. That water can also be driven farther into the wall by heat from sunlight.

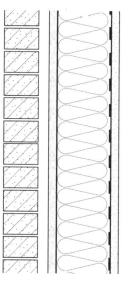

cules happen to find the hole to exit through. That is a painfully slow process. It appears that one underestimated detail may turn out to be quite important—the opening at the top of the wythe. Research under way seems to indicate that where the top of a brick wythe is open, air currents may appear and greatly accelerate the drying of water that enters with rain.

There is a growing concern for *solar vapor drive,* which occurs when the sun is allowed to bake the brick (or stucco, or other moisture-storage cladding material) and the cavity behind the cladding. The water in the cavity is evaporated quickly at a temperature well below the boiling point of water. The resulting vapor travels wherever it can, including toward the inside. We discuss the effect of solar vapor drive into the cavity in Chapter 6.

Wood Frame

Consider a wood frame wall assembly with 1×6 pine sheathing, the style done up to the introduction of plywood (Figure 4-32). It would typically be covered with building paper and have wood clapboards. The wood is painted and may be back-primed. Water lands on the paint surface of the siding. Any imperfections in the paint allow water to penetrate the wood. Water that runs down a continuous painted surface reaches the bottom of a clapboard and runs across. With sufficient water volume it may drip off. If the clapboard is back-primed, then the mating surfaces between the two boards are likely to stay dry. If it is bare wood, the water is likely to enter into the wood. Detailing, wind, and air pressure differences can move water to the back side of the siding. When the sun comes out, the water behind the siding is evaporated. Painters back then used to recommend painters' wedges to allow drops of water to drain and to permit easy diffusion through

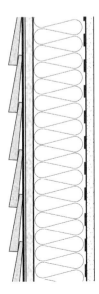

Figure 4-32
Wood cladding on wood frame construction. Rainwater may collect at the back side of the cladding and moves laterally along the tops of the cladding boards. It dries by drainage and by air exchange with the outdoors.

the open crack. The building paper used was typically asphalted felt or rosin paper. The role of these papers was primarily to block drafts of air from passing through the cracks in the shiplap or tongue-and-groove sheathing. In Chapter 3 we saw how the introduction of insulation into wood frame construction led to paint peeling and then to the moisture control regulations currently in place. But prior to the placement of insulation, the water performance of this type of construction was quite good. After the placement of insulation was widely adopted, most homes moved to exterior finishes that were more water resistant than painted clapboard.

External Insulation and Finish Systems

Consider external insulation and finish system (EIFS) cladding. It is composed of rigid board insulation (usually, expanded polystyrene) that is adhered or mechanically fastened to the substrate, then mesh reinforcement added to which is applied polymer stuccolike coatings (Figure 4-33). When I practiced architecture in France in the 1980s, EIFS construction applied to concrete or block structures was the old standby. It worked beautifully when applied to masonry and concrete substrates. That changed when it was applied to sheathing panels in the United States and Canada. An early commercial installation might have consisted of sheathing-grade gypsum panels fastened to the framing mechanically, then expanded polystyrene panels simply adhered to the paper facing of the gypsum with construction adhesive. For residences, an EIFS was applied to plywood or OSB (oriented strand board) sheathing, again using construction adhesive. In all cases, the exterior was completed with reinforcing mesh and several coats of polymer finish. The problem was simple: Water leaked in at windows and other de-

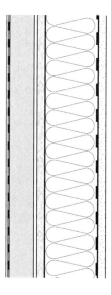

Figure 4-33
Exterior insulation and finish system (EIFS) on frame construction. Rainwater that enters at poorly flashed details is removed only by provision for drainage at the back of the exterior foam insulation. Interior vapor retarders preclude effective drying to the interior.

tails and had little or no means to dry to the outside. The airspaces in the system were small and didn't permit evaporation and mixing and moving of air that is often associated with drying. Episodes of EIFS failure in Wilmington, North Carolina and Vancouver, British Columbia, two cities with different but severe rain problems, led to large lawsuits. When water leaked in, it softened the paper facing and caused deterioration of the sheathing materials. With masonry and concrete, the small quantities of water were more evenly distributed through the larger mass of material; because the substrate was inorganic, rotting microorganisms could not get much of a foothold.

In response, companies that sold EIFS systems took different tacks. Some improved their standard details and wrote stronger language to enforce their use. Some developed "drainage plane" systems to allow the evacuation of water that gets behind the foam. Some developed guidelines to associate system design with anticipated rainfall. Some companies folded and some reorganized. The outcome of all this is some consumer reluctance to rejoin a system that has seen so much courtroom activity. On the other hand, EIFS lends itself to wide design variation, and the insulation on the outside of the structure is ideally situated. Exterior insulation generally performs much better than interior insulation, as we showed in the example from the National Gallery of Australia.

Vinyl Siding with OSB Sheathing

Consider a wood frame wall with sheathing of OSB, a weather barrier, and vinyl siding (Figure 4-34). Vinyl siding contains small holes at the underside to allow water on the back side to drain out. To its great credit, vinyl

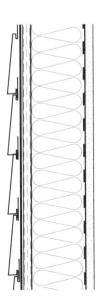

Figure 4-34
Vinyl siding with oriented strand board (OSB) sheathing on frame construction. Rainwater freely enters through the vinyl siding and also drains freely back to the outdoors. Since OSB degrades at high water content, it is important to provide a weather-resistant barrier (WRB) behind the siding, and it must be detailed to shed water with correct shingle lapping.

siding probably sheds almost all of the water that is sloshed against it in a rainstorm. The water that does get behind the siding is able to move laterally and find its way to any of the drainage holes with ease. When the sun hits the wall after a rainstorm, the evaporated water escapes easily through all the cracks and holes in vinyl. For many years, many residences (millions, perhaps) were constructed with vinyl siding, OSB, or plywood sheathing, and no weather-resistant barrier. What consequences might we expect?

The wood panel product OSB is not so much a product as it is a specification for the structural properties of a product. It was introduced into U.S. construction around 1990. Any product that complies with the structural and dimensional properties may qualify. Note from Figure 3-8 the range of vapor permeabilities possible with this product (as with plywood). So it is hard to pin down the future moisture performance of a product when these properties receive no mention in the product specification. We know that the material is produced from chipped wood and adhesives under great heat and pressure. The resulting product is dry and quite stiff for its thickness. Concrete gets better with age; some make the same claim for kiln-dried hardwoods. OSB should be expected to relax from its manufactured state, with some relaxation of wood chips and some loss of adhesion around the outermost chips. Manufacturers often wax the panels to forestall water effects on the outermost layer. These are the layers on which the engineering properties of the material rely most heavily, much like the flanges in a steel member. No one has yet put a time line on the expected long-term performance of these products. For many products, such as paint and roofing materials, laboratories use accelerated weathering tests. (Many in the industry are suspicious of such tests—my colleague Don Brotherson used to say that any material that passed was at least useful as a liner for the test apparatus.) For such results to be meaningful, they must offer some semblance of actual conditions at an accelerated pace, they must show a measurable form of degradation, and some criterion that marks the end of service life should be presented. To our knowledge, that work has not been done with OSB.

With proper maintenance, a home of earlier generations of materials would be expected to be maintainable into an indefinitely long future. The stave churches of Norway, made of wood framing and cladding, have lasted nearly a millennium. The generation of Victorian homes should be capable of the same (absent economic forces that make dilapidation occasionally desirable). The present generation of wood frame construction, using engineered materials, may not cooperate as well with such long-term aims. The aim of building science has been to help assure long-term durability or at least to point to the steps necessary for its achievement. It would be unfortunate if the aims of building science had to be refocused toward a shorter term.

If we strip the siding from a vinyl-sided, OSB-sheathed house, we would expect to see varying water effects: teardrop shapes of discoloration beneath the lower corners of windows in particular, and discoloration and pulping at intersections of walls with fascia, balconies, and so on. If the material had been rained on during construction, signs of that might be evident. At this point, there are no standards that would permit us to rate those conditions for seriousness. Such conditions should be corrected when they are found to occur. Can the wetness that occurs simply by virtue of being cold on the outside of insulated assemblies lead to chronic deterioration of these materials? That question remains to be answered.

WINDOWS

Windows were long the test of a carpenter's skill. The sill was dadoed into the jamb and if the joint was tight, well painted, and well maintained, the amount of water entering at that joint was easy to accommodate in the long run. Poorer-quality windows, poorly painted, with poorly maintained sills led to water leakage problems described above. As site-built windows gave way to factory units at the middle of the century, and as those gave way to flange-mounted windows in the latter part of the century, leaking into the frame opening appeared to become more problematic. In response the industry has begun to address window installation more seriously. ASTM has produced ASTM E2112–01, "Standard Practice for Installation of Exterior Windows, Doors and Skylights."

This standard seeks to ensure that all of the water-shedding layers at the exterior of the building are integrated, shingle-lap fashion, with the elements of the windows, and it provides that the framed openings into which window units will be placed will be flashed. Flange-mounted windows may

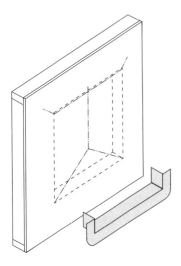

Figure 4-35
Window openings require flashing. Flange-mounted windows can be flashed into openings as shown, with "inverted martini glass" cuts in the WRB and adhesive membrane flashing at the sill.

have openings flashed with membranes (see Figure 4-35), whereas non-finned windows are to be panned. Pans are typically of rigid material. In both cases the critical element of window opening flashing is the upturn terminations at each end of the sill flashing. Note that this provides a triple-point condition at the front and perhaps at the rear of the flashing or pan. The drawings to describe any three-dimensional geometry should be three-dimensional. Two-dimensional drawings that show panning of a window opening fail to show the upturning of the ends, which is the most critical part of the detail. Jacques Rousseau, formerly of the Canada Mortgage and Housing Corporation, contends that instead of three-dimensional drawings we really need four dimensions, including sequencing of placement. This task may be easy enough in advisory drawings but may encounter the "means and methods" objection in traditional contract documents. In other delivery systems, such as design-build, means and methods of construction may be shared between designer and builder.

Special flashing may be necessary at ganged window units, as they are quite prone to water movement between units. In short, windows should be installed in a way that manages the rainwater. All of the layers involved—WRB beneath the cladding, the cladding itself, and the details of the window—should provide water shedding to the outside.

SUMMARY

Decide where the water is supposed to go. Design all conducting elements so that it goes there.

- Roofs need good geometry. They should be simple and should avoid dead valleys and plugged valleys.
- Concentration and funneling are the principal determinants of where leaks will occur. Design for maintenance of zones of high water concentration.
- In the case of ice dams, identify and correct vagrant heat loss.
- Design the gutters. Integrate the gutters with the facade.
- Design to reduce wetting and to enhance drying of all assemblies.
- Design for water shedding at all exterior elements.

5 Soils and Foundations

The purpose of water management in soils is to prevent saturation conditions in soil that is in contact with a building foundation. The purpose of the rainwater management of the roof and facade, described above, is to shed water horizontally, to prevent bulk water entry into the living space or past the weather barrier. What we know about roofs may be very helpful in working with soils.

Let's review some material from Chapter 2. Water is a polar molecule. It coheres to other water molecules, forming hydrogen bonds. It adheres more strongly to any other molecules or parts of molecules that have an unbalanced charge, which are anything but absolutely neutral. Water adheres strongly to ions—charged particles such as the components of dissolved salts. This attraction to unbalanced charges in molecules or parts of molecules may be considered chemical or mechanical and is termed *osmotic*. Consider pure table salt. It is *deliquescent*; that is, molecules from the air, if they have the misfortune to collide with crystals, become attached and unable to reevaporate (on average, of course). They accumulate over time. Over a long enough time, so much will accumulate that a saltwater soup is formed, and the resulting solution is in equilibrium with the surrounding air. The salt ions, say, sodium and chlorine, are so electrically strong that they affect the physical properties of water. Because of its high osmotic potential, salt lowers the freezing/melting point of snow. Why? Water molecules are more strongly attached to the liquid solution state than they would be to an ice crystal lattice that excludes the ions. Salt raises the boiling temperature of water, although very slightly compared to the freezing point depression. An ounce of salt raises the boiling point by only 1°F at atmospheric pressure (McGee, 1984). Osmotic potential in a solution lowers the vapor pressure.

The sodium and chlorine ions in a salt solution are mobile. But if the molecular surfaces have unbalanced electrical charges but are immobile, water may and can attach to those surfaces as well. The resulting condition—water attaching itself to a surface—seems, in many respects, like a solution. Like the attachment of water to mobile ions, the attachment of water to charged surfaces results in elevated boiling points, lowered freezing points, and lowered equilibrium vapor pressures, compared to those same values for pure liquid water. The water that attaches itself to wood finds the unbalanced radicals (parts of hydrocarbons), particularly hydroxyl (OH⁻) radicals, as binding sites.

Sand is made up primarily of oxides of silicon. The crystals are not very electrically active (until turned into computer chips). So the binding energy of water to sand is small, and thus the sorption water of sand is small. Clay, on the other hand, has a most peculiar molecular structure (see Figure 5-1). It is composed of layers of silicon and oxygen in a flat array, and these are sandwiched with layers that are rather flat crystal arrays of aluminum, magnesium, oxygen, and hydroxyl ions. The resulting mineral shape is quite flat. However, it is electrostatically very active, with a net negative charge that appears at the lattice edges. It is so active that for one thing, the plates do not stack but are jumbled as if to maximize the open space between them. For another, the exterior edges of the crystal lattices are very electronegative, so that the lattice maintains a "swarm" (Hillel's term) of positive ions, cations, that are attracted to the strong negative charge but are entirely unattached and capable of being replaced with ease. This fact is of considerable importance to maintaining plant life in soil. As you might imagine, water can attach itself quite strongly to both the lattice and the free cations in the clay matrix.

Figure 5-1

Schematic of a clay crystal (montmorillonite) with aluminum-based octahedron layer sandwiched between two silicon–oxygen (tetrahedral) layers and a cation swarm.

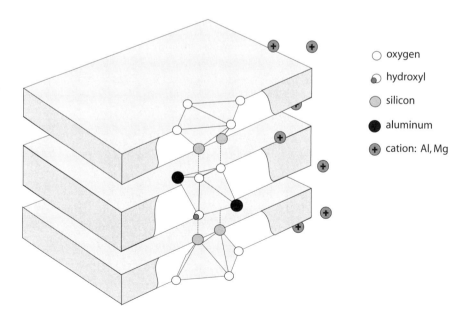

○ oxygen
◗ hydroxyl
◔ silicon
● aluminum
⊕ cation: Al, Mg

WATER IN SOIL

Soil is a matrix formed by solid particles, with void spaces between. The voids may contain air or water. The porosity is the percent, usually by volume, of void space (i.e., nonsolid space) compared to the volume of the total matrix. The porosity of sand is usually less than 50%, so more than 50% of sand is solid. But the porosity of clay is greater than 50%, and for a clay such as bentonite, the porosity may be as great as 85%. We think of clay as being impermeable to water flow and may be inclined to attribute this to density of solids. It is not. The relative impermeability of clay is due to the strong chemical reactions with water that occur in otherwise wide-open voids of the mineral.

The water that attaches itself in the first few layers to molecules, ions, or chemical radicals with unbalanced charges is very difficult to remove. This small amount of bound water must be considered fixed, as it can be removed only by heating. The adsorbed layer, a "phase" to itself, can assume a thickness of about 10 to 20 angstrom units. Its structure may be icelike. This layer has mechanical properties quite different from the properties of ordinary liquid water at the same temperature. The water of adhesion that binds to the surfaces of material may be thicker or thinner depending on the humidity conditions in the air that surrounds the materials, and the moisture content of the material may vary somewhat with the ambient humidity. This range of moisture contents, which varies with changes in ambient relative humidity, is called the *sorption range*.

Figure 5-2 also shows a thickening of the water mass where two surfaces come into close contact. This is capillary water. It is present in a soil matrix for the same reasons that water rises in a capillary tube. Recall that water rises in a capillary tube because of the attractive forces between water and surfaces and because of the surface tension of water. There is a strong attractive force between the glass surface and the water molecules. That attraction is strong enough to lift water molecules upward. But surface tension distributes that attractive force to the entire affected surface, resulting in the concave meniscus shown. Thus, a force acts on the area of the water surface. A force acting on an area is usually considered a pressure, but in this case, the force pulls rather than pushes the surface. It may be considered as a pressure with negative sign, it may be considered a "suction" pressure, or it may be considered a stress. In either case, the units are pressure units: pascal (Pa) in SI units, or any of the myriad pressure units in I-P: psi, in.Hg, in.H_2O, and so on.

The capillary pressure may be calculated. The surface tension of water is γ. At room temperature $\gamma_{water} = 0.0728$ J/m^2. The water surface makes an angle θ with the vertical surface of the glass. This is the contact angle.

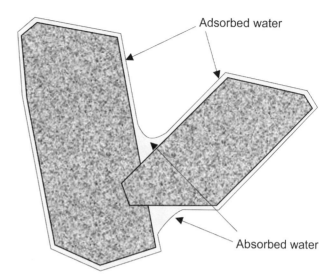

Adsorbed water

Absorbed water

Figure 5-2
Adsorption of water onto surfaces, and absorption where the proximity of surfaces provides matric potential.

The surface tension acts in the plane of the meniscus, so it operates at the contact angle all along the perimeter of the meniscus. But we are interested in the vertical force in the capillary tube, so we need to know the vertical component of the surface tension. That is $\cos \theta$. The force acts all along the perimeter of the meniscus, which is the circumference of the tube, $2\pi r$. Thus, the vertical force is $-2\pi r \cos \theta$ (the negative sign indicates a pull upward). The pressure is the force acting on the area of the meniscus, which is πr^2. So the pressure is the force over the area:

$$P = \frac{-2\gamma \cos \theta}{r} \qquad (5\text{-}1)$$

How high can a capillary tube lift water? To lift anything requires a pressure of $\rho g h$, where ρ (rho) is the effective density of the material being lifted, g is the acceleration of gravity, and h is the height. Substituting the required pressure for the capillary pressure above, we find that

$$h = \frac{2\gamma \cos \theta}{r \rho g} \qquad (5\text{-}2)$$

In clay soils, most soil mixtures, brick (which is made of clay), and most porous organic material, such as wood and paper, the contact angle is effectively zero. So in the equations above, we may replace $\cos \theta$ with 1.

Wood is made up of tubes called *xylem*. But if we applied this equation to the height of water in xylem, we would never begin to approach the height actually found in nature, where we know that water from the ground does make it all the way up to the leaves. Water is lifted much higher because for the life of the plant, the xylem never contains air. Other constituents in the sap prevent *cavitation*, the formation of vacuum cavities when the height exceeds the Torricelli height of water or about 32 ft. Soil, however, is not made up of tubes. It contains mineral particles that are flat in the case of clay and more spherical in shape (not in surface texture) for silt and sand. Capillary water resides in the nooks where the proximity of particle surfaces allows local menisci to form.

Capillary water in one location typically arises because of proximity to a greater density of capillary water immediately below. That is, a vertical section through soil may show a gradient in the zone immediately above the water table, where the soil becomes slightly drier with elevation above the water table. The water characteristics of the capillary fringe depend on the fineness of the pores (smaller pores leading to higher capillary rise) and on the uniformity of the pore structure. Where the moisture content of the pores is less, the air content in those same pores is greater by the same measure.

However, another, perhaps more significant form of soil wetting occurs from above. Rain falls on soil and it percolates through the soil. It displaces air, fills pores, and operates to some extent as a slug of water moving downward through the soil matrix. If we have two samples of soil in equilibrium, with one wetted from below by capillarity and the other wetted from above, then even after the drainage is complete, the second sample may be significantly wetter than the first. Why so? Figure 5-3 represents the *inkbottle effect*. Look at a capillary tube (radius r_1) that contains a bulge (radius r_2, larger than r_1). If a dry tube is placed into a water container, the water will rise to the underside of the bulge through capillary suction. If, on the other hand, the tube is filled with water, then immersed into the container, water will drain down. But if the capillary suction can support the weight of the water beneath, the final meniscus may well be above the bulge. These two tubes will be in equilibrium but will have very different moisture contents.

The ink-bottle effect is one contributor to hysteresis. Hysteresis is any difference in results of a process, depending on the direction and history of that process. We expect no hysteresis in thermal processes: A glass of hot

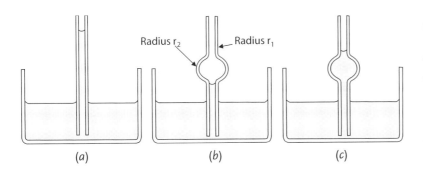

(a) (b) (c)

Figure 5-3

Ink bottle effect. If the capillary tube is straight, water will reach equilibrium as in (a). If there is a bulge in the tube and if water rises from below, it will reach equilibrium as in (b). If water fills from above, it will reach equilibrium as in (c). This is one of the components of hysteresis.

Radius r_2 Radius r_1

water and a glass of cold water, left on the counter, will eventually wind up at the same temperature. But hysteresis has a very strong effect in the determination of moisture content in porous and hygroscopic materials. Figure 5-4 shows a schematic version of hysteresis in wood. (See Figure 5-15 for measured values of hysteresis in concrete.) To get a sense of hysteresis in soils, imagine what happens to air in the soil. If the water table rises, the capillary fringe rises as well, and air is displaced upward, toward the site of greater air concentration. A void with an increasing amount of capillary water may lead to a captured air bubble. But if a slug of water passes down through the soil, the head of water above the drainage front may drive air out of voids and pores. In short, water that enters soil from above may lead to higher moisture contents than water that enters soil from below.

Figure 5-5 shows the percent by volume of solid, water, and air components of possible samples of sand and clay. The single-sample values presented do not represent the wide range of values that are possible for all soil types. The figure shows that much of the water contained in sand is drainable and only a small amount is fixed; clay, on the other hand, has a high percentage of fixed water and a relatively small amount that is drainable. The figure indicates representative values in sand and clay for field capacity, permanent wilting point, and air-dry conditions. Field capacity is a roughly defined value intended to represent the stable wetness in soil that remains after drainage. Permanent wilting point is a soil characteristic that represents transition between adhered and absorbed water. The permanent wilting point for agronomists corresponds to the fiber saturation point for wood scientists. Air-dry soil is soil in equilibrium with local dryness conditions, often around 20% relative humidity.

We would like to model what happens in soil in order to determine how water moves and where. A change in conditions is driven by a change in *potential*. Something must drive change, some motivating force that applies as

Figure 5-4

Hysteresis in wood. As wood goes from drier to wetter, it tends to be dry compared to wood going from wet to dry. Two samples at the same relative humidity may have different equilibrium moisture contents.

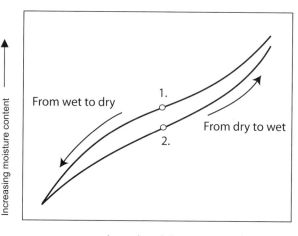

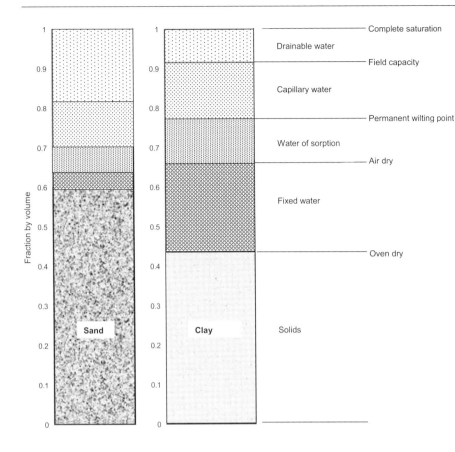

Figure 5-5
Amount of solid, water, and air in samples of sand and clay. Values are not representative of the entire range possible for the two soil types. (Data from Hillel, 1982.)

well to sand as to clay. Obviously, water content will not do, in that water content is strongly a function of soil properties (see Figure 5-6). Two soil samples of different type may be in equilibrium but have widely different water content values. Instead, suction pressure is commonly taken as the driving potential for moisture content, at least in the drainable and capillary regions. Suction pressures are continuous from one material to another.

Imagine taking a sample of soil that is completely saturated and suspending it, intact, in air. It may not drain because of the surface tension holding the water at the outermost pores. Put the sample in a pressure plate apparatus with two different air chambers separated by a ceramic plate that lets water pass through but not air, keep the sample at ambient air pressure, and apply a vacuum to the other side of the plate. This apparatus, in effect, sucks water out of the sample. Suction pressure could be applied to bring the samples to approximately field capacity. At this point, sand and clay would be at differing volumetric water contents (see Figure 5-5). Vacuum suction can be applied only in the range 0 to 1 atm. For higher suction pressures, a positive pressure is applied to the sample side of the pressure plate apparatus, effectively pushing the water molecules out of the sample matrix.

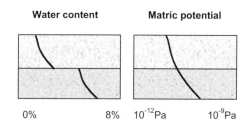

Figure 5-6
Same sample of two soil strata. Moisture content measurements are discontinuous, but pressure (suction) measurements are continuous.

This approach works in the drainable and capillary regions. But it is practically impossible to achieve pressures that represent conditions in the drier sorption range. Nevertheless, the same units of suction pressure can be shown to have an equivalence with relative humidity. The Kelvin relation (ASHRAE *Handbook—Fundamentals*, Chap. 23) states that

$$\ln \phi = \frac{P}{\rho_w R_w T} \tag{5-3}$$

where $\ln \phi$ is the natural logarithm of the relative humidity; P the suction pressure, from equation (5-1); ρ_w the density of water; R_w the universal gas constant for water vapor (not the gas constant for air); and T the absolute temperature.

Figure 5-6 illustrates the value of using pressure as a potential rather than a more easily measured value such as moisture content. Moisture content values are discontinuous at discontinuities in material, but pressure values are continuous. This is a very convenient choice of units, because it permits a smooth continuity between the capillary and sorption ranges. It allows either set of units to be considered as the driving potential for wetness calculations. Künzel (1995) has shown measurements that demonstrate the continuity between the capillary and sorption regions. Using suction pressure units is clearly indispensable for the drainable and capillary regimes. Table 5-1 shows a comparison of RH and suction values for water, at room temperature, in the presence of a surface at a 0° contact angle. The Kelvin relationship described above depends on the assumption of water as an ideal gas (see Chapter 2). Water is not an ideal gas, however, so these results derived from the formula vary from measured values.

The use of pressure units allows us to view the continuity not only between the capillary and sorption regions, but also between the drainable and capillary regions. The force that drives drainage in the hydraulic head is gravitational and is measured as $\rho g h$ (units are described above). The force that drives capillary movement is termed *matric pressure* or *matric suction*. The force that provides for moisture content in equilibrium with ambient air (sorption range) or oven-heated air (fixed range) may be termed *osmotic pressure*. The magnitude of each of these three potentials (i.e.,

Table 5-1 Relationship between relative humidity and suction pressure values		
	Suction Pressure	
RH	atm	MPa
20	2167.0	221.0
50	933.3	95.2
80	300.4	30.6
90	141.9	14.5
95	69.1	7.0
98	27.2	2.8
99	13.5	1.4
99.9	1.347	0.137
99.99	0.135	0.014
99.999	0.013	0.001

gravitational, matric, and osmotic) is dependent on the properties of the soil or other porous material, and, of course, on the moisture content of the material.

We have an intuitive sense of what pressure is; we know that pressure can rise several times the pressure of the atmosphere. Suction is somewhat intuitive—we all know of suction as negative pressure helping get liquids up a soda straw. But the intuitive nature of suction begins to break down when the suction exceeds −1 atm. How can this be? It can be simply by changing the sign of positive pressure, for one thing, although we decouple it from its intuitive hook in so doing. Another way to imagine a very strong negative pressure is to imagine removing water from a block of material using a centrifuge. As the block is spun around, water is moved toward the outside and may be removed if the shell of the centrifuge is perforated to let water pass through. We can imagine a plane of the material that is normal to the radius of the centrifuge. A mass of water in the material accelerates away from the plane. *Force* is mass × acceleration, and if the water is distributed uniformly with respect to the plane, the (negative) force acting on the plane represents a negative pressure. We know that a surface of liquid water will sponsor water vapor at the saturation (100% RH) book value at 1 atm of barometric pressure. We can then picture dry materials as sucking the water right out of the air and thereby reducing the relative humidity. The suction pressure necessary to do this is precisely what is given in the Kelvin relationship above.

HYDRAULIC CONDUCTIVITY

We have shown how the moisture content of soils may differ among soil types and as a function of surrounding wetness, but the rate at which water moves through soil may vary as well. The hydraulic water conductivity in clay is low, allowing water to pass only with great difficulty. In sand, the conductivity is relatively high.

A drainage pattern of water through soil can be seen in Figure 5-7. In Figure 5-7a, an example of water draining through sand, the vertical gravity component of the drainage is strong, while the omnidirectional component associated with matric potential is low. In Figure 5-7b, an example of water draining through clay, the vertical gravity component is small while the omnidirectional component (matric suction) is great. Note that a soil such as clay has a low hydraulic conductivity, so water that lands on the surface may flow along the surface without penetration. Clay changes vol-

Figure 5-7
Drainage patterns of water through sand, clay, and clay with macrocracking.

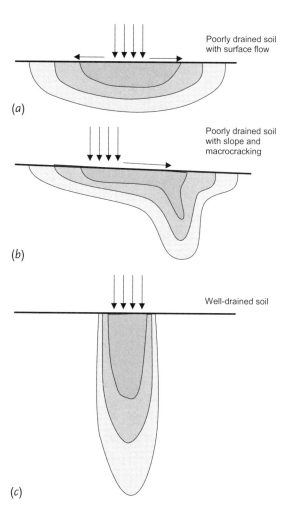

Poorly drained soil with surface flow

(a)

Poorly drained soil with slope and macrocracking

(b)

Well-drained soil

(c)

ume as a function of wetness. We are all familiar with the large macrocracks found in clay-containing soil in periods of dryness. Those same cracks may play a major role in water penetration, because they become discrete locations where the hydraulic conductivity of clay, presumed to be low, actually conducts water rapidly and with great ease (Figure 5-7c). In building foundations this may become a dominant factor: often the largest crack found in clay-containing soils is the crack between the soil mass and a vertical foundation wall. Water penetration may be easiest and greatest in precisely the location where it is least desired.

The type of soil and moisture content of the soil will also affect belowground horizontal flow. Water moves easily through strata of sand and gravel. Clay layers are often impenetrable. In many areas, soil contains varying strata of high and low water conductivity. A perched water table occurs where a clay stratum occurs in otherwise drainable soil, leading to a locally high water table. Similar strata can be found in urban areas as well, where several levels of street overlie one another, creating alternating sequences of high and low water conductivity. Figure 5-8 shows a suction pressure distribution through soil, from the groundwater at atmospheric pressure to the drier surface soil at greater suction pressure.

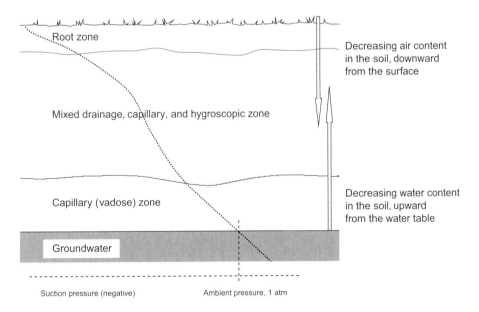

Figure 5-8

Suction pressure distribution through the upper layers of soil. The groundwater is at atmospheric pressure. That water imposes a hydraulic (positive) pressure on the water beneath the level of the water table. Soil above is at (negative) suction pressure.

SURFACE FLOW

Recall that the aim of water management in the soil is to prevent water accumulation up to the point of saturation in the soil that is in contact with the building foundation. Wherever the surface soil has low water conductivity, or where it has become saturated, a water load from above cannot penetrate, so it flows along the surface. The rate of flow depends on the roughness of the surface and the slope of the surface (Figure 5-9). If the surface is smooth, water may run quite freely. It may flow as a sheet or it may carve rivulets for flow, provided that there is some slope. If the surface is rough, water may accumulate in that roughness and flow will be impeded. Plants are generally beneficial for rainwater management. They will absorb some quantity of rainfall, depending on the mass and type of vegetation and on its water deficit. Bushes in particular can buffer large amounts of water flow and help keep the moisture content of the surrounding soil at a comfortable level.

For soils of medium hydraulic conductivity, including most soils that contain mixtures of clay and sand, and for surfaces of medium roughness (e.g., turf grass), an appropriate soil slope for water management is 5%. Most model U.S. building codes contain requirements for a minimum 5% slope in the soil surface away from a building, with that slope requirement imposed on the first 10 ft away from the building. Some code changes lowered this minimum slope to 2%, which would certainly facilitate compliance with accessibility requirements for buildings. In general, a 5% slope should be considered satisfactory for most rainwater management, while a 2% slope should be considered unsatisfactory for surface drainage, in my opinion.

A soil surface is a roof. Rather, water is managed on the soil surface in much the same way that water is managed on a roof. To design a soil surface for rainwater management, think of that soil surface as a roof. The de-

Figure 5-9
Water flow on soil surface from a downspout.

signer should know what to keep dry—the soil in contact with the foundation—and where the water should be delivered. Water may be taken to the water table below via percolation through the soil, it may be taken to neighboring soil surfaces, or it may be taken to the street. If the site slopes, the building may need an uphill swale, much as a chimney requires an uphill cricket. Concentration is greatest in valleys. Ridges or high points are naturally much drier than valleys or low points. Low areas can be quite troublesome, particularly if water is allowed to collect in sand or gravel layers. A common area where water collects, but often remains unseen, is in the gravel or sand base beneath appurtenances such as concrete patios, stoops, porches, walkways, or driveways. Such areas are much like low ponding areas on roofs with ballast and pavers—the ponding may not be visible on cursory inspection.

DRAINS

Below-grade drains for rainwater management were brought to the United States by Henry French of Exeter, New Hampshire, in the 1850s. He authored *Farm Drainage,* in which he explained the principles of below-grade water management for U.S. agricultural purposes. His work was based on European, particularly British work, which predated his own.

He proposed drainage to lower the water table in land that became agriculturally useless due to constant or seasonal flooding. For French, the principal concern was groundwater. So the tiles he proposed were open at the bottom, including one profile that was simply an inverted U-form. Once the water hits the level of the tile, it is carried laterally to the outfall by the modest pitch of the tile. The pipes are not likely to clog, as sediment would drain out of the tile at least as easily as it may drain into the tile. He showed how to construct drainage systems for all different terrains. He described collector tile with perforations at the bottom, and conduit tile with no perforations. Collectors lead to conduit, which leads to outfall, to daylight . . . at least in moderately hilly areas such as New England.

He included with the chapter "Drainage of Cellars," which appears to be the basis for more than a century of basement drainage design. He begins the chapter as follows:

> No child, who ever saw a cellar afloat during one of these inundations, will ever outgrow the impression. You stand on the cellar stairs, and below is a dark waste of waters, of illimitable extent. By the dim glimmer of the dip-candle, a scene is presented which furnishes a tolerable picture of "chaos and old night" but defies all description. Empty dry cases, with cider barrels, washtubs, and boxes ride triumphantly on the surface, while half filled vinegar and molasses kegs, like water-logged ships, roll heavily below. Broken

boards and planks, old hoops, and staves, and barrel heads innu-
merable, are buoyant with this change of the elements; while floating turnips and apples, with, here and there, a brilliant cabbage
head, gleam in the subterranean firmament, like twinkling stars,
dimmed by the effulgence of the moon at her full. Magnificent
among the lesser vessels of the fleet, "like some tall admiral," rides
the enormous "mash-tub," while the astonished rats and mice are
splashing about at its base in the dark waters, like sailors just
washed, at midnight, from the deck, by a heavy sea. (French, 1865)

The drainage approach described by French involved placing collector
drainage tile at the inside of the footing for the perimeter, and conduit tile
leading through the base of the wall outward, at a slight pitch, to daylight.
Clearly, this is possible only on rather sloped sites, where the threatening
groundwater can be drained to a lower spot that is not threatened. Groundwater roughly follows surface contours, although on a small building site it
is best represented as being as flat as a sea surface. The collector tile inter-
cepts rising groundwater in the most strategic location, inside the footing.
There is no need for gravel in tiles designed only to intercept rising groundwater, and French spoke heartily against the use of stones along with tiles.
A footing tile on the outside of the footing may not be quite as effective an
interceptor of water that threatens the basement, but this detriment would
be weighed against the ease of running the conduit directly to the outfall
rather than through the footing or base of the foundation. Over time, storm
drains became the preferred outlet for footing drains.

Old tile was of low-fired clay. At present, some perforated collector tile
is made from rigid plastic conduit tile by drilled holes. Other collector drain
tile is corrugated plastic with perforated slits around the perimeter of the
tile. All of these tiles are usually placed in excavations surrounded by
gravel. So for the collector tile actually to collect water, the gravel base beneath the tile must be filled with water. The collector tile will distribute
water along its length before discharging any water to the intended outlet.

But presently, drains are thought of as collectors of water coming from
above, not just from below. They are designed with gravel not just beneath
the tile but also above the tile. Filter fabrics and graded stone are used to
prevent the infiltration of fines into the drain tile. Perforated tile, of course,
will not convey water unless the gravel beneath the tile, up to the underside of the tile, is full of water. Designers of drain systems should be aware
that simply drawing a tile in a foundation section does not ensure that
water will flow at that surface level. More care should actually be placed in
the preparation of the soil at the base of the excavation into which the drain
will be placed, as that is the water-conveying surface for water coming from
above.

Water will not flow by capillary suction from a matrix of small pores to a matrix of larger pores, so water in the capillary regime will not naturally drain to a gravel base beneath. If the water is in the gravity-drainable regime, it can and will drain into gravel or sand below. But all liquid drainable water may contain salts in solution and fine soil particles in suspension. As water drains downward, it carries the fines along. Movement of fines may be lessened by:

- Reducing the actual amount of liquid flow
- Using graded gravel, where each layer from fine soil to coarse gravel differs in diameter by a factor of 5 (i.e., each successively coarser layer should have an average diameter that is five times greater than the average diameter of its finer neighbor)
- Using a filter fabric

If there is a strong source of concentrated water, such as the downspout discharge of a large roof section, together with an effective sink for the water to go to, one can imagine how a path can be carved by the water between these two points. Once a trickle flow path is established in soil, it can be expanded easily by erosion along the path. I once investigated a home with a crawl space section attached to a basement foundation. The crawl space section was large, and all of the roof runoff for one side of the house landed in a puddle at the base of a single downspout. The house had an effective footing drain system at the level of the basement footing that delivered water to the indoor sump pump. The crawl space foundation had settled by several inches. In the course of my inspection, I discovered that the eroded path from downspout to footing drain included a section of path that ran exactly along the underside of the crawl space footing. I was able to feel the very clean underside of the concrete footing, as it was suspended about 1 to 2 in. above the soil below. A hazard associated with the movement of fines in draining soil is the risk of undermining the structural support system that the soil provides.

Water that lands in a collector drain needs a place to go. The common outlet sites are (1) to daylight on sites with a strong slope, (2) municipal storm drainage, or (3) a sump pump. Of course, with a sump pump, an outlet for that discharge needs to be identified. Unfortunately, it is common for sump pump discharge to be handled haphazardly, leading to a cycle of discharge and more or less direct reentry of the same water into the sump pump.

The soil that is in direct contact with the foundation deserves special consideration. It is composed of backfill, which may be similar to the excavated soil or may be selected and specified for other properties. Generally, backfill is poorly compacted, as contractors are wary of applying too much lateral pressure to green (fresh) concrete or masonry. Lateral pressure is not a concern, of course, at outside corners of foundations which resist lateral loading simply by virtue of their geometry. Construction that anticipates having concentrated water discharge at the outside corners of the buildings (downspouts are often located there) may choose to have better compaction at outside corners where concentrations of water deposit are expected.

Settling backfill may need to be corrected. Builders should anticipate having to make this correction a year or two after construction, by avoiding permanent plantings and by anticipating settlement in the pinning of porches, stoops, and walkways to the foundation of the building.

If the backfill contains expansive clay (e.g., montmorillonite), during dry spells, the soil may retreat from the foundation leaving a crevice. For the duration of the dry spell, plant and soil materials may accumulate in the crevice. When wetness recurs in the soil, it will swell to its original dimension plus the additional increment of accumulated surface debris. This leads to high soil pressures, often sufficiently high to cause an inward bulge in foundations of unreinforced block. A study we conducted with the Illinois State Geological Survey showed that in a building with a 1-cm inward bulge, the first 1 cm of soil in contact with the top of the wall was identical to the materials of the A horizon (the first few inches on the soil surface). It was utterly unlike the soil just 4 cm into the backfill. Figure 5-10 illustrates this finding.

Designers of foundation drainage often use a drainage layer product with filter fabric placed against the foundation wall. Drainage layer products require an effective collector system at the base. They also require care

Figure 5-10
As clay soil shrinks and swells, soil from the A horizon (the topmost soil) can enter the crack between the soil and the foundation during dry seasons and can contribute to lateral soil pressure during wet seasons.

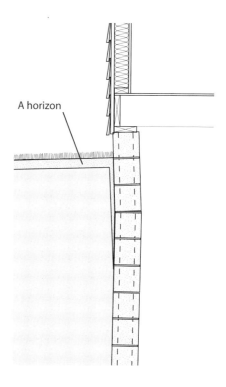

A horizon

at the top termination to ensure that appropriate, not excessive amounts of water are conveyed via the drainage layer. In general, the top of a drainage layer should be kept well below the soil grade, and it should be capped with flashing material to prevent silting.

The soil surface may be considered a roof, as described above. When a roof meets a wall, it is commonly flashed so that water that might otherwise penetrate at the joint between the two surfaces is diverted away. The same concept has been used for building foundations and how they meet the surrounding soil. Gunston Hall, the family home of George Mason in Lorton, Virginia, was an early site of below-grade "flashing" for water management (see also Rose, 1997). Water-impermeable sheet materials such as polyethylene or rubber can be fastened to the foundation at grade, taken downward a foot or so, then flared outward for another 2 to 4 ft at a downward slope, say, 20% (see Figure 5-11). Ground flashing has several advantages:

- Covering the crack between the soil and foundation that often forms (as described above) with clay-containing soils
- Working with exterior foundation insulation strategies, in particular the frost-protected shallow foundation
- Buffering the moisture content in the soil, perhaps moderating the moisture swings that lead to soil movement in expansive clay soils
- Providing umbrellalike protection for termite treatment chemicals in the soil, which might otherwise be leached by downward flow of water in the soil
- Providing an effective site for a below-grade collector tile at the outward end of the flashing; the tile in this location is at a high elevation (providing better outlet options) and is protected against freezing by insulation at the flashing

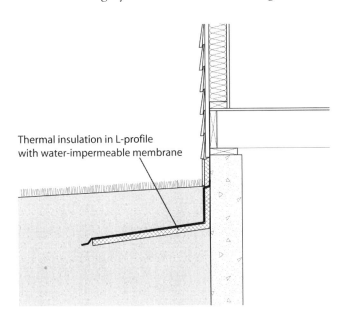

Thermal insulation in L-profile with water-impermeable membrane

Figure 5-11
Insulation in the L-profile shown can reduce heat loss. The water-impermeable membrane above "flashes" the building into the ground and helps prevent saturation of the soil beneath. (Modified from the insulation profile shown in Labs, et al., 1988.)

A gravel or sand base is often prepared in an excavation prior to setting a concrete slab, whether for a walkway, driveway, garage, porch, stoop, or patio. The purpose of the base is to provide material that can easily be leveled and to serve as a capillary break. Concrete has small pores, so it would be a natural accumulator of water if it were in contact with capillary material beneath. Concrete over a sand or gravel base provides a very good capillary break unless the base collects water. If that happens, and the bottom of the concrete is in contact with the liquid water in the base, the moisture content of the concrete may move to the top of the capillary range. Good practice is to provide drainage from any gravel or sand base and to avoid any concentrated rainwater flows into the gravel base.

In cold climates, concrete slabs in garages or other unheated spaces near sites of water concentration may suffer from cracking due to frost heave. The condition shown in Figure 5-12 is unfortunately quite widespread. The saturated soil at the base of the downspout turns to ice at the surface. This ice attaches itself tightly to the edge of the slab. As cold weather continues, water beneath the ice freezes, expands in volume, pushes against the stable soil beneath, and raises the edge of the slab. A corner that is elevated cannot bear the weight of the slab and the contents of the garage, so the corner of the slab can crack. Frost heaving requires a continuing contribution of liquid water to the site of the heave. Downspouts are usually able to replenish the water even during cold weather because of snow melt from the roof when exposed to the sun.

An idealized version of attachment frost heave is shown in Figure 5-13. Imagine a container of fixed volume that contains water and a solid block that is free to move upward. Cold temperatures at the top permit the first layer of water to turn to ice. That ice attaches itself to the block. As subsequent layers of water beneath the original ice turn to ice, the volume of each layer is increased by 8%. If the lowest resistance to volume change is offered

Figure 5-12
Crack in garage slab. This occurs during cold weather at unheated slabs in contact with saturated soil.

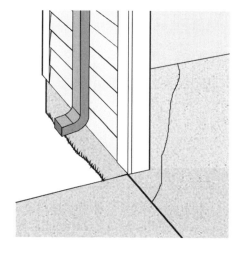

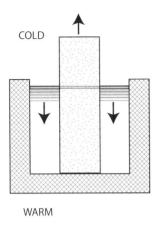

COLD

WARM

Figure 5-13
Attachment frost heave. The water at the surface attaches to the center post, which is free to move upward. As freezing continues, the volume change cannot act against the incompressible water below, so, it lifts the post.

by the ice above, it moves upward and takes the block with it. When 1 ft³ of water increases in volume to 1.08 ft³ (the volume change associated with change to ice), each side of the cube will be incremented by about $\frac{3}{8}$ in. If the entire volume change is taken up in one dimension, say upward, the upward growth will be about 1 in. It is common to see uninsulated building piers being racked and heaved by winter, especially if downspouts discharge water nearby. The amount of resistance offered by the soil surrounding the pier depends, of course, on peculiar site conditions.

Frost heave generally follows this pattern. First, the soil must be saturated: If the soil contains air, expansion of the water will act against the air, not against the surfaces. If the soil is well drained, either by good pitch on the surface or by granular soil type, frost heave is unlikely. Second, the soil must be capable of freezing. Soil that is in contact with the foundation of a heated building is unlikely to freeze unless the thermal insulation in the basement wall is considerable. Extending foundation materials down to *frost depth* provides no guarantee against frost heave, because attachment heaving is still possible with saturated frozen soil. Extending foundations down to frost depth does provide greater friction against heave, of course, provided that the foundation has tension connection between the upper section that is lifted and the lower foundation wall that resists lifting through weight and friction.

Another ice event that is rare but interesting is the formation of ice extrusions in soil (see Figure 5-14). These occur during cold weather and cold soil surfaces with liquid water beneath. Hydraulic pressure is exerted on the water by water uphill or the weight of the frozen soil above or by the volume expansion of ice against a confined volume of water. This pushes the water upward through openings in the surface soil. Pure water freezes at 0°C. Salts, we know, depress the freezing point of water, so it is reasonable to expect that water that is bound to soil particles may also have a lower freezing point. At just the right temperature, pure water under pressure may

Figure 5-14
Ice crystals extruded out of the soil during cold weather.

freeze while the bound water remains unfrozen, and this may lead to a small amount of "lubrication" as the ice grows upward from the water beneath.

BASEMENTS

Basement construction typically consists of footings, walls placed on the footings, and a floor slab. The footing should be placed on stable, usually undisturbed soil. The wall is typically constructed of masonry (block or brick) or precast or cast-in-place concrete. A small number of basement walls are of treated lumber. A growing number are of insulated concrete forms into which concrete is cast. The basement floor slab is typically concrete over a gravel or sand base.

Let's investigate the properties of concrete in order to see how water can move through basement foundation assemblies. The following data are from IEA, Annex 24 (1996), *Heat, Air and Moisture Transfer in Insulated Envelope Parts*, Final Report Task 3: Material Properties:

- *Dry density:* 2200 ($\pm$ 100) kg/m^3
- *Heat capacity:* 840 to 940 J/(kg·K)
- *Porosity:* ~0.15 (m^3/m^3)
- *Sorption curve:* Figure 5-15
- *Curve of permeability:* Figure 5-16

Note that the maximum amount of water in the concrete on a volume basis (porosity) is 15%. The density of concrete is 2200 kg/m^3, whereas the den-

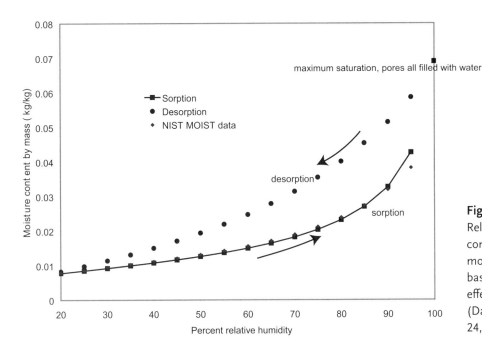

Figure 5-15
Relative humidity of concrete compared to moisture content (mass basis). Note the strong effect of hysteresis. (Data from IEA, Annex 24, 1996.)

sity of water is much less, 1000 kg/m³. So on a mass basis, the maximum amount of water that can be retained in concrete is around 7%.

Look closely at the sorption curve (Figure 5-15), which compares the relative humidity to the mass-base moisture content. Concrete is a material with very small pores, so it is more like clay than sand; that is, it retains great quantities of water in the sorption range, while the amount of drainable water is very small. The water is bound tightly to surfaces and within the small pores. The amount of air in a sample of normal concrete (not air-entrained concrete) is small, so moisture movement as vapor is small.

Note that concrete shows very strong hysteresis, that is, it shows a great difference in water content depending on whether the specimen is in the process of wetting or drying out. The most accurate way to measure the water content of concrete is by oven drying. It is much simpler simply to place a small hole in the concrete, cover the hole, and measure the relative humidity of the air in the hole. This method introduces some errors. For one thing, it averages any water content gradient that may occur in the depth of the hole. For another, it does not account for the hysteresis effect, which, in the case of concrete, is considerable. Suppose that the relative humidity meter indicates 80% RH. If the concrete was first wetted, the water content may be as high as 0.045; if it had been dry, the water content might be half that amount. The two concrete samples would be in equilibrium. This twofold difference in water content may translate into a tenfold difference in vapor permeability. Figure 5-16 shows one order of magnitude

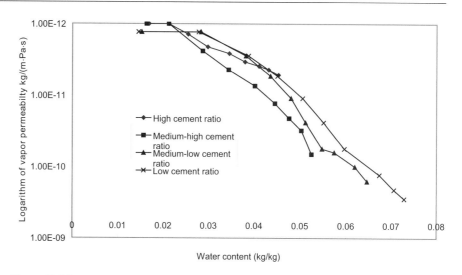

Figure 5-16
Permeability of several concrete samples compared to moisture content. (Data from IEA, Annex 24, 1996.)

difference in vapor permeability between samples at 0.2 and 0.4 water content, for example. Such differences make it very difficult to predict with precision the drying behavior of concrete.

Water may come into contact with the foundation through the wall and from the footing (see Figure 5-17). In clay soils, water may accumulate in the top layers of soil, causing it to swell and blocking flow to a footing drain. Footing drains may be blocked or missing. This water may enter through cracks in the foundation by hydraulic (gravity) pressure, where the height of the water forms a hydraulic head. The saturated soil could lead to saturation in the wall, at least in the absence of dampproofing applied to the wall. If the wall is of block (with cores) rather than cast-in-place concrete, the water would probably penetrate the cores. Usually, block cores are interconnected at the bottom of the wall where it rests on the footing, so that water can be redistributed along the length of a wall even from a point source of water. In any case, water that appears as leakage through foundation walls is associated, in almost all cases, with rainwater that is concentrated in the soil near the site of the leakage. Water that leaks through a floor slab or from the corner where the slab meets the foundation wall may be associated with rising groundwater, but the water table would, in this case, have to be elevated some distance above the elevation where water enters.

Dampproofing usually consists of a trowel-applied or spray-applied coating of bitumen or parging concrete with additives to reduce water penetration. Dampproofing helps concrete to resist wetting from occasional contact with saturated soil. Dampproofing interrupts capillary flow from

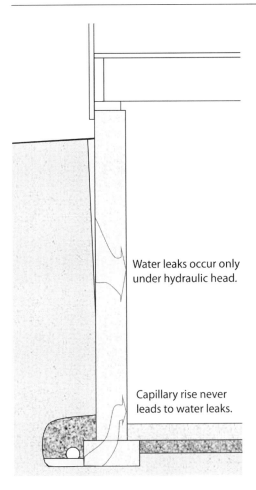

Water leaks occur only under hydraulic head.

Capillary rise never leads to water leaks.

Figure 5-17
Means of water entry through basement elements.

moist soil. It is often argued that dampproofing acts as a *vapor retarder* preventing wetting of the concrete from transport via vapor in the air. Neither clay soils nor concrete has enough interconnected pore volume for this claim to have much merit. In soil and concrete, water vapor diffusion would be very minor and very slow.

If we did need to know the water vapor pressure in the air contained in the soil, we could calculate it from the soil wetness and the temperature. In saturated soil, either following rains or at the water table, the soil is saturated, so the temperature of the saturated soil, or well water, represents the dew point temperature, and vapor pressure can be calculated from the dew point.

Since soil temperature is usually colder than room temperature, perhaps 50°F, the vapor pressure may be surprisingly low, and it may be at the same level as room air at 50% relative humidity. That leads to rather balanced vapor pressures. With balanced vapor pressures on either side of a wall, a vapor retarder is not necessary. The benefits of dampproofing are that it serves as a capillary break and provides some resistance against water entry from saturated soil. However, it retards drying of concrete and forces drying to occur toward the interior of the building.

Foundations may also be designed and engineered for waterproofing, a technique that uses liners with sealable joints together with drains that are strategically placed depending on the anticipated water loading. Water may also collect in the gravel that surrounds the footing drain, beneath the bottom of the excavation and the outflow of the drain (see Figure 5-17). That water can saturate the footing. Some have argued for placement of a capillary break between a footing and a wall. I prefer (1) improved design of the footing drain system, (2) reducing the amount of surface rainwater that reaches the footing drain, and (3) minimizing the depth of water that can accumulate there.

We saw earlier in the work of Henry French that a drain system at the interior of the footing is the best protection against rising groundwater. In all cases where rising groundwater poses a threat, the water must be collected and evacuated. Evacuation can be done by gravity on sloped sites and where stormwater collection systems are deep enough to collect water from footing drains. In many cases, however, water must go to a sump pump. A sump is a pit that serves as a gravity collector, a low point to which water may drain. It should be pierced at the bottom for direct entry of rising groundwater.

The sump pump must have a designed site of discharge. It is sadly quite common to see sump pump discharge pipes so short that the water recycles back into the foundation, causing erosion and silting with each cycle. Or the pipe may be so long that it is easily dislodged, interferes with traffic, and may present a circulation hazard. A solution often used is for a below-grade connection to the street or to daylight, with an inspectable connection to the sump pump discharge (see Figure 5-18).

Insulation of Basement Walls

Historically, basement walls have been uninsulated. Only in the last few decades have materials been provided that perform as thermal insulation in below-grade spaces. These include extruded polystyrene and borate-treated expanded polystyrene. There have been several attempts to estimate heat loss through building foundations (Labs et al., 1988). Air is the principal insulator in the soil–water–air matrix, and estimates of the quantity of air in the soil are very difficult to make, given varieties of soil types and variation in moisture content. The thermal resistance of dry soil is considerably greater than the thermal resistance of wet soil for all soil types. Nevertheless, many energy codes require insulation of building foundations, although ensuring dry foundations may be as effective or more effective in reducing heat transfer.

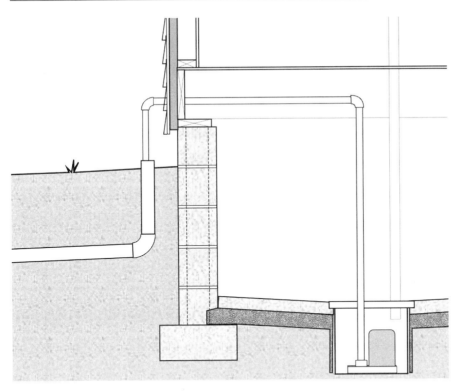

Figure 5-18
Sump pump connection. Care must be taken to ensure safe discharge of water from sump pumps.

Exterior insulation is generally the best approach, although the long-term durability of insulation materials in ground contact is a persistent issue. With exterior insulation, the mass of the building foundation remains warm. Thus, the concrete can remain rather dry and consequently have a low rate of moisture transfer. If insulation is placed on the inside, several concerns arise. The foundation materials will be cold during cold weather; if they are in contact with water-saturated soil and the exterior climate is severely cold, the foundation could be subject to heave. Also, if the concrete or block is cold, it tends to be wet. If wet, it has a high permeance, so it can convey water toward the interior more quickly.

How should the interior of a basement wall be insulated? Canada Mortgage and Housing Corporation conducted a study that compared several strategies (Forest and Ackerman, 1999). Two were proprietary systems, one using prefinished polystyrene panels and one using prefinished high-density fiberglass panels. They also studied interior framing, with wood and metal studs. The framed systems used fiberglass insulation, gypsum wallboard at the interior, and polyethylene in two locations, behind the gypsum and between the framing and the foundation wall. The study used loading typical for basement walls: a quantity of water was poured between the foundation and the framing, and water was brought into the basement to a height of several inches for one day. The outcome was that the proprietary systems survived the loading well, but the framed systems all developed mold growth. This points to the importance of selecting correct loading for engineering design of systems. Polyethylene is often introduced into insulated frame wall systems as a vapor retarder. But the load in this case is not vapor, but liquid water. Obviously, water comes from the soil or rises up on the floor. Systems designed to prevent wetting from vapor were not successful, as they failed to provide for drying of liquid loads.

In summary, a dry basement occurs whenever the soil that is in contact with the foundation remains free of saturation. With saturation, concrete materials become wetted, dry slowly, and have increased vapor and liquid transport properties. Both rainwater and groundwater can lead to soil saturation. Good rainwater management is essential, particularly on the soil surface. Building sites should be selected away from high groundwater tables. Where rising groundwater does threaten a basement, perimeter drainage to a sump, storm drain system, or daylight is the only solution. The best site for insulation is the outside of the foundation. Insulation located at the interior should be able to pass the "smell test." That is, if there are any signs of wetness or bad odor at the basement walls, the interior finish should be inspectable and repairable.

CRAWL SPACES

Crawl spaces are under-floor foundation areas that are much stubbier than basements. Prior to World War II, most buildings in the north had basements, and many of the buildings in the south were built on pier foundations. Around the Great Lakes, many homes for immigrants were built in areas with high water tables, so they had crawl spaces. One common variant was a *Dutch basement* (other regional terms abound), which was largely unexcavated except for a central area that usually held the boiler or gravity furnace. Many buildings had a full or partial basement that was open to an unexcavated area under a porch or part of the house. Federal Housing Administration documents from the 1930s mention "basementless spaces" (incidentally, with stern warnings about the likelihood of water problems), but crawl space construction did not become widespread until the postwar housing boom. A January 1942 FHA document, *Property Standards and Minimum Construction Requirements for Dwellings,* contained the first requirements for the ventilation of crawl spaces. It required an area of ventilation to be at least equal to 1/150 of the footprint of the house. This same document was the source of the first requirements for vapor barriers and attic ventilation.

In 1948, Ralph Britton, a researcher with the Housing and Home Finance Agency, which oversaw the FHA, inspected a group of 72 apartment houses in Arlington, Virginia, which were on crawl spaces and had terrible water problems. He noted several things. Water got in directly through vent openings that were too close to the ground. It also evaporated into the building from exposed soil, as much as 100 lb/day per 1000 ft². Once water was in the crawl space, it severely damaged the steel and wood floor framing members. It passed upward through the buildings, through chases and furring cavities that even bypassed the living space, up to the attic (see Figure 5-19). The water from the crawl space severely damaged the attic sheathing. Britton recommended improving the drainage to keep water out of crawl spaces. He recommended using ground covers, except that roll roofing, the one membrane available (polyethylene didn't come into residential construction until the early 1950s), was known to become brittle from ground contact. He recommended generous crawl space vent openings, 1/150 of the floor area (he may have been the author of the 1942 requirements) and he recommended attic ventilation. What he noticed, largely overlooked today, is that with vent openings at the level of the foundation and also the

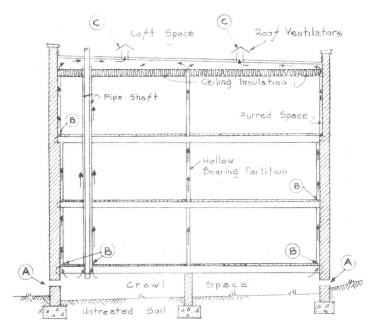

Figure 5-19

Britton (1948) recognized that moisture in attic or loft spaces comes from foundations, through plumbing chases and furred spaces. He recognized that crawl spaces were very wet and he recognized that humid crawl space air can be carried up to the attic when crawl space and attic vents are open.

· T Y P I C A L   C R O S S   S E C T I O N ·
· A P A R T M E N T   P R O J E C T ·

Ⓐ = Inadequate wall ventilation

Ⓑ = Openings in floor ⅛" ±, continuous

Ⓒ = Roof ventilation misplaced unless vents are also in side walls above top ceiling floor

→ → Arrows indicate path of warm humid air

attic, air is likely to move between the two if any pathway is provided. He pointed out that attic venting may be able to be reduced tenfold if pathways for humid crawl space air into the attic are eliminated. He recommended providing roofing material to cover the soil of a crawl space as well as ventilation. Of these recommendations, the crawl space venting recommendations were the ones that were measurable and verifiable by a building inspector. (Model building codes were first introduced in the same year, 1948.) So venting regulations became the cornerstone of moisture control regulations.

How Crawl Spaces Work

It is often said that a building cavity has "gotta breathe," and this leads many to a simple faith in the efficacy of vents. The common understanding of venting efficacy runs like this: Some water will evaporate from the soil; to prevent that humidity from affecting a building, we dilute the crawl space air with outdoor air. Wintertime is considered the critical moisture control season, so the dilution air is presumed to be dry. Most building codes have deviated little from the first formulation of the venting requirement and call for vent openings that measure in area 1/150 of the crawl space area. The required area needs to be doubled if covered by screen but can be cut down by a factor of 10 if the soil of the crawl space is covered with a vapor-impermeable ground cover. Vents, they say, are to be placed within 3 ft of corners.

However, the effectiveness of ventilation and dilution depends primarily on the strength of the contaminant source. It is not hard to imagine a water load that will overtax any vent ratio and any resulting rate of dilution. Why are vents the focus of current crawl space regulation? Probably because they are verifiable and code enforceable, whereas other, more important factors, such as downspouts, rainwater discharge, soil slope, and ground cover, are not.

Let's run some numbers. Suppose that water is the principal concern. We begin by choosing an estimated design load, the amount of water we estimate will evaporate from the soil. Britton suggests that we use 100 lb/day from a crawl space of 1000 ft^2, with no ground cover and a water table about 3 ft below the soil surface. Later researchers support this estimate. With a ground cover, the amount of water evaporating from the soil will be greatly reduced. But if rainwater can find its way onto the top of the ground cover, we're back up to a load on the order of 100 lb/day. Can we dilute 100 lb of water per day with ventilation? Under ideal conditions, yes. Suppose that the air coming out of the vents is at 70°F and 65% RH. Such air contains about 1% water by mass—it has a humidity ratio of 0.01. So we would need to exhaust 10,000 lb of air, not accounting for the humidity of the incoming air, and maybe 20,000 lb of air per day if we account for the incoming humidity. That's about 14 lb of air per minute or about 200 ft^3/min. On the top of a hill on a windy day, with the vents wide open, one can imagine airflow through the vents of about 200 ft^3/min. At the bottom of the hill, with still air and with vegetation growing around the vents or with grass clippings blown against them, it's hard to expect any airflow at all. In my opinion, it is inappropriate to apply the same venting requirements to buildings in exposed sites and buildings at low elevations or in dense sites. And isn't it true that we opt for crawl space foundations for low-lying areas where the water table might be high? These are precisely the sites where the wind can be least effective.

There is another problem with ventilation: During summer, especially when air conditioning is in operation, vents are more likely to let moisture in than let it out. Many vents are operable, but there is no manual on how they ought to be operated. Many homeowners keep them closed. There is another problem: the crawl space provides very valuable space for running mechanical services. If the outdoor extremes of temperature and humidity are allowed to come in contact with water supply pipes and ductwork, the chances for damage are high. Most ductwork has air loss, leading to energy loss; why not keep these losses within the conditioned space?

Which leads us to the importance of source reduction. Good rainwater management at the outside of the building should reduce the moisture source from a crawl space down to a tiny fraction of the 100 lb per day that is possible. To dilute 1 lb/day, one might need only 2 ft^3/min. A water contribution that small could easily be bundled in with the anticipated moisture generation rate of 20 lb per day for a family of four.

Needless to say, the vent should not admit water into the crawl space. This is a very common problem. It occurs because homes in the United States are expected to show little more than 8 in. of exposed foundation. With increasing requirements for accessibility and visitability of buildings, it is expected that the vertical separation between outdoor grade and indoor floor level will not be increasing. Vents are designed to be installed in place of a concrete block. With only 8 in. of exposed foundation, clearly the bottom of the vent opening will be at grade. The term *vent* should be changed to *sluice* or *weir*.

Crawl spaces are often used because they form convenient service spaces for running utilities. These utilities cause penetrations through the floor. Typically, the floor system that separates the crawl space from the living space is perforated and there is exchange of air between the two spaces. This can be troublesome. The air contained in the soil is termed *soil gas*. Soil gas may contain chemicals from the soil, such as agricultural or industrial chemicals, depending on site uses nearby, and it may contain odors coming from organic compounds, fungi, and bacteria. Musty smells are usually fungal; earthy smells are typically from bacteria. These are contaminants and they should not be allowed into the living space. Soil gas tends to leave the soil during times of low barometric pressure. This causes any stored smells, such as agricultural smells, to be more pronounced, and its effect can be felt in crawl space homes.

In most climates, if the crawl space is vented, the floor system must be insulated. It is very common for insulation to be placed within floor framing and for gravity to have its way, so that batts lie collapsed on the floor of the crawl space. For one thing, insulation must be secured in place. If insulation is secured in place and wood framing members are exposed to the crawl space, the exposed wood surfaces may darken from mold growth. This occurs because the floor of the crawl space may be cold during the summertime. Indeed, it may be chilled by evaporation of moisture from the surface. When two planar surfaces are parallel and extend broadly, they tend toward the same temperature from radiant exchange. The floor of the crawl space will, in effect, chill the underside of the insulated floor framing system. During summer, when the crawl space air tends toward a high dew point, the exposed wood may see a considerable amount of time above 80% surface water activity, leading to mold growth. Generally, wood should be covered in insulated floor assemblies.

In 1954, the Housing and Home Finance Agency researched moisture migration from the ground. They found that with suitable ground covers that effectively reduced moisture evaporation from the soil, the vents could be closed (Russell, 1954). This finding was seconded by the University of Illinois Small Homes Council in its circular *Crawl Spaces* (SHC, 1959). That publication described how to build a successful crawl space without reliance on ventilation. It stressed the importance of good drainage and of having a good ground cover in place. If those two conditions are met, the circular stated, the vents can be closed and the perimeter walls of the crawl space can be insulated against heat loss.

Is this a good idea? Judging from inspections of crawl spaces in the Midwest (where people followed the recommendations of the Council), those that do meet the drainage and ground cover requirements have floor framing that is in good shape. Those that didn't were the houses where we found damage. Some inspectors pay scant attention to the presence or absence of vents (they are usually blocked with lawn clippings anyway), but pay very careful attention to drainage and ground covers. This issue was reviewed at an ASHRAE symposium in 1994 (American Society of Heating, Refrigerating, and Air-Conditioning Engineers). Only one of the resulting articles demonstrated the benefits of venting, and that was with large 1/150 vent openings. The other articles stressed the importance of drainage and access and the overriding importance of ground covers. The summary article concluded that "there is no technical basis in the literature for the venting requirements." Those conclusions have been incorporated in the 1997 and later editions of ASHRAE *Handbook—Fundamentals*. Discussions are under way with code bodies to revisit the issue of venting requirements for crawl spaces.

General Strategies

Crawl spaces should be dry spaces. They should not support the growth of mold.

- Rainwater should be kept out. The crawl space floor level should be well above the historic high water table elevation. Careful attention should be paid to rainwater management at the outside of a foundation, including good grading of the soil and providing for discharge of any collected water.
- The crawl space should be an inviting place to visit. It should be as tall as possible within the constraints of economy, preferably five blocks or 40 in. It should be completely free of clutter and construction debris. It should have easy access and good lighting. The floor should be designed not only to prevent evaporation, but also for comfort in getting around for inspections and repairs.
- Penetrations in the floor framing should be kept to a minimum. Subcontractors should be told not to make oversize cuts and to close up openings after themselves.

Crawl spaces should be cleanable. I was asked to investigate for moisture 32 homes with identical crawl spaces, and an industrial hygienist made concurrent samples of air for mold spores. We were astonished to find that the number of spores was *inversely* proportional to the wetness (measured by testing the moisture content of the floor framing). This puzzling finding made sense once it was realized that the dry crawl spaces were dusty, and dust may contain mold spores and mold material. Also, careless investigators may disturb the dust.

Vented Crawl Space

To build a vented crawl space correctly, designers and builders might take a lesson from the manufactured housing industry, because their floor systems stand up quite well. Manufactured homes use an insulated floor and they integrate the mechanical system into the insulated framing rather than have it suspended below. They use a belly paper or belly board, which is a plastic or bitumen membrane that does not allow water or water vapor to pass through. The great advantage of having a continuous membrane on the underside of the framing is that it avoids the common problem in insulated floor systems of having exposed wood facing the crawl space. The disadvantage of using a continuous membrane at the underside of a floor system is that water spills from the living space above have nowhere to go but to sit for what could be a very long time in the framing. The solution to this, of course, is to lance the belly board here and there, especially in locations where spills are likely to occur, such as the kitchen and laundry room.

The belly board (say, 10-mil polyethylene sheet) is a good way to keep insulation in place; another is to use rigid panels of foam insulation. Of course, this works only for new construction—full rigid panels might have a hard time making it through the crawl space opening. Using wire or plastic construction fencing can be helpful for keeping insulation in place, but simply stapling kraft paper probably will not work for the long term.

We hear in the construction industry to "install the vapor barrier on the warm side." In fact, this is shorthand for "install the vapor barrier on the side with the high vapor pressure." In a crawl space, the belly board can be installed on the underside of the framing and fully comply with the vapor pressure requirement.

The foundation may be designed as a perimeter wall with large openings or a pier foundation with skirting. Vent openings of 1/150 of the floor area are a good starting point. Good site drainage is very helpful. This type of construction effectively isolates occupants from having soil gas mixed with their breathing air; this is a great advantage in potentially contaminated sites (see Figure 5-20). Note in the figure that the vent openings are located well above the outside grade. Note, too, that there is no mechanical equipment located in the crawl space. If mechanical equipment were installed, the requirements for airtightness and continuity of insulation might make this approach uneconomical and difficult to execute.

Figure 5-20

Details of a vented crawl space. Note that mechanical equipment in a crawl space and penetrations of the sealed insulated floor system could compromise the effectiveness of this system.

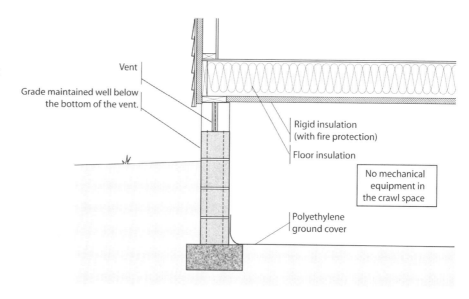

Vent

Grade maintained well below the bottom of the vent.

Rigid insulation (with fire protection)

Floor insulation

No mechanical equipment in the crawl space

Polyethylene ground cover

Crawl Space Without Venting

My preference is to think of the crawl space as a stubby basement, as another room in the house (see Figure 5-21). The first chore in the design is to make sure that the floor stays dry. It is common practice to level the dirt floor. Instead, I recommend installing a sump pump wherever the future wet spot may be, usually on the side of the house that faces uphill. Then slope the crawl space soil toward the sump pit at a 2 to 3% slope and tamp it. I recommend adding 3 in. of pea gravel on top of the soil. To improve further the drainage of the floor, a collector pipe system may be installed in the thickness of the pea gravel. A good choice for a sump pit would be one with a tight lid so that the sump pit could be used, if needed, for radon control. Extracting air from the sump pit and the gravel layer may be good for overall indoor air quality.

Some people recommend covering the soil with polyethylene sheeting. I recommend a thin (2- to 3-in.) slab of concrete for cleanability. If there are smells that come from the crawl space, all of the surfaces should be able to be cleaned and bleached if necessary.

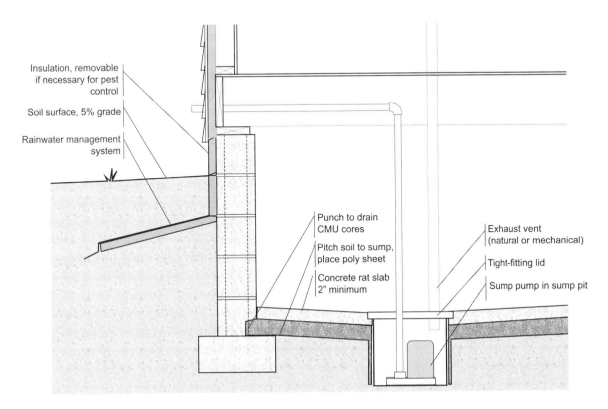

Figure 5-21
Crawl space designed without ventilation.

Although insulation of expanded polystyrene on the interior of the crawl space wall has been used, I recommend exterior insulation. The choice of insulation material, location, and covering may hinge on fire safety considerations.

The band joist area is often insulated in cold-weather areas. If exterior insulated sheathing is used, that may be sufficient. Fitting panels of rigid foam insulation may work except that the unprotected ends of the joists may be cooled to risky low temperatures. Commonly, the band joist area is usually stuffed with fiberglass insulation, another risky practice because the crawl space humidity can occasionally creep up. Spray foam insulation from the interior may work, but it may raise fire concerns. With risk of water accumulation in the crawl space, I would strongly recommend exterior insulation, and we might consider no interior insulation at the band joist, only in cases of foundations that are exceptionally wet.

Of course, the furnace (and other mechanical equipment for that matter) should be kept out of the crawl space. Furnace filters in crawl spaces are simply never changed.

Some builders in the Midwest install operable vents to meet the minimum requirements of the local building code. They advise owners to go ahead and close the vents and install blocks of foam insulation behind the vents once the owners are comfortable with dry conditions in the crawl space. The only down side to this practice occurs with poor drainage, when the vent becomes the hole that lets the water in.

Perhaps we should think of venting for emergencies rather than day-to-day concerns. In case of flooding, a major plumbing leak, a dead animal, or if someone wished to remove mold with bleach, having the capacity to power flush the crawl space air would be very desirable.

SLAB CONSTRUCTION

Concrete slab construction began in industrial buildings with the introduction of the Portland cement industry, beginning in the United States in Pennsylvania's Lehigh Valley. Residential slab construction began immediately following World War II.

Slab construction had several strong benefits. It was inexpensive, of course, obviating the need for substantial excavation. It lent itself to the development of construction in the southern United States because of the low frost depth. Homes after World War II were built much lower to the ground than those immediately prior to the war. The reason for this is the source of some speculation. Some say it was due to the influence of architects such as Frank Lloyd Wright, with emphasis on horizontal lines, and represented a rejection of classicism (with its rusticated base) in favor of modernism. The most convincing argument I've encountered notes that the social area of a house moved from the front porch to the rear patio, with only at most a one-step difference between the patio height and the indoor floor height. This would argue strongly for slab construction. The obvious disadvantage of slab construction is the inaccessibility and inflexibility of the service functions of the floor system. Below-grade ducts were possible but frowned upon because of the possibility of water entry. Hydronic systems could be fixed, and repairs were difficult. The floor could not be used for electrical distribution as it could with basement and crawl space construction. When problems appear in the service functions of a building with a slab foundation, usually those services are moved to overhead.

The best slab construction ensures that there is an air gap between the top grade surface and the underside of the slab (see Figure 5-22). This helps to ensure that water cannot accumulate in the gravel base beneath the slab and reside in contact with the concrete. Where this rule is broken, wet slabs are quite common.

In the 1950s and 1960s, the Building Research Advisory Board studied slab construction. They cited the need for an air gap and they predicted poor performance for any slab that could permit water to sit against the underside. They planned for a series of moisture studies to include swelling pressures, stabilization and, a curious term, *thermal osmosis*. This seems to refer to the migration of water toward cold materials, described above in the work of Teesdale (1937, p. 59).

The earliest slab construction consisted of a perimeter foundation to frost depth, often designed to act as a beam in case of minor soil movement, and a horizontal slab cast in place over a sand or gravel base. The base

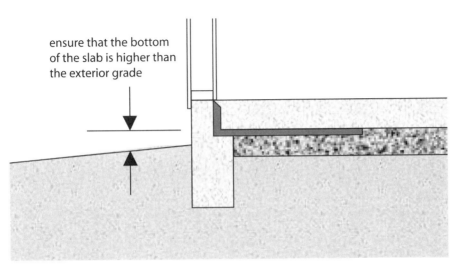

ensure that the bottom of the slab is higher than the exterior grade

Figure 5-22
Slab construction. It is important to maintain an air gap between the top of the outdoor grade and the underside of the slab.

served as a capillary break. The air contained in the gravel base was also a sink that permitted drying to below. As long as the concrete could dry to both above and below, and as long as it was never subject to liquid wetting, the concrete could reach the sorption side of the hysteresis difference (see Figure 5-15) and remain quite dry.

Polyethylene sheet material was introduced into the construction industry in the 1950s. The introduction of polyethylene meant that, in principle, the isolation of a concrete slab from water effects in the soil beneath was complete. There are two possible water effects: first, capillary water, which should be very low through a gravel base, low through a sand base, and could be quite high if the concrete is poured directly onto silt or clay; and second, liquid water rising through the base to the underside of the concrete. In the first case, polyethylene may be unnecessary over gravel or sand but would be very helpful with more water-active soils. The sand or gravel base is retained in practice because it permits more accurate leveling of the excavation, as well as serving as a capillary break. In the second case, if water rises through the base to the underside of the concrete, then wherever the polyethylene is intact, wetting is prevented. But poly has joints and the joints are practically impossible to seal, so the potential remains for wetting at the edges and joints of polyethylene. The importance attached to good rainwater management around and beneath a slab is not diminished by the use of polyethylene.

The downside of polyethylene was the reduced drying potential through the underside of the slab. With overly wet concrete, this could be quite detrimental, but with a dry mix (and concrete needs to be formed with as little water as possible) this does not represent much difficulty.

Insulation is often used beneath slabs. Extruded polystyrene appears to be the insulation material of choice. The capillary and wetting effects are similar to the use of polyethylene; foam may retard drying, it may serve as a capillary break, but hydraulic wetting is still possible at joints and edges. Insulation does reduce heat loss and helps ensure that the mean temperature of the concrete is warmer during cold weather. This helps speed drying and may help keep insulation material at drier conditions than a comparable slab without insulation.

Slabs may contain radiant heating elements, and these will certainly accelerate drying. Indeed, the drying may be sufficiently rapid to impose an unexpected moisture burden on the interior of the building, at least until the water content of the concrete reaches equilibrium with normal conditions. Generally, insulation will be used beneath radiant-heated slabs. Rainwater and groundwater management is essential with all slabs, but the importance is doubled with radiant-heated slabs. If the slab is wetted with a constantly renewable source of water, the effect of heating may simply be to increase the rate of evaporation from the surface, and the water can be replenished continuously. As a general rule, heating a concrete surface that is wetted by sorption or by capillary moisture will result in a slab or wall that is drier and has reduced transport toward, and evaporation from, the surface. On the other hand, heating a concrete surface that is wetted hydraulically may leave a surface that may appear dry but may have greater surface evaporation than an unheated surface.

The nagging question in slab construction is this: When is the slab ready for the application of a floor finish? The answers are quite contentious and subject to varying points of view. The American Concrete Institute (Standard 302) has adopted the flowchart shown in Figure 5-23 in an attempt to address this question. There is more to the standard than this chart of course; refer to the standard for more information.

The flowchart presents three types of slabs and gives conditions for the use of each. Of these three, the assembly with the membrane beneath the dry granular material is the most questionable. The makers of the flowchart seem to acknowledge the importance of keeping water out of any granular material between the membrane and the concrete. I would point out that the building may need rainwater management through the life of the building, not just attention during construction.

All water transport may involve salt transport. *Efflorescence* is the deposit of salts on surfaces of building materials. *Subflorescence* is the deposit just beneath the surface in the case of more porous materials where evaporation occurs from beneath. The transport occurs as liquid or bound (capillary) water with dissolved salts wicks upward, then evaporates. The concentration of salts left behind increases the osmotic potential at that surface, so the surface is not only discolored but is wetter. Water transport of salts through floor slabs, given a salt strength below, can affect floor coatings and finishes.

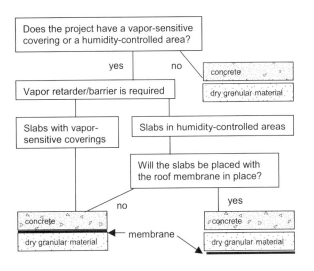

Figure 5-23

Decision tree regarding the use of a vapor retarder membrane in slab construction. (From the American Concrete Institute standard 302.)

In summary, slabs are constructed with a gravel or sand base beneath. As a capillary break, the base is quite effective. But if the base can fill with water, the damage to the slab and to the indoor environment may be substantial. Two strategies for ensuring a dry base are (1) an air gap between the outdoor grade and the underside of the slab, and (2) good rainwater management on the outside of the building. If polyethylene or insulation is used, its placement up against the underside of the slab is preferred; placing poly under gravel may lead to unwanted water collection in the base.

6 Walls

INTRODUCTION

In Chapter 3 we noted that moisture control since the 1930s has meant management of indoor humidity. In Chapter 4 we discussed shedding water to the outdoors from facade elements. How much water comes from outside, how much from inside? Figure 6-1 shows some of the paths that water may take as it begins outside and affects the interior of a building. It may enter building cracks and cavities as liquid water and require drainage or evaporation. In the author's experience, many buildings with moisture problems have wet foundation areas, and that loading is shown in Figure 6-1.

But the humidity from indoors cannot be ignored (see Table 6-1). The table contains figures that may look exact, but they represent artificial estimates for the input values, to illustrate that under certain assumptions, humidity from indoors may be comparable to outdoor moisture. The assumptions in this table are that $\frac{1}{2}$ in. per year of rain is applied to the vertical wall surface, and 2% of that amount gets through the weather-resistant barrier. For vapor transport the assumption is four months of outdoor temperatures averaging 20°F. Other assumptions lead to other conclusions, of course, and of course these are just numbers that represent the rate of loading—the assemblies would be expected to dry out during this period.

The water that enters into building assemblies and cavities past weather-resistant barriers is never uniformly distributed across a surface. It is concentrated at openings where the water gets in and on sides of the building where the weather load is greatest. Those who inspect for water problems in buildings would readily agree: Water problems in walls occur locally. They make patterns that can be interpreted to determine source of the water, source strength, weather conditions under which the damage occurred, and how recently the problems occurred. One of the elements of the pattern is a gradient, where there is likely to be a point or a line or an area that has

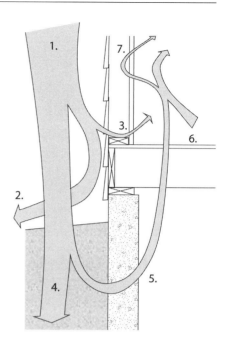

Figure 6-1
Paths along which water enters walls.
The largest amount may be from outside
(3). The foundation area can be a large
contributor to building humidity (5).
A relatively small amount enters walls
as indoor water vapor (7).

the densest deterioration: usually, mold growth, discoloration, or corrosion. The zone of greatest density is ground zero for the water source.

If the wall gets wetted by rainwater leakage, then it must be helped to dry. Several factors can assist in drying. First, heat. Recall the *rule of material wetting*. Building materials that are warm will dry much more quickly than those left at cold temperatures. Vapor pressure over water or over materials is an exponential function of temperature. For each increase in temperature, the vapor pressure increases—more vapor in the air, less water in the materials. Recall the shape of any of the RH curves on the psychrometric chart and that the moisture content of materials tracks relative humidity rather closely. If materials can stay warm, they are likely to stay dry. Heat enhances drying. We may use the terms *thermal wetting* and *thermal drying* to refer to the fact that at the same vapor pressure, cold porous materials are wetter and warm materials are drier.

The second factor that assists in drying is airflow. The site of water leakage has a wetness that is out of equilibrium with either indoor or outdoor air. To dry, it must give up vapor molecules to the air. If the airstream is replenished constantly, the wet spot can move more quickly to a condition in equilibrium with the indoor air or the outdoor air, depending on which direction the air is coming from. The value of airflow (and heat) in drying is not a mystery to anyone who has done laundry or housecleaning.

Third, there should be no barriers to drying. Once water vapor molecules leave the wet spot with no intention of returning, they have to migrate outward from the wet spot as freely as possible. Airflow certainly is very

Table 6-1 Water accumulation in frame cavities from rain compared to moisture accumulation from indoor humidity	
How much rain?	
0.5	Incident rainfall on a wall surface, in./yr
2%	Percent that penetrates the weather resistant barrier
0.01	Inches of water into the assembly per year
0.0008	Cubic feet of water into the assembly through 1 ft^2/yr
62.4	Pounds per cubic feet
0.052	Pounds per square foot per year from rain
How much "condensation"?	
0.14	Average vapor pressure difference (70°F, 50% RH in, 20°F, 70% RH out)
1	Permeance to the possible "condensing" plane, perms
0.14	Rate of moisture accumulation, grains per hr-ft^2
4	Number of months in the year with these conditions
2880	Number of hours at these conditions
403.2	Accumulation in grains per year per square foot
7000	Conversion: grains per pound
0.058	Pounds per square foot per year from vapor transport

important, but so is the absence of any membranes, materials, or films that would strongly impede the outward migration of the unwanted water.

Drying takes time. If we wish to model drying, we would have to use a model that accounts for time. We could never, of course, use a steady-state model. Let's review these four aspects of moisture management in walls: thermal wetting and drying, solar vapor drive, airflow, and the vapor barrier.

THERMAL WETTING AND DRYING

If we take a closer look at how cold materials tend toward wet and warm materials tend to be dry, we can begin to measure the relative contribution of indoor humidity and thermal wetting to the moisture content of exterior materials. We can quantify the effect using the profile method that was developed and used by the three researchers cited just above.

Recall from Chapter 3 the steps in the profile method: (1) Select building materials and list their thermal and moisture transport properties; (2) select indoor and outdoor temperature and humidity, and calculate those two vapor pressures; (3) calculate the resulting thermal profile and the resulting vapor pressure profile; and (4) correct the vapor pressure profile if it ex-

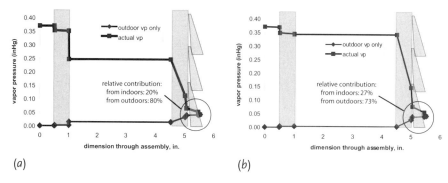

(a)   *(b)*

Figure 6-2
Steady-state profiles of frame construction (*a*) with and (*b*) without a vapor retarder. See the text for how the profiles were constructed. The circled area shows the comparison of vapor contributed to the siding from the outdoors and from the indoors.

ceeds saturation, noting the accumulation rate. This fourth step came about in the 1950s, when it was noted that a profile chart with actual lines crossing represents a rarity.

Any building profile can be seen as the sum of two profiles: one from actual vapor pressure indoors to zero vapor pressure outdoors and another from zero vapor pressure indoors to actual vapor pressure outdoors. The sum takes us from the actual vapor pressure indoors to the actual vapor pressure outdoors, but it allows us to see the relative contribution of indoors and outdoors.

Figure 6-2 and Table 6-2 provide an example. If we compare the overall contribution of outdoor vapor pressure to the actual vapor pressure for the entire assembly, it is quite small. But for the outermost materials, the contribution of vapor from the exterior may be quite high, as we see in the percentages of the tables. If only 20% of the water in the siding comes from indoors, there is a 20% limit on the effectiveness of any interior vapor retarder strategy as a means to prevent paint peeling. The researchers of the 1930s had the tools to reach this conclusion, and they did not.

SOLAR VAPOR DRIVE

ASHRAE *Handbook—Fundamentals* (2001, sec. 24.8) discusses what happens when cladding material such as brick is wetted by rain and then is struck by the heating effect of sunlight. It reports findings from NRC Canada in which an insulated furred cavity directly behind brick was found to be wetted as solar gain on a wall elevated the brick temperature, causing the sorbed water to evaporate. Recall that warm material is dry and that dry material has lower vapor permeability. The net effect of this heating is to cause the water to evaporate along any path it can, but much of the water moves in the more permeable (colder and wetter) direction, that is,

Table 6-2   Percent contributions from indoors and outdoors, for the setup shown in Figure 6-3[a]

Component	Contribution from outdoor air	
	Vapor barrier	No vapor barrier
Indoor air film	0	0
Paint	1	1
$\frac{1}{2}$-in. drywall	1	1
Vapor barrier	6	1
Fiberglass insulation	6	1
OSB sheathing	30	21
Felt paper	61	51
Wood shakes	80	73
Outdoor paint	100	100
Outdoor air film	100	100

[a] Note that vapor control strategies such as vapor retarders can affect only the contribution from indoors.

inward. The result was an accumulation of water within the insulation. According to ASHRAE *Handbook—Fundamentals*, the problem was stopped with the use of building paper between the brick and the insulation.

Other researchers contend that the effect may be so strong that moisture can be driven in significant quantities past not only very permeable building wrap materials but also through felts and wood product panel sheathing materials. The driving force is vapor pressure. Recall the previous discussion, which pointed out that capillary sorption can drive water into masonry materials, but capillarity itself cannot drive water back out. Only air or water pressure can drive water through a masonry layer such that it reappears as liquid water on the other side. If the quality of masonry work and the exposure of the masonry face to both water and wind permit liquid water to accumulate in the cavity behind the brick, then indeed, upon heating, the vapor pressure in the cavity may be very high. Of course, such loading of cavities from solar vapor drive will be episodic—it will happen only with the right conditions of rain, wind, and sun. But the possibility of significant solar vapor drive is causing rethinking of the use of vapor retarders.

AIRFLOW IN WALL ASSEMBLIES

The shouts are "A building's gotta breathe!" and "Build it tight; ventilate right!" Let's try to bring some order to the discussion.

For energy conservation purposes, tight building envelopes are desirable—the tighter the better. During the heating season of winter, all infiltration, exfiltration, or air change comes at an energy cost. Buildings must provide fresh air to occupants, so we willingly pay that cost. Ventilation in commercial buildings is established by standard (ASHRAE 62.1). Ventilation in residential buildings is much more contentious. Up to the present it has been hit or miss, but a new residential ventilation standard (ASHRAE 62.2) has been put in place. It contains a requirement for mechanical ventilation of new residential buildings. Air-to-air heat exchangers can lower the energy cost of providing fresh air.

It is during the period of air-conditioner use during summertime that the benefits of airtightness are most fully realized. Chapter 8 describes the relative importance of temperature and humidity in providing comfort. Imagine running an air conditioner in the car with the windows cracked compared to running it with the windows tightly shut. That is an indicator of the value of airtightness in air-conditioned buildings.

How desirable or undesirable is airtightness for the durability of building envelope assemblies? Let's look at airflow-induced moisture failure in building envelopes. This occurs when humid air meanders along building component surfaces that have been chilled.

The classic condition in heating climates occurs at a parapet (light-gauge steel construction) as described earlier (see Figure 4-24). Imagine a commercial steel-frame building with wintertime humidification and pressurization. Museums, for example, add wintertime humidity for artifact stabilization and they pressurize to prevent the unwanted infiltration of unfiltered air. The airflow paths from the interior, across the top steel beam, and into the parapet area are most likely. Once the air is in the parapet, it courses along looking for an opening, usually at the coping for escape. The parapet is cold and serves as a condensing surface for the meandering exiting air. It deposits its water on the inside surfaces of the parapet. The solution for this is to create an airtight joint from the wall sheathing to the roof deck. Incidentally, if the exiting air path is short, the heat of the exiting air may warm up the surface sufficiently to keep the pathway dry. That appears to be the case in exiting air leaks in triple-wythe brick loft buildings with leaky wood windows. This also explains why long, meandering pathways for exiting air are the most dangerous—they have certainly given up any heat they might have used to warm the surfaces along which they pass.

The classic condition that leads to moisture problems in cooling climates occurs in buildings put under negative pressure, say a hotel or motel with continually running bathroom exhaust and insufficient makeup air. The air conditioner can create cold spots on the wall. Outdoor humid air during the summer may filter in, pass along the back side of the interior gypsum wallboard, and wet this material from the back. This occurs primarily where drywall cannot dry to the inside, especially with vinyl wall coverings. It often occurs at walls that separate individual rooms, where the exterior finish permits air entry at the exterior end of the wall.

Notice that in both these cases, the buildings are mechanically pressurized (northern heating climates) or mechanically depressurized (humid south). If the pressure across the building envelope is neutral, rather small quantities of air will pulse back and forth through the openings in the envelope. This may lead to occasional accumulations, but is unlikely to lead to serious damage. A tall building with openings at the floor level may invite buoyancy flow in the building. The persistence over the winter season of this unidirectional flow (in at the bottom, out at the top) can lead to stronger flows than wind-driven pulses, although they are not likely to be as strong as those induced mechanically. Often, such buildings will show window frosting at the upper floors but little or none on lower floors, an indication of the direction of flow on each of those floors caused by buoyancy.

Openings in exterior walls may be fine, provided that (1) they are not costly in terms of heating or cooling energy, (2) the building is well compartmentalized if tall, and (3) there are no meandering airflows in mechanically pressurized or depressurized buildings. Once a building is constructed, it is difficult to decrease the area of infiltration. Weather-stripping and testing for major leaks may be useful. Tightening the ceiling is certainly possible (see Chapter 7). Modulating the pressures is usually the best approach to solving problems of ice or water formation in building envelopes. See Chapter 8 for ways to modulate building pressure.

For new buildings, the design and installation of an air barrier system may be very useful, particularly in tall buildings and buildings with mechanical pressurization or depressurization. Some energy codes are moving toward mandating an air barrier system. Materials used for vapor retarders typically make poor air barrier components. The elements of an air barrier system should be rigid and the edges of discrete materials should be made sealable. Air typically leaks in or out of a building at individual areas, each of which must be detailed for the air barrier approach to be successful. Those areas include the following joint areas:

- Top of the foundation
- Wall–floor junction
- Wall–ceiling junction
- Window sill, jamb, and head
- Balcony
- Parapet or overhang
- Junction where a partition joins an exterior wall
- Control and expansion joints
- Mechanical penetrations through exterior walls

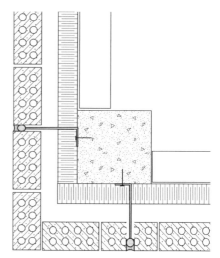

Figure 6-3
Plan detail showing the use of vertical flanges at the corner in single-wythe brick veneer construction. Without such protection, air pressure differences on the two sides of the building could produce airflows that could degrade the thermal insulation at the corner. (From CMHC, 1997.)

Excellent guidance on the design and execution of air barrier systems is available from the Canada Mortgage and Housing Corporation's *Best Practice Guides* (CMHC, 1996, 1997, 1999, 2001). These guides also address air movement in the cavities behind single-wythe brick veneers. It is presumed that air movement here is detrimental to the insulation value of the sheathing–insulation system. Canadian researchers note the difference in pressure between the windward side and the other sides of a building and recommend providing air blocking at corners. See Figure 6-3, a plan detail of brick veneer, for the Canadian approach to this problem.

VAPOR BARRIERS: COMPACT AND CAVITY ASSEMBLIES

Before entering into a discussion of vapor barriers let's distinguish two types of building envelope assemblies: cavity and compact assemblies. A *cavity assembly* is any assembly that contains one or more significant air layers, such as a layer of material such as fiberglass through which air can pass rather easily. A *compact assembly* is one that has no such layer. A compact assembly is a sandwich of rather dense materials, dense enough to effectively stop airflow through the assembly.

The interface between two rather dense materials is rarely the site of a problem. An exception to this rule might be the interface between sheathing and exterior insulation, where water problems have occurred and drying has not. But setting aside the deposition of liquid water at the interface between two solid materials, water problems at the interface are practically nonexistent. Recall the pass–fail criterion developed earlier from International Energy Agency Annex 14—prevention of surface water activity below 0.8 on a monthly mean basis. This criterion relates to a *surface*, defined as an interface between a material and air. Every assembly has an inside and outside surface. Compact assemblies have only those two, so if the inside and outside surfaces of a compact assembly are fine, the assembly is fine.

Cavity assemblies have extra surfaces, the interstitial surfaces, the surfaces that line the cavity. The construction industry relies on its building scientists to advise it regarding interstitial conditions. It may be tempting to exaggerate interstitial problems—building scientists seem to err in that direction. But in fact, problems of interstitial accumulation are quite rare. The materials that line a cavity are quite porous, so sorptive, so they reach 80% surface relative humidity only after a lot of time, a high moisture load, or an accident.

VAPOR RETARDER

Recall from the earlier discussion of vapor retarders that they were the principal product of the era marked by the introduction of insulation into building cavities. When the cavities got wet, painters blamed the insulation companies, and insulation companies countered that if the assembly got wet, it must be due to the lack of a vapor retarder. The discussion above shows that the wetness of exterior-most materials is independent of conditions indoors or a lack of vapor retarders indoors. So the call for vapor retarders to solve the paint peeling problem was disingenuous at best. The vapor retarder also seems to have served yeoman's duty in keeping the thoughts of the public and the construction industry off the subject of thermal wetting, wetting due only to the introduction of insulation into building envelope assemblies. T. S. Rogers, director of publications for Owens-Corning Fiberglas from 1939, provided excellent graphic material in support of the vapor barrier, from his seminal article in *Architecture Record* (1938) to his beautifully illustrated text *Thermal Design of Buildings* (1964).

Do compact assemblies need vapor retarders? Some examples of compact wall construction might include:

- Concrete masonry unit construction with or without adhered rigid foam insulation
- Cast-in-place or precast concrete wall construction, with or without adhered rigid foam insulation
- Solid masonry construction, brick or stone, with or without adhered rigid foam insulation
- Structural insulated panel (SIPS) construction
- Insulated concrete form (ICF) construction
- Urethane-foamed cavity construction
- Solid log construction

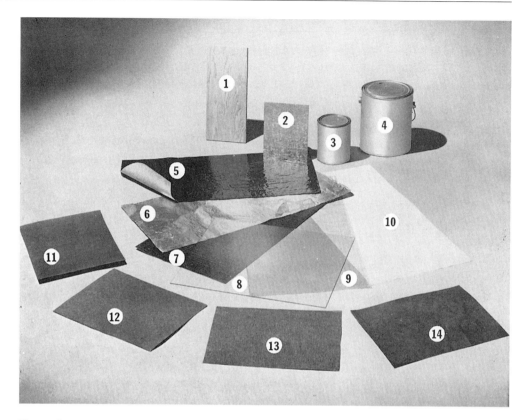

Figure 6-4
Selection of vapor barrier materials. (From Rogers, 1951.)

The materials in such construction themselves have measurable vapor permeance, and in each case, that permeance is 1 U.S. perm or less. In other words, the material can be said to "have" a vapor retarder because it "is" a vapor retarder. Moreover, all of these materials have the beneficial property of varying permeability with wetness, so, no, one need not add a vapor retarder to wall assemblies such as these. For proof, we need go no further than a steady-state profile analysis. For thick materials, if we assume uniform conditions, the vapor pressure gradient is considered linear through the material thickness. Same for the thermal conductivity. Now the vapor pressure is considered less than the saturation vapor pressure at both the inside and the outside. Connecting those two with straight lines, we see that the lines cannot cross, and if, as we stated earlier, the steady-state profile method overpredicts moisture problems, we have determined that there is a substantial margin of safety. If we assume nonlinearity for vapor permeance, with the wetter side being more permeable than the drier side (so that side has higher vapor pressure), we must note that thermal conductivity also increases with wetness. The outcome is that although curved, the lines tend to track one another and still not cross.

For a sandwich of nonhomogeneous materials, the gradients must be calculated, but most compact assemblies can be determined to be safe even by steady state, under wetting conditions from indoor vapor. The results of transient modeling of compact assemblies are generally quite good, as most transport is in the sorption and liquid transport regimes. Airflow is restricted in most assemblies. However, in panel assemblies such as SIPS, conditions at the joint may be particularly pernicious. What happens when liquid water gets to the interface between solid materials, such as in EIFS construction or in a low-slope roof with a leak, is anybody's guess. Small amounts of water which may be harmless in an EIFS over concrete or CMUs (concrete masonry units), could be disastrous in an EIFS over wood product or gypsum sheathing.

The steady-state profile method cannot replicate the effects of liquid water applied to assemblies (of the transient analysis programs available, MOIST cannot, WUFI can). Those programs that use only vapor load tend to magnify the effect of vapor loading on building envelope assemblies; by the same token, those programs understate the effects of liquid loading. Under vapor loading, the profile method appears to make a strong case for vapor retarders in all or most cavity construction. As we have discussed before, that conclusion arises in some cases because it is correct, but it occurs in many others because the profile method is used in its abridged form (no second round of calculations), because the inputs were selected as overly extreme, or because the output of water accumulation was interpreted too harshly. Let's try to peer through the assumptions and methods to make some rough decisions about vapor retarder use by climate. Note that these recommendations are intended to help control moisture diffusion. They are not intended to address airflow; for that, see below.

- For very cold climates, an interior vapor retarder is desirable.
- For cold climates, including Minneapolis, Chicago, and Boston, for example:
    - With compact construction there may be no need for a membrane barrier in addition to the material itself, or the material itself with an interior paint layer.
    - With cavity construction, a vapor retarder may be desirable. Use of a polyethylene vapor retarder should oblige design and construction professionals to take extra care in exterior rainwater management. Use of a higher-permeance vapor retarder system such as kraft facing of insulation may be more forgiving of occasional water entry events.
- For mixed climates such as St. Louis, Washington, DC, or Seattle, Washington, for example:
    - With compact construction there is no need for a membrane

barrier in addition to the material itself or to the material with an interior paint layer.

- With cavity construction, a vapor retarder may be dispensable. Use of a polyethylene vapor retarder should be avoided. A higher-permeance vapor retarder system such as kraft facing of insulation may be used.
- For hot dry climates such as Phoenix, no vapor retarder.
- For hot humid climates such as Houston, Miami, or Charleston, South Carolina, no interior vapor retarder and no low-permeance finishes such as vinyl wall covering on interior surfaces. High-permeance interior finish materials are available for such climates.

The answer to questions about the need for vapor retarders should not be relegated to checklists such as this, but should be made professionally based on experience as well as analysis.

DESIGN FOR DRYING OR AGAINST WETTING?

Recall the predicament described earlier in this chapter. If water comes from inside, good design dictates (1) thermal insulation, (2) restriction of airflow, and (3) barriers against wetting. If water comes from outdoors, good design dictates (1) conduction of heat to building components, (2) enhancement of airflow, and (3) elimination of barriers to drying. There are several ways to handle this dilemma.

The first way is the way that it has been handled for 50 years. Assume no wetting from outdoors, that is, assume that the only humidity load used in design calculations is the indoor humidity during cold weather. Those who laid the groundwork for this approach concerned themselves with humid air reaches chilled surfaces only during cold weather. During warm weather, they supposed back in the 1950s, the humid south would not present surfaces so chilled that they would be below the dew point temperature of the outdoor air. We may say that they succeeded—of all the forms of water damage that have occurred, very little of it is due to excess accumulation of indoor vapor on outer surfaces, where the mode of transport was vapor diffusion. It's a Pyrrhic victory, of course. Walls do have severe water problems, but those problems are not of the type envisioned by those who formulated the diffusion paradigm.

A second way involves tweaking this first approach. Design the exterior with world-class rainwater management. In dry climates this is quite easy. In wet climates it involves (1) simple roof designs; (2) wide overhangs; (3) excellent flashings at the roof, windows, porches, balconies, and so on; (4) inspection, maintenance, and repair; and (5) rainwater management at the base of the building. If the rainwater load is indeed reduced to almost nothing, the designer and builder have wide latitude in vapor control methods. One might say that if a designer or builder opts for a vapor retarder or airtight construction in walls, they are obliged to provide world-class rainwater management.

A third way might be the bathwater and baby approach. If our water problems are associated with excessive insulation (e.g., buildings that are too tight and lined with polyethylene), dump it all. According to this approach, one might remove the insulation, pierce the coverings that don't "breathe," and forgo all these membranes, which were never that appealing to drywall installers anyway. Such buildings might be just fine in a very mild climate, one where the roof takes care of the rain and the temperature takes care of itself. In such areas (e.g., tropical), walls themselves are a bit superfluous. In Mediterranean climates, thick uninsulated walls, with openings that catch the breezes, have no need of vapor protection for the assembly. But in climates with extremes, such an approach is impractical. Warm exteriors of walls means, inevitably, colder interiors of walls. This is not only likely to lead to water spotting and worse on the walls, it is uncomfortable and wastes energy.

A fourth way is through moisture engineering, which is the subject of this book. Moisture engineering was described earlier. It requires the designer to (1) determine the appropriate moisture loads to the building, (2) use those loads as inputs to calculate thermal and moisture transfer and distribution through the assembly in a way that mirrors physical reality, and (3) check the output of the calculations against a respected threshold that distinguishes acceptability from unacceptability.

The fourth approach is the approach recommended here. However, it is underdeveloped for the design professions. A designer may use the profile method, MOIST, or WUFI, of course. All three programs are good to excellent in dealing with heat transfer by conduction and radiation, and with moisture transport by vapor or bound-water transport. If airflow occurs through the assembly, or if liquid condensation can occur, the results are suspect. Recall the three elements of moisture engineering: loads, analysis, and criteria. A designer may adopt two of the three engineering requirements, loads and criteria, and simply provide the best seat-of-the-pants analysis keeping these in mind. Vapor retarders and airflow have been discussed in general above, and they are discussed with particular application to walls below. Keeping the anticipated loads in mind and being aware of the form of failure will provide excellent design guidance.

People ask: Do I need a vapor retarder here? The best answer is: Don't know yet, let's run the numbers. But we are still waiting on improvements in the hygrothermal computer models. Meanwhile, what is the best guidance regarding vapor retarders and airtightness of building assemblies?

To restate from above: Wetting from outdoors (and perhaps from the soil) is the principal water source for building walls. This wetting is greater than the wetting by water vapor from indoors. Once wetted, the wall must be dried. Drying is achieved by (1) keeping wetted surfaces warm, (2) enhancing airflow, and (3) avoiding the use of any barriers that might inhibit drying. Calculations of drying over time are the only suitable modeling approach.

The current paradigm is different from the preceding in several important regards. Wetting occurs from outside. Outside wetting needs to be able to dry. Airflow may be helpful toward drying incidental water entry, but it is not at all helpful in summertime, when it brings a substantial latent load, or in commercial buildings, which carry a risk of allowing humid air to be pushed mechanically along paths lined with cold materials.

These two paradigms of moisture control are sharply at odds with one another. Do we design to prevent wetting or to enhance drying? The correct answer lies in using good assumptions about the nature and magnitude of loads, using tools to predict outcomes most accurately and using accepted criteria against which to measure the outcomes. The answer is to do moisture engineering.

There are two additional issues to contend with in wall design: the insulation of historic buildings and rising damp.

INSULATING HISTORIC BUILDINGS

Should historic buildings be insulated? The National Park Service in 1975 instituted a series of *Preservation Briefs* that were intended to guide preservationists in the most appropriate techniques and materials for preservation. *Preservation Brief 3* (1978) addressed energy in historic buildings. It advised readers to insulate. Such advice would make sense given that its date of authorship was in the midst of the energy crisis.

A better approach might be to review the overall energy use by the subject building and make changes that are appropriate. The changes might include reducing air-conditioner use, reducing summer solar gain through windows, reducing the quantity of ventilation air, adjusting the temperature set point seasonally, adding ceiling insulation, adding shades and shutters, keeping doors and windows closed, and others. Adding wall insulation might find itself far down on the list and may have a very small payback. But would adding insulation to the walls of historic buildings be harmful?

Yes, indeed it might. From the foregoing discussion we can see that adding insulation to the interior will render the exterior materials much colder during winter and much warmer during summer. Those temperature swings may exceed the expected range of expansion and contraction that the building has seen historically. But more important, the range of moisture contents will be greater, in particular, the materials will probably stay much colder for much longer periods of time. For masonry buildings this may mean more water in cracks, higher overall moisture content, higher capillary rise of soil water, and a greater risk of icing and spalling. *Preservation Brief 3* contains repeated warnings regarding the importance of vapor barriers. It leaves the impression that wetness in insulated buildings is due only to the failure to provide proper vapor protection. It is hoped that the foregoing discussion points out the fallacy of that viewpoint. Vapor retarders may help reduce the moisture contribution from inside, but in well-insulated walls during cold weather, the extent of that contribution may be small.

Energy savings should be balanced against the risks to the durability of fabrics. Since the energy crisis, energy savings have received attention that should now be directed toward durability.

RISING DAMP

Another form of water damage in walls appears much more as a European problem than an American problem: rising damp (see Figures 6-5 and 6-6). The problem is usually interpreted as capillary rise of water from the soil through porous stone and brick masonry materials. Figure 6-5 shows that the extent of rising damp is closely associated with wetness in the soil. Those familiar with the problem also know that rising damp is a problem much more in cold buildings than in heated buildings; in fact, one can sometimes determine whether or not a building is heated by the amount of capillary rise. This is consistent with our understanding of capillary rise in tubes from before: Warm surfaces are more hydrophobic than cold surfaces, so warm surfaces spend more of their energy popping off vapor mol-

Figure 6-5
Rising damp in an unheated masonry train shed. The extent of the rising damp is a function of the concentration of water, with the greatest amount of rising damp at the center of the downspout.

Figure 6-6
Rising damp (Pierrefonds, France).

ecules and less energy attracting surface layer water. It is the attraction of surface layers that pulls water up a capillary opening. Rising damp is as much a chemical as a physical phenomenon. It is usually seen with efflorescence, indicating a source of salts. It is worth noting, for example, that rising damp is quite rare among buildings that are right at the side of freshwater waterways. Flowing fresh water may leach out salts that would otherwise appear as efflorescence (see Figure 6-7).

What can be done about rising damp? There are several strategies that do not work (see the Knapen siphons in Figure 6-8). These are simple metal tubes, triangular in section, that point downward and reach from the center of the wall toward the outside. They are marketed on the principle that "cold, moist" air will flow down and out of the tube, to be replaced with warmer drier air (see Gratwick, 1974, p. 82). Readers who have paid attention to the material in this book will note that while cold air is indeed denser than warm air, moist air is less dense. The opening into the stone may help dry out the core of the stone. That may have some merit in reducing the total amount of flow and height of flow, but rising damp itself remains a problem. Let's hope that the users of this strategy do not again

Figure 6-7
Stone foundation near a freshwater pond. The fresh water at the base of the stone helps prevent the buildup of efflorescence in the stone.

Figure 6-8
Knapen siphons. These devices may increase the total amount of drying surface area; otherwise, their claims of siphon effect cannot be realized.

hope to challenge the rule of capillarity, figuring that water will run from the small pores to the large Knapen openings and drain outward.

Electroosmosis has also been proposed as a solution, in which an anode grid and cathode grid are strategically placed in the building and in the surrounding soil, and (so the fantastic claims go) water leaves the building fabric for the surrounding soil. This principle has had excellent application in work with soils, notably by making steel drill points much less susceptible to caking when drilling through clay. Certain problems with electroosmosis as a means of preventing rising damp in building foundations include:

1. The pure activity of water, soil, and electric field have not been sufficiently elucidated to demonstrate the effectiveness of applications.
2. Salts in the soil may confound any electrolytic plans.
3. Variations occur in the concentration of water at the base of the wall.

Electroosmosis has been explained as *reversing capillarity;* that is, electricity is used to neutralize the binding sites that water would otherwise take. I've been asked if electroosmosis can prevent the flooding of basements. Recall that the flooding of basements can never occur from capillarity (capillarity takes water only from larger to smaller pores), so reversing capillarity cannot address the causes of flooding. Flooding is caused by hydraulic head and gravity flow.

Oliver (1997, p. 199) notes that electroosmosis systems do not have official approval from either the British Research Establishment or the British Board of Agrément. He disapproves of the systems as well. Gratwick (1974, p. 152) is a supporter. Case studies proclaim loudly how successful they were, but to my knowledge, none have chosen to provide physical proof of the effectiveness of the intervention alone.

Effective solutions usually consist of introducing a dampproof course into the thickness of the wall at some level just above grade. The course may be a low-porosity masonry material, lead sheet, through-the-wall metal flashing, or an injected material, usually polymeric, that forms a continuous layer. Of course, reducing the water load would work well; one strategy for doing that may be the flashing approach described in Chapter 4. Also, leaching the salt out of the masonry would greatly reduce the solute suction of the wall. A common method of removing salt is by poultice, with an exchange ion basis that is more water soluble than the salts in the wall. In addition, the wall would benefit from heat and would suffer if any barrier membranes were used in the wall.

7 Attics

INTRODUCTION

Managing water in attics is actually rather simple. Recall from earlier that all things being equal, hot spaces and hot materials tend to be dry spaces and materials. Attics are strongly affected by sun, so they tend to be dry. The sun bakes moisture from sorptive wood and other materials. If material gets wet, then given enough sun, sheathing materials can dry quite readily. If there are moisture problems in attics, we may consider that they are due to a strong excess moisture load, a lack of sunlight, or both. Of all the parts of a building, the easiest to keep dry is the attic. You may recall from childhood that attics in older homes are places rich with smells. This is because the dryness of attics and the high heat tends to volatilize hydrocarbons in wood, clothes, or whatever is stored there and leave behind higher concentrations of these aromas than we would have in closets in the living space, which is at cooler temperatures.

Attic spaces are the unconditioned building cavities beneath roofs. There are some roof constructions that have no cavities. Low-slope roofs, for example, are of compact sandwich construction. We know from commercial construction that for the most part, they perform quite well. Trouble occurs when they leak, as the insulating materials may become soaked, lose their insulating value, and contribute to corrosion of metals or mold growth on organic building elements.

If the structural and insulating members are packed together in compact construction, there is no cavity, so there is little or no opportunity for the type of damage that can occur in cavities. Tobiasson (1986) showed that low-slope roof system should not be constructed as vented cavity assemblies, as the difficulties in actually getting flow through a horizontal cavity by natural means are considerable. If we take a compact low-slope roof system and turn it up at an angle, making a cathedral roof section, the same rules must apply. Of course, roof leaks can be quite damaging in any type of roof assembly, whether of compact or cavity construction.

Given the beneficial effect of the sun, you might think that it is difficult to create moisture problems in attics. You'd be right for the most part. So it sounds odd to hear people (building code inspectors, roofing product manufacturers, consultants, and others) talk about "proper venting" and achieving a 1/300 vent ratio. A *vent ratio* is the ratio between the net free area of a vent device and the horizontally projected roof area. Such language gives the impression of a target value, a bull's-eye, that must be hit in order to have good performance from an attic system, while anything other than a bull's-eye leaves one open to worry. If we simply look around, we see a wide variety of attic designs and attic venting approaches, hardly any of which hit the bull's-eye, yet the attics seems to be faring quite well for the most part. The approach I wish to suggest to the material in this chapter is to set aside predispositions about attic performance and see if the background and discussion lead to a refreshed understanding about attics.

There may, however, be valid reasons why adding attic vents is either impractical or undesirable. Wildfires are the most pertinent current example— it is important to strictly avoid roof vents in wildfire-prone areas. Architectural details or geometry may be such that effective attic ventilation is improbable in all or part of the roof. In some areas the danger of snow blowing in through the vents has rendered attic vents unsuitable. Attic vents may also be undesirable for aesthetic or historical reasons—the original roof may not have had ventilation, so why start now? Closing vents may be desirable for sound mitigation, especially near airports. Vents may not be desirable in hurricane-prone areas. In addition, venting rules for attics have been extended to apply to cathedral ceilings, but the validity of that extension was never truly demonstrated. The current universal requirement in the United States for ventilation of all attics and cathedral ceilings in all climatic regions is long overdue for review.

HISTORICAL BACKGROUND

Vent devices on roofs first appeared as steeples, towers, or cupolas, which assisted buoyant flow upward through a building. This was common in barns, mill buildings, and any buildings subject to buildup of odors or contaminants. It was also common in buildings in hot climates to assist comfort by increasing airspeed across the skin.

Most early roofing material, such as wood shingle, slate, or tile, was applied to spaced wood lath. Continuous roof sheathing began to appear in the late nineteenth century in some construction because it allowed the application of asphalt felt underlayment for additional protection against rainwater in addition to the additional resistance it offered against lateral structural loads. In quality construction in northern climates, nails were sized so that the points did not penetrate the underside of the sheathing.

The use of longer nails that penetrated through the sheathing probably represented low-quality construction when it appeared in the first decades of the twentieth century. Penetrating nail points were the site of frosting in the first insulated buildings, and roof frosting was one of the first arguments for attic ventilation.

During the Depression of the 1930s, the use of asphalt shingle roofing materials on continuous 1×6 sheathing became the norm for one- and two-family construction. To what extent was ventilation practiced prior to the 1930s? It is difficult to provide an answer because reroofing often involves reconfiguration of venting. Thus, it may be necessary to state only that roof systems both with and without ventilation were used up to the 1930s. Those persons who introduced the practice of regulated attic ventilation are the same familiar names involved in the diffusion paradigm (see Chapter 3).

F. L. Browne, senior chemist with the U.S. Forest Products Laboratory, cited the lack of ventilation in unused attics as one of the conditions associated with moisture problems of paint peeling. His ventilation discussion reads in full:

> *Lack of ventilation in unused attics.* During cold weather water may condense beneath the cold roof and drain down toward the cornice. If the top course of siding is placed below the frieze board the water is directed between siding and sheathing, coming directly in contact with the backs of the painted clapboards. (Browne, 1933)

Browne claimed that water condensed on the underside. From the earlier discussion we know that water sorbs into wood or frosts on the surface, and could condense only on the nail points. If water were to "drain" toward the cornice, it would require some sort of interior channel or gutter.

In his moisture and attic studies, Larry V. Teesdale states:

> Roof condensation is reported far more frequently than sidewall condensation, not necessarily because it occurs more frequently but rather because it is more likely to be seen by the occupants. For example, in a pitched roof house having, say, fill insulation in the ceiling below the attic, condensation may develop during a severe cold spell on the underside of the roof boards, forming as ice or frost. When the weather moderates, or even under a bright sun, the ice melts and drips on the attic floor, leaks through and spots the ceiling below. Often such spots are assumed to be roof leaks and cause owners and contractors considerable unnecessary expense in attempting to waterproof a roof that is not leaking. If the attic has adequate ventilation little or no trouble will occur but adequate ventilation is sometimes difficult to attain, and tends to increase the heat loss. (Teesdale, 1937)

The article contains no other mention of attic ventilation until the final page under "General Recommendations": "For new construction it is recommended that a suitable vapor barrier be installed on the side wall studs and below the ceiling insulation and that some attic ventilation also be provided." The overall emphasis of the article is the importance of reducing indoor humidity.

Tyler S. Rogers, the architect who promoted the use of insulation, publicized moisture control strategies in a March 1938 *Architectural Record* article. In the section titled "Attic and Roof Insulation," he wrote:

> Principles that apply to wall construction apply with equal force to ceilings, attics and roofs, but somewhat different techniques are needed to meet the conditions encountered. A vapor barrier undoubtedly should be employed on the warm side of any insulation as the first step in minimizing condensation; venting to the cold air is an equally desirable second step. Either one may suffice; both are desirable.
>
> Venting of roof areas above insulation may be accomplished by various means, according to the construction involved. Unoccupied attics or loft spaces, above insulation installed at the ceiling below, should be vented by louvers in gable ends or side walls at the highest possible point, or by ridge ventilators or false chimneys. Wood shingle roofs applied on spaced shingle lath without vapor resistant papers provide sufficiently free vapor movement to make additional venting unnecessary, but roof decks of any kind which are covered with vapor-resistive materials should have special vents. (Tyler, 1938)

He showed three diagrams of venting (Figure 7-1).

The following month, an article, "Condensation," appeared without author attribution in *Architectural Forum* magazine (Anon., 1938). It stated:

> The single exception to [rare frost formation] has been the poorly ventilated attic. Such frost often takes a curious form known in some sections as "walnuts"; balls of rust-colored ice which gather on nail-ends projecting through the roof boards which—since they are colder than the wooden parts of the roof—attract the water vapor. Such ice or frost seldom damages the roof structure, but if quickly melted by sun shining on the roof or a sudden rise in temperature may drip on the ceilings below and cause discoloration and even disintegration of the plaster.

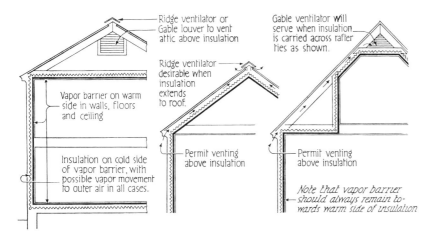

Figure 7-1
Three roof venting strategies. (From Rogers, 1938. These drawings reappeared in *Architectural Graphic Standards,* 4th ed., Ramsey and Sleeper, 1951.)

This article concludes: "Condensation in attics is best prevented by providing adequate ventilation, supplemented where necessary by a vapor barrier on the underside of the attic joists." There is strong reason to believe that the author was Teesdale.

In January 1939, Rowley et al. (1938) reported on a study conducted along five lines of investigation:

1. A further study of vapor barriers
2. Ventilation of walls through exterior surfaces
3. The effect of vapor barriers on the drying of wet plaster
4. The effect of attic ventilation on the accumulation of moisture and frost within the attic and on attic temperatures
5. The effect of vapor pressures on the rate of vapor travel through materials

They constructed three "doghouses" within a climate-controlled chamber at the University of Minnesota. The setup is shown in Figure 7-2. One had no intentional ventilation; one had "natural" ventilation (i.e., small holes in each of the two gables), and one had mechanical ventilation. The sheathing was removable to gain access to a small aluminum plate which could be weighed for frost accumulation. The significant test for natural ventilation was conducted with an indoor temperature of 70°F, an indoor relative humidity of 40%, and an outdoor temperature of −10°F. In one test the gable holes (presumably two such holes, one in each gable) were $\frac{1}{4}$ in. per square foot of ceiling area in size. In a second test, the gable

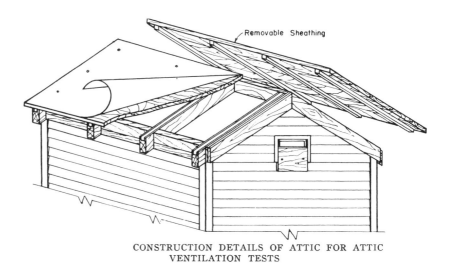

CONSTRUCTION DETAILS OF ATTIC FOR ATTIC
VENTILATION TESTS

Figure 7-2
Setup of Frank Rowley's University
of Minnesota attic research. From
ASHRAE Transactions 1938.
© American Society of Heating,
Refrigerating, and Air-Conditioning
Engineers, Inc., www.ashrae.org.

holes measured $\frac{1}{8}$ in. per ceiling square foot area in each gable. Although
Rowley did not use such expressions, we might say that the vent ratio in the
first test was 1/288 and the vent ratio in the second test was 1/576. No
vapor barriers were used in these assemblies.

Rowley found that there was no condensation in test 1, but test 2
showed a frost accumulation of 0.16 g per square foot of ceiling area per
24 hours. The case with no ventilation, under the same conditions, showed
frost accumulation of about 3 g/ft² in 24 hours. Based on this finding, Rowley's conclusions regarding attic ventilation are these:

4. It is possible to reduce the rate of condensation within a structure
by ventilating to the outside. This method may be particularly ef-

fective in attics where the condensation occurs on the underside of the roof. Adequate ventilation may be obtained without serious loss of heat.

9. For cold attic spaces it is desirable to allow openings for outside air circulation through attic space as a precaution against condensation on the underside of the roof, even though barriers are used in the ceiling below.

How legitimate are these conclusions? Conclusion 4 seems to follow from Rowley's findings, as he was able to demonstrate condensation on the aluminum plate in two cases and not in one other. But how significant is the rate of condensation that he did find? Assume that the sheathing is $\frac{1}{2}$-in. pine. One square foot of southern pine (density 36 lb/ft^3) weighs 2.3 lb or about 1000 g. Under dry conditions (10% moisture content) it contains 100 g of moisture. Under wet conditions (say, 23% moisture content) it contains 230 g of water. The difference is 130 g of moisture. Rowley showed that for an unvented attic to go from dry conditions to incipient wet conditions at −10°F would require 130/3 or 43 days. For an "undervented" attic of 1/576 vent ratio to go from dry to incipient wet conditions at −10°F would require over two years (130/0.16 = 812 days). It is difficult to conclude that the rate of accumulation Rowley found could, in any way, justify a need for attic ventilation for moisture control, and it certainly does not support the need for 1/288 rather than 1/576 venting.

Conclusion 9 does not follow from his findings. He did not study roofs with barriers in place. He provides no basis for concluding that allowing openings for outside air circulation is desirable.

In January 1942, the *Property Standards and Minimum Construction Requirements for Dwellings* of FHA was revised. It contains the following section.

209 LIGHT AND VENTILATION

K Attics (Includes air space between ceiling and flat roofs) Provide effective fixed ventilation in all spaces between roofs and top floor ceilings, by screened louvres or by other means acceptable to the Chief Architect.

Net ventilation area for each separate space to be not less than 1/300 of horizontally projected roof area. Where possible, locate vents to provide effective cross-ventilation.

Use corrosion-resistant screening over openings, mesh not less than 12 per inch.

This document is the source of the fabled 1/300 ratio. It appears in this document with no citation and no references. The vent ratio 1/300 is an arbitrary number. It has no significance in the physical performance of buildings.

It may have been selected by FHA because it cuts between Rowley's 1/288 and 1/576. Rogers (1951) confirmed the dependence of 1/300 natural ventilation on Rowley's work. Rogers used the mechanical ventilation findings of Rowley, where an airflow rate of 105 ft^3/min led to no condensation at 40% RH and $-10°$F outdoors. From this, Rogers recommended 2 to 3 air changes per hour in an attic, down to 0.5 air changes per hour if a reasonably good vapor barrier is present. At the time of adoption of 1/300 by FHA, all that could faithfully be deduced from the research record is that under the conditions of Rowley's tests, approximately three years of bitter cold temperatures would be necessary for attics with 1/576 venting ratio to reach significantly high levels of moisture in attic sheathing.

Incidentally, the page on which 1/300 first appears also contains the first mention of the need for ventilation in "basementless spaces." The following page contains the first mention of the need for vapor barriers with measured permeance.

Following World War II, Ralph Britton was the principal investigator with the Housing and Home Finance Agency (HHFA). Britton contracted with Pennsylvania State University to test the condensation performance of various wall and roof assemblies (Britton, 1948). Britton may have had a hand in the initial formulation of the 1/300 vent ratio, as indicated by his decision to use 1/300 as the vent ratio in his 1947 tests. The first report began with a curious remark under "Test Procedure": "When this program started there was, to the best of our knowledge, no past experience to serve as a guide in setting up a test procedure." It is odd to imagine that Rowley's work had been ignored. If that is so, FHA's selection of 1/300 appears all that much more arbitrary.

The results were in two phases. The first phase gave results that were expected: With 1/300 venting, attics with facing or film vapor barriers did fine. In the second phase, increasing the venting to 1/100 led to problems, and taking out the ventilation, of all things, led to problems. Of course, the results were inconclusive, but the money ran out and this very important study, which was designed to confirm 1/300 but might have undermined it, came to an end.

Britton also wrote an extended report (the first of its kind) on crawl spaces. He made several significant findings in this report, including the finding that air from wet crawl spaces moves upward along furring chases and plumbing chases up into the attic, bypassing the living space.

Note: Where an effective vapor barrier is assured in the top-story ceiling, loft or attic space ventilation specified above may be greatly decreased. Such decrease may well be as much as 90% where controlled construction is assured and walls or crawl space do not contribute to moisture supply in the attic or loft space.

This conclusion is important because it highlights the importance attached by Britton and HHFA to moisture loads from a foundation. It leads to speculation that if Britton's thinking had been pursued, a primary means of regulated moisture control for attics might have been air tightening at the ceiling plane, and 1/300 venting could have been reduced to 1/3000. In a survey of moisture damage to homes (Rose, 1987), severe damage to roof sheathing was found only in buildings with flooded or excessively wet crawl spaces. Vent openings in the crawl spaces, vent openings in the roof, and openings that connect the crawl space to the roof may be a recipe for a large number of the roof sheathing problems found to date.

Britton wrapped the conclusions from his wall–roof studies and his crawl space investigations into an important article, "Condensation Control in Dwelling Construction: Good Practice Recommendations" (Britton, 1949b). This article became the August 1949 HHFA bulletin *Condensation Control in Dwelling Construction* (HHFA, 1949). This publication was widely distributed and used for much postwar housing. A diagram from this brochure is shown in Figure 7-3.

Jordan et al. (1948) took moisture readings in three attics in Madison, Wisconsin, during winter. Only one house, where humidity in the living space was high, showed condensation in the attic. The importance of indoor humidity was also evident in a recent survey of moisture levels in attics (Buchan, Lawton, Parent Ltd., 1991), where "high attic moisture content was not found in the absence of high house humidities."

HIP ROOF, ENCLOSED RAFTERS

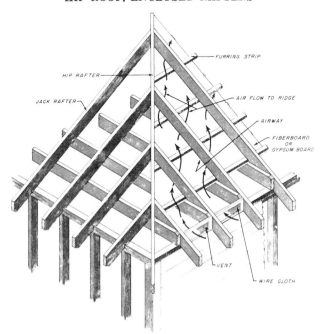

Figure 7-3
Hip roof venting.
(From HHFA, 1949.)

Early attic moisture studies generally concluded that ceiling vapor retarders were effective in lowering attic moisture levels. Hinrichs (1962) noted that air infiltration through the ceiling into the attic was the major source of condensation, and he therefore concluded that a vapor retarder was not a dependable means of attic moisture control. Dutt and Harrje (1979) posed the question more directly, and based on his calculations, argued in favor of an airflow retarder in the ceiling in addition to a vapor retarder. Samuelson (in ASHRAE, 1994) demonstrated that if there is no air moving from the living space to the attic, unvented attics are drier than vented attics, because of higher temperatures in unvented attics. However, he states that in order to guarantee no indoor air movement into an attic, the ceiling has to be airtight and the attic air needs to be at a higher pressure than the indoor air (i.e., pressurized attic or depressurized living space).

What Do We Learn from this Historical Summary?

- Attic ventilation was recommended by the Forest Products Laboratory as a means of reducing frosting on nail points in insulated attics.
- A single data point in a single piece of research predated the introduction of attic ventilation as a strictly (i.e., numerically) regulated practice. That data point did not make a convincing case for attic ventilation as a broadly applied practice.
- The famous 1/300 ratio was first expressed in a document from FHA, without citation and without justification.

A designer must ask this: If compliance with a poorly supported practice does not ensure good performance, what does? But before we answer that question, we have to note that once attic ventilation was introduced as a regulated practice, other justifications began to piggyback on the practice. If it was hard enough to address attic ventilation with one set of obscure moisture research results, imagine how difficult it becomes to help refine good practice with all this piling on. The items piggybacking on attic ventilation practice are:

- Moisture
- Prevention of ice damming
- Enhancing shingle service life
- Reducing heat loss during summer

Each of these items results from the influence of several factors. Attic ventilation is one of those factors, but it is down the list away from primary importance for all the items.

MOISTURE

Recall from above that attics tend to be dry spaces because of the heat they encounter. Moisture problems in attics arise simply because of the unwanted movement of humid air from beneath up into the attic. It is always preferable to reduce an excess moisture source than to presume its existence and hope to dilute it with outdoor air. The first way fits into good engineering practice. The second is a crapshoot. It just doesn't look like a crapshoot because that number 1/300 is so damned specific.

Protruding nail points may become frosty during cold weather, and as the early researchers recognized, this frost may melt (before it sublimates) and create droplets. The density of frost is very low if the source of moisture is only from outside. Imagine a gust of nighttime air on a cold clear night. It is most likely to deposit its water on the coldest surface that is most directly in its flow stream. That is much more likely to be your car window or mine than for it to be the relatively warmer surface of the underside of roof sheathing, especially given the tortuous path the air must follow to get there. Figure 7-4 shows a photo of frost on the underside of an attic, and the pattern the frost makes is a very clear indication that it is excess, unwanted leaking airflow that causes severe frost problems.

The three most effective measures to lower attic moisture conditions (assuming cavity construction and porous insulation) are (1) ensuring airtightness at the ceiling plane, (2) indoor humidity control, and (3) attic ventilation. Most moisture damage to attic sheathing occurs in cold climates, and it occurs in locations near a major pathway for humid air to escape into the attic. Sealing these pathways blocks the flow of humid indoor air and, incidentally, greatly improves the fire performance of the building.

The air may come from the foundation area. Recall Figure 5-19, which showed the flow of humid air from crawl spaces up into the attic space, bypassing the living space. In a series of 670 home inspections reported by this author, there were 42 cases of deterioration of attic sheathing; every single one of those cases occurred on a home with a wet crawl space.

The air may come from a humidified indoors. Indoor humidity control is beneficial to the entire building envelope and should therefore lead the list of recommendations. In cold climates indoor humidity control is most easily accomplished by reducing excess moisture loads such as runaway humidifiers, as well as by ventilation of the living space, which also improves indoor air quality. Excess humidity is also a product of poorly vented or unvented combustion heating appliances.

The air may come from the mechanical discharge of humid air into attic cavities. Bathroom vents and dryer vents are the common culprits. Such vents should always be discharged to the outdoors, not into the attic.

Figure 7-4
Frost on wood truss members. The frost is centered above an opening through the ceiling that joins the attic to a humidified room below. The frost is due to both convective flows through the opening as well as diffusion.

It is clear from the research that unvented attics in cold climates can perform well if indoor humidity is controlled, and thus there should be no objections to unvented attics as long as there is assurance that winter indoor humidity will remain low. In the case of rehabilitation of historical buildings or other building, this can often be judged from the building's previous performance. In new buildings as well as existing buildings, humidity control can be assured by properly designed house ventilation systems.

Recent, as yet published, changes in the International Residential Code allow the use of air-impermeable insulations right up against the underside of roof sheathing if the space below is unconditioned. There are enormous energy benefits for attics containing ductwork or air-handling equipment that can be reaped if measures are taken to place the insulation at the roof plane rather than at the ceiling plane. Taking measures to prevent meandering airflows from a humid indoors should suffice as a moisture control strategy for most of the United States. The necessity (or not) of interior vapor protection can be determined rather easily (steady-state or transient analysis) for envelope assemblies that do not permit airflow. In general, some vapor protection for the northern United States is desirable for cavity construction without intentional vents.

Cathedral ceiling construction is inherently more prone to moisture damage than attic construction, because cathedral ceiling construction creates isolated conditions in each rafter cavity. While providing effective ventilation to attics with simple geometries is relatively easy and inexpensive, providing effective soffit and ridge ventilation to each individual cavity in a cathedral ceiling is far more difficult, and the advantages of roof vents over normal soffit air leakage are slight. Wind washing of the insulation, especially near the soffit vents, is another common problem with ventilated cathedral ceilings, as it is any time that airflow is allowed to pass across unprotected low-density insulation such as fiberglass. On balance, the case for vents in a cathedral ceiling is much weaker than for attic vents. Indoor humidity control, combined with an airtight ceiling plane with a vapor retarder, should provide reliable moisture control in an unvented cathedral ceiling.

The discussion of moisture conditions in attics and cathedral ceilings seems to be monopolized by the case of a framed cavity with a porous insulation material such as fiberglass. Other constructions deserve attention, too, notably roof systems with foam thermal insulation which is relatively vapor impermeable. When foam insulation is used in walls and low-slope roof systems it generally demonstrates good moisture performance. In a sloped roof assembly, equal moisture performance should be expected. There is no moisture performance advantage to venting a well-designed foam insulation roof system. Indeed, given the recent damage in wildfire areas, allowing vent slots that are bounded by flammable foams is out of the question.

The early studies all were performed in cold climates or simulated cold climates. More recent data on attic ventilation in wet, cold coastal climates provides a different perspective. In such climates the moisture in the outside air, carried into the attic by ventilation, is a major source of moisture in the attic. Forest and Walker (1993) found with computer model simulation that in coastal climates high attic ventilation rates resulted in higher sheathing moisture contents than lower ventilation rates. The higher ventilation rates produced colder attics without sufficiently lowering attic water vapor pressures, resulting in high attic RH and moisture contents in the sheathing.

No claims have ever been made that attic ventilation is needed for moisture control in warm, humid climates, where the outside air is much more humid than the inside air, which is cooled and dehumidified by air-conditioning equipment. In such climates attic venting tends to increase rather than reduce moisture levels in the attic. Cooling ducts are commonly located in the attic space, and attic ventilation with humid outdoor air may therefore increase the danger of condensation on the ducts. When a ceiling is not airtight, attic venting may also increase the latent cooling load in the building. In short, if attic ventilation is required or recommended in warm humid climates, it must be based on considerations other than moisture control.

ICE DAMMING

To follow up on the discussion of ice dams from Chapter 4, early requirements for attic ventilation were based entirely on prevention of condensation in cold climates, not on preventing ice damming. The 1949 publication *Condensation Control in Dwelling Construction* (HHFA, 1949) did not even mention prevention of ice dams as a potential benefit of attic ventilation, but recommended installation of heavy roll roofing felt or sheet metal under the shingles over the eaves. Latta (1973) recognized the importance of air leaks and recommended attic ventilation, but only after "blocking all passages by which warm air can leak into the space below the roof." An important recent study of ice dams to date was conducted by Tobiasson et al. (1994). They observed that ice dams seldom occurred when outdoor temperatures were above 22°F (−5.5°C). Ice dams also do not occur when the attic air temperature is below freezing, and thus they arrived at a "window" of temperature conditions that lead to ice dams. Conversely, ice dams can be avoided if attic air temperature can be kept below 30°F (−1°C) with an outdoor temperature of 22°F (−5.5°C).

The ability of vents to prevent ice dams on cathedral ceiling roofs is more questionable than on roofs over attics. The amount of airflow needed to maintain the necessary cold conditions on the top of the roof is difficult to achieve with vents. Mechanical ventilation of cathedral ceilings is not a practical option. Thus, ice dam prevention on cathedral ceiling roofs should focus on optimizing roof insulation and minimizing penetrations of the insulation and the roof.

As mentioned in Chapter 4, preventing ice dams in roofs requires preventing excess and vagrant heat loss in attics, from chimneys, poorly insulated ducts, leaky ducts, mechanical equipment, and "bypasses" (i.e., openings in the ceiling connecting the indoor air to the attic). These are most common at plumbing and mechanical chases.

Designers seem unsure about the consequences of placing waterproofing underlayment beneath asphalt shingles. Waterproofing underlayment is self-adhering membrane of modified asphalt. It is recommended at any locations where ice damming might occur. Recall from Chapter 4 that ice dams produce lenses that extend several feet up the roof. In general, it would be appropriate to place waterproofing underlayment wherever future ice dams may be likely to extend. This may involve extensive use over much of or the entire roof. That can be done safely wherever the level of protection against air movement and vapor movement is good (i.e., using materials and practices similar to those used in low-slope roof assemblies).

SHINGLE DURABILITY

Many asphalt shingle manufacturers offer warranties with a clause requiring "code-level" ventilation. Their rationale is that shingles on unvented roofs are hotter. It is quite plausible that higher shingle temperatures accelerate aging, but does ventilation significantly reduce shingle temperatures? The short answer is no, not significantly.

Shingle color is a very strong determinant of shingle, sheathing, and attic temperature. In the University of Illinois laboratory comparison of white versus dark shingles (Rose, 2001), the white shingles were about 25% cooler than black (meaning that the white-shingle solar increase in temperature was 25% less than the black-shingle solar increase). A comparison of framing type, truss-framed flat-ceiling open attics versus cathedral ceilings, showed about a 6% cooling effect due to the open attic. Venting in truss-framed flat-ceiling attics had only about a 3% cooling effect on the shingles. Venting had a curious cooling effect in cathedral ceilings: Vents were able to have a powerful cooling effect low on the roof, but the cooling effect diminished to almost nothing at the top of the roof. This is because thermal buoyancy or the density difference between hot air at the top and cool air at the inlet drives air strongly up the slot. In other words, in a vented cathedral ceiling, venting can cool shingles in the lower part of the roof; it cannot cool shingles high in the roof.

Shingles are made of asphalt, and asphalt is a soup of hydrocarbons of different length and volatility (which is often proportional to molecular length). The vapor pressure of these hydrocarbons is a function of the absolute temperature of the material to the fourth power. So higher temperatures can indeed cause evaporation of the short-chain hydrocarbons, and this can lead to brittleness. Brittleness is one form of failure for an asphalt shingle. So higher temperatures never *improve* shingle durability. As long as shingle manufacturers ignore the effects of shingle color as a determinant of temperature, they may be admonished for asserting so strongly the importance of venting to control temperature. Of those manufacturers who hide poor product quality behind the 1/300 defense, the less said the better.

In short, on the basis of currently available information, attic ventilation is only marginally beneficial to shingle durability. Attic ventilation does not deserve the attention it has received in relation to shingle durability.

SUMMER COOLING

In both summer and winter, ventilation tends to lower the temperature of attic air and the air in the lower part of cathedral ceilings. So, on the surface of it, attic ventilation could be expected to lower summer cooling energy bills and to raise those bills for wintertime heating. For much of the United States, the net effect of those two might sound about like a wash, and it probably is.

Research on this subject really began with the publication of results at a National Bureau of Standards [now the National Institute for Standards and Technology (NIST)] workshop in 1978. Its title was *Summer Attic and Whole-House Ventilation* (NBS, 1979). One finding was that although attic ventilation did indeed cool the attic cavity considerably, that made little difference across a sufficient thickness of attic insulation. The ceiling heat flux is "a very small part of the house air-conditioning load" (Dutt and Harrje, 1979). They also stated that "any difference between the air conditioner use between houses with and without attic fans is not discernible from other factors which lead to house-to-house variation in air conditioner use." That was from New Jersey; results from the deeper south may be different.

Comparing energy use for air conditioning between two cases is rather difficult. In our studies we might have tended to have slightly higher energy use in the vented conditions, but the results were never outside the range of measurement error. Actually, I might expect higher energy use in houses with attic venting. With this reasoning: energy load is composed of two components: sensible cooling and moisture removal. The sensible cooling load is probably lower when the attic is cooler, even with R-30 or R-38 insulation. But ceiling planes are full of holes, and if the attic is open to the outside, the gusts associated with wind and the pulls associated with buoyancy will tend to move air across the ceiling plane. Air exchange with the outdoors on a hot muggy afternoon or evening brings along humidity; and humidity is air-conditioning load. So it makes sense that in some cases at least, a vented attic system, at least one with some holes in the ceiling plane, will lead to greater air-conditioning use for moisture removal, so higher summertime energy bills. In other systems there might be savings.

VENT DESIGN

Many vent devices, called *static devices* to distinguish them from mechanical powered devices, are rated for net free area (NFA). The NFAs of vent devices are usually provided by the manufacturer, and the industry that oversees static devices is the Home Ventilating Institute. The definitions and tests are not very strictly defined, nor are they applied uniformly. Code officials and those who give shingle warranties attach importance to NFA because of its importance in 1/300 calculations. Nevertheless, if there are vent devices out there, we might expect that they would offer more or less resistance to airflow and that the rating would somehow reflect this resistance. Jeff Gordon of the University of Illinois Building Research Council conducted research to test the NFA of vent devices. He began by asking: Exactly what is NFA? We might imagine that what we mean by NFA, in the absence of a common definition, is this: The *net free area* of a vent device is the sum of all the openings to airflow such that the resistance offered by those openings is equal to the resistance offered by a rectangular orifice of roughly equal height and width dimensions of that opening area. In other words, a 2 in. × 2 in. hole in a piece of sheet metal should have 4 in² of net free area; and any device that offers that amount of resistance to flow should have an NFA rating of 4 in². Gordon constructed a length of ductwork with a variable orifice at one end and a place for a vent device sample at the other. He used a variable-speed fan to draw air through the duct, and flow straighteners (bundles of soda straws) upstream of both the orifice and the sample. He measured the pressure drop upstream of both orifice and sample, as well as at a developed length downstream. He tested the test apparatus and found that a 3 in. × 6 in. rectangular metal sample came in within 0.25% of 18 in². Not bad.

Then he tested the samples. Some came very close to their rated NFA. These were the ones with punched openings with a minimum $\frac{1}{4}$-in. dimension in metal. Others had filter fabric put in place to help prevent snow entry, and the filter fabric added resistance to airflow. Some devices used fabrics and screens and matrix materials to confuse the snow that might enter with the air. These had NFA measurements much lower than their NFA ratings, in some cases lower than 20% of their rated value. Anyone who wished to estimate what the measured NFA of a vent device might be may just picture the tortuosity of an air path that passes through the vent. If it's open, the NFA rating might be fine. If the path appears to be restricted, it probably is, and the rating might be an overstatement.

These measurements are not to argue for a reintroduction of calculations into attic design, not at all, but rather to argue for some recognition that taking vent calculations to their conclusions involves a sequence of absurdist adventures, such as NFA.

TRUSS RISE

We cannot leave the matter of attic construction without addressing truss rise (Figure 7-5). During cold weather, the top chords are cold and the bottom chord is warm. At the same vapor pressure, some wood has a greater length when wet, whereas drier wood has a lesser length. The apex of the triangle of the truss thus moves upward. The web members attach the top

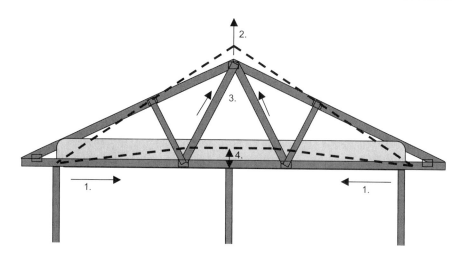

Figure 7-5
Illustration of truss rise. (1) Heat from below causes the bottom chord to dry out and shrink slightly. (2) The shrinking in the length of the bottom chord causes the triangular shape at the top chords to change. (3) The lift in the top chords draws the web members upward. (4) The upward pull by the web members causes the bottom chord to bend and lift upward from the partition below.

chord to the bottom chord, so the bottom chord is arched upward. This creates a gap at a partition on the inside of a building.

This is a natural phenomenon associated with properties of the wood and the geometry of the truss. It is claimed that longitudinal expansion and contraction occurs with *reaction wood,* wood with embedded stresses associated with its growing conditions. The problem is *not* solved by cutting web members, of course. Usually, it is solved by not having fasteners in the ceiling drywall within 16 in. of the partition and clipping the edge of the ceiling drywall to the drywall at the partition.

SUMMARY

- Indoor humidity control is the primary means to limit moisture accumulation in attics. By this author's experience, the strongest moisture source into attics is from wet foundations such as crawl spaces.
- To minimize ice dam formation, it is important to identify and rectify excess and vagrant heat sources in the attic. Venting may be necessary against ice dams in severely cold regions only. Ice dams are most likely in valleys.
- Venting should be a design option, the way that a choice between hip roofs and gable roofs is an option. Hips and gables can both be

done well or poorly; vented and unvented roof designs can be done both well and poorly. An easy design for a roof system without vents is a roof system that is satisfactory for low-slope roofing—a compact or sandwich assembly—turned at the roof angle.

- Architects and designers should develop a palette of both vented and unvented designs that work for the climate.

Mechanical Systems

COMFORT

Air is a mixture of many different gases. For every 100 molecules of air, about one is a molecule of water. The average molecular weight of air is 28.9. The molecular weight of water, you may recall, is 18. The humidity ratio, recall, is the ratio of the mass of water vapor to the mass of dry air. If an air sample at 72°F, say, has one water vapor molecule out of 100 air molecules, we can calculate the humidity ratio: approximately 0.0065. We can check a psychrometric chart and find that the relative humidity of our air sample is 40%. At that temperature and 80% RH, two molecules of 100 would be water vapor. Relative humidity of 40% is quite comfortable, some would say ideal. Relative humidity of 80% is high. In fact, 80% RH right at a surface forms a rough threshold above which mold may begin to grow on surfaces.

The point is this: The quantity of water in the air is small. The difference between having one molecule of 100 and two molecules of 100 makes a big difference as to what happens at surfaces such as our skin and the surfaces on which mold might grow. It makes a big difference in human comfort. Whether it makes a difference in health is the subject of Chapter 9.

Warm-blooded animals such as ourselves maintain an internal temperature higher than the ambient temperature that surrounds us, so heat flows from us to the environment. The rate at which we deliver metabolic heat outward depends on several factors. The most important is our activity. ASHRAE uses the unit *met,* where 1 met = 18.4 Btu/hr-ft² of body surface. A person seated quietly generates 1 met. Sleeping generates 0.7 met. House-cleaning: 2.0 to 3.4. Calisthenics: 3 to 4. Competitive wrestling: 7.0 to 8.7.

An adult male has a body surface area of about 20 ft². So a seated person generates about 360 Btu/hr or 107 W.

Metabolic heat is expelled by:

- Sensible heat loss from the skin, as regulated by the thermal insulating value of clothing, the ambient air temperature, and the convective heat coefficient due to the stillness (or not) of air at the skin surface.
- Evaporative heat loss from the skin, which depends on the wettedness of the skin, the vapor pressure at the skin, the vapor pressure in the ambient air, the evaporative heat transfer coefficient (analogous to the convective heat transfer coefficient), and the vapor permeance of clothing.
- Respiratory losses from exhaling warm air. Bohren and Walker (1987) point out that under some colder temperatures, dog breath may be foggy even when human breath is not. This is because dogs may have warmer mouths (and tongues) than humans, allowing them to have greater heat expulsion by panting. The respired air is typically at near-vapor saturation conditions, so hotter exhaled air has a higher dew point.

In general, at comfortable humidities, about 80% of a person's metabolic heat is discharged thermally and 20% is discharged evaporatively, through the skin and through respiration. In warmer conditions, and with brisker activity, the proportion of evaporative losses is increased.

The Comfort Zone

ASHRAE has maintained, over the years, Standard 55, which defines the *comfort zone* in terms of temperature and humidity (see Figure 8-1). The comfort zone is defined in terms of dry bulb temperature on the horizontal axis and moisture concentration on the vertical axis. This allows the comfort zone to be superimposed on a psychrometric chart.

The comfort zone is usually shown as two zones, somewhat overlapping, reflecting the difference in conditions between wintertime and summertime. We dress differently in those two seasons, thus the comfort zone is defined differently. It is intended to describe the conditions that 80% of sedentary or slightly active persons find thermally acceptable. The sensible temperature boundaries are defined in terms of effective temperature rather than dry bulb, but they correspond within 2° (plus or minus) to the following:

- Wintertime: 68 to 75°F
- Summertime: 73 to 80°F

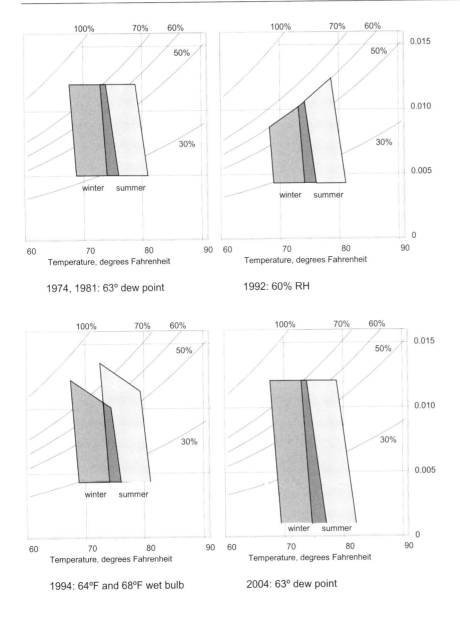

Figure 8-1
Comfort zone from ASHRAE Standard 55. The definition of the upper humidity bound has varied over time. Humidity ratio is indicated on the y-axis.

How low a humidity is too low? The first people to answer that question are usually those with contact lenses, who may find relative humidity below 25% to be irritating. At that low a humidity, certain shoes walking on carpet may cause sparks and static electricity. Harriman et al. (2001) has an excellent discussion of how static charges are built up as surfaces pull away from contact and of the role of moisture on those surfaces that conducts charge imbalances back to neutral. He shows a very strong increase in capacitance at relative humidity below 35%. Others may complain of sinus or bronchial irritation, dry nose, dry throat, dry eyes and skin. ASHRAE standard 55–1994 recommended a dew point temperature above 36°F, which lies between 25 and 30% RH, depending on the dry-bulb temperature. ASHRAE standard 55–2004 has no lower limit of humidity.

How high a humidity is too high? We all know it when we feel it, but it has been difficult to draw an upper humidity bound to the comfort chart. In 1974 and 1981, ASHRAE Standard 55 drew the upper limit at 63°F dew point or a humidity ratio of about 0.012. No comfort reasons were cited for this selection. In 1992, the upper bound was changed to 60% relative humidity. Again this reflected physical conditions in buildings—the attempt to prevent mold growth (more on that in Chapter 9)—rather than to pinpoint a threshold between comfort and discomfort. In 1994, again reasons outside human comfort led to a redefinition of the upper bound. The upper bound was taken at the wet-bulb lines of 64°F (winter) and 68°F (summer). These correspond to 18°C and 20°C. According to Harriman et al. (2001) the change to the 1994 chart was seen as being less restrictive as to the use of evaporative coolers (swamp coolers). These devices are common in the U.S. southwest where the outdoor humidity is low. Water is chilled by evaporation into the outdoor air, and that cooling effect is circulated into the house. The resulting coil temperatures are quite high compared to coil temperatures in a refrigerant unit, so the potential for dehumidification is low. Human disposition may support the 1994 upper limit: At high temperatures our skin is less supportive of high humidity. For 2004, the principal change is not the reversion to a flat-top upper humidity limit, but rather, the inclusion of an alternate adaptive model for buildings in which occupants open and close windows. In three of these mutations of the comfort zone, indoor RH over 80% appears allowable at low temperatures. I do not concur.

So what does give the sensation of too much humidity? The outer layer of the skin is made up of dead squamous cells which readily absorb and lose moisture. With high humidity these cells swell and soften. Studies by Gwosdow et al. (1986) indicate that the stickiness of fabric to the skin may play a large role. He took strips of fabric and pulled them across the skin and measured the friction between the skin and the fabric. He did this at several skin wetness levels, and naturally, the friction increased with wetter skin. He found that most fabrics, including burlap, wool, linen, and cotton, had the same effect, except for silk. Silk had a much lower friction at the full range of skin wetness levels. Based on this study, Harriman suggests that retail clothing stores might do well to maintain low humidity levels as people come in from a muggy street and try on clothes from the store.

HUMIDITY STANDARDS FOR MUSEUMS

Humidity standards for human comfort help reduce complaints. But stronger claims are made for the need for humidity control. Some manufacturing processes need strictly controlled humidity. So do operating rooms, with the risk of explosion in an oxygen-rich environment if any sparks occurred.

Museum conservators and curators claim a need for humidity control to ensure the preservation of artifacts under their care. This claim merits closer inspection. J. P. Brown, a conservator at the Field Museum in Chicago, has written about the history of humidity standards in museums (Brown and Rose, 1996), and the historical material he uncovered can be summarized here.

Historical Development

Toward the end of the nineteenth century, museums were unlike the shiny scoured places they are today. The urban environment was heavily polluted by the burning of coal and of coal gas for street lighting. Paintings needed to be covered with glass to create a surface that could be wiped clean before visitors arrived. Reflections in the glass were bothersome to visitors, of course. When electricity replaced coal gas for lighting, the environment became considerably cleaner, but it was not until after World War II that soot stopped being part of urban life. By the beginning of the twentieth century, water washers were introduced. Museums discovered first that regulation of the water temperature could humidify indoor air in the winter; later they discovered that if water was naturally or artificially chilled, it could dehumidify summer air as well. The Huntingdon Building of the Boston Museum of Fine Arts installed a central humidification and air washing system in 1908, and, after a two-year experimental period, according to an article by McCabe in *Museum News* in 1931: "It was found that the humidity best adapted for paintings and other works of art ranged from 55 to 60 percent regardless of the temperature or the time of year" (McCabe, 1931, p. 7). Brown notes that this is the first humidity set point described in the literature. The Cleveland Museum of Fine Art followed suit in 1915 or so, with double glazing to control condensation and humidification set at 50 to 55% RH.

The National Gallery of London had a full air-conditioning system designed in the late 1920s, but the cost to install was prohibitive. MacIntyre, an engineer in HM Office of Works, studied museum humidity in 1934–1935. He concluded first that "optimum conditions for any particular class of paintings must be more or less arbitrary" (p. 16); nevertheless, like McCabe, he proposed 55 to 60% for paintings on wood or canvas, at a temperature of 60°F (Courtauld, 1954). At the Orangery at Hampton Court Palace, the site of damage to Mantegna's cartoons from humidity fluctuations, MacIntyre tried to design a system of air conditioning that involved running heated, humidified air through 1740 lb of canvas hose, given the still-too-high cost of refrigerant systems.

In the United States, Brewster of the Forest Products Laboratory measured moisture content in wood furniture in the United States, noted that

British furniture had a higher moisture content, and showed how a coating such as varnish provides a lag time for humidity buffering (Brewster, 1931). He recommended a lower humidity limit of 40%, with occasional excursions down to 35%. He got there by working backward, to a recommended RH level from what the common moisture contents were in the furniture that he measured (see Figure 3-12).

During World War I, works from the British collections were stored in the London Underground system, where they suffered damage from uncontrolled damp. During World War II, the British collections were stored in quarries, where they survived remarkably well. The National Gallery's collections went to the Manod slate quarries in Wales. Conditions in the caves were constant 47°F (8°C) at 95% RH. The caves were heated to 63°F (17°C), which brought the RH down to 58%. Before the war, a technician had been employed eight months per year to correct cracking and blistering in panel paintings. During the first year in Wales, his work was reduced to one month, and by 1945 there was no work to do on the paintings. When they were returned to the essentially uncontrolled environment of the National Gallery, an epidemic of blistering, warping, and cracking broke out.

In 1947, Parliament commissioned the Weaver Report. Its authors cited the story of the Manod technician as striking evidence of the importance of maintaining humidity at 60% RH. This report failed to consider the benefits of stable temperature and stable ($\pm 2.5\%$ RH) humidity. In 1956, Plenderleith's *Conservation of Antiquities and Works of Art* became the "official textbook on the conservation of museum objects." The author retold the story of the Manod technician and stated that the lower safety limit should be fixed at 50%. He warned against damage if relative humidity at 45% persisted. He offered no proof of his damage predictions.

Plenderleith's recommendations for a 50% minimum RH were restated in Garry Thomson's *The Museum Environment*, first published in 1978, and they became a fixture of belief among a generation or two of art conservators. Thomson was scientific advisor at the National Gallery of London. He knew how weak the basis for humidity specification was:

> No one who reads this book will fail to end with a realisation of our general ignorance. We have a very uneven knowledge of how things in a museum change [i.e., deteriorate] and what causes these changes, and yet we have to erect this framework of preventive conservation before rather than after our research has reached a dignified level of completion. (Thomson, 1978, p. ii)

He also knew the practical difficulties of maintaining humidity levels. He stated that his specifications were "$97\frac{1}{2}\%$ specifications," where they might be expected to be exceeded about nine days per year. He knew that equipment design offered no guarantee of good equipment operation. In the second edition of *Museum Environment* in 1986, Thomson cited two tiers of museum environments: class 1 (50 or 55% ±5% RH year round) for major national museums and all new important museum buildings, and class 2 (40 to 70% RH) as a cost-effective alternative. Brown and Rose (1996) point out that "class 2" became synonymous with second class.

Stefan Michalski of the Canada Conservation Institute (1993) asked just what damage might actually occur with variations of ±15% RH around the midpoint. He wrote:

> For collections dominated by rigid organic materials (wood and paint), we must accept that data supports common sense, not magic numbers. Safe RH is a broad valley. . . . Overall high risk begins outside the range 25%–75% RH. Slight mechanical damage will accumulate on highly vulnerable assemblies at ±20% RH but this is virtually eliminated by ±10% RH in wood, ±5% RH in paint. (Michalski, 1993, p. 628)

In 1994, researchers Erhardt and Mecklenburg at the Smithsonian Conservation Analytical Laboratory (CAL) further challenged humidity *flatlining*, as Thomson's recommendations (without his qualifiers) came to be known:

> It is easy to see how RH values around 50% have become so widely accepted. It is only when less obvious forms of damage are considered, such as the slow but continuous [chemical] degradation of organic materials, that lower values of humidity seem more desirable. In fact, the reduction of mechanical damage is the only major factor that would seem to argue against all but the lowest values of relative humidity, those below 25–30% RH. This conflict—mechanical versus chemical degradation, form versus content—is the main consideration in choosing a suitable RH, and one for which there is no obvious resolution. (Erhardt and Mecklenburg, 1994, p. 37)

Throughout the course of these discussions of artifact safety, that is, throughout the twentieth century, others were asking what the effect of elevated humidity levels will be in the buildings that house these environments. The questions arose most forcefully among U.S. and Canadian researchers, whose museums are subject to colder winters and greater risk to the building envelope than in Europe, especially the British Isles. Their concerns culminated in 1991 in the New Orleans Charter, which assigned value to both collections and buildings, and sought to find environments that minimized the total amount of damage. This charter was a joint product of the Association for Preservation Technology and the American Conservation Institute.

In 1999, ASHRAE published a handbook chapter on environmental conditions in museums, libraries, and archival spaces. It was prepared with the recognition that collections were not particularly threatened by slow seasonal variation in humidity set point. Table 6 in the ASHRAE *Handbook, Applications,* Chapter 20, taken from the work of Conrad (1995), produced a definition for a class A museum environment. It allows a seasonal ±10% RH variation in set point about a fixed value, and also a short-term variation of ±5% RH to account for spatial variations in a room and for the operating range in the control equipment. So a class A environment may have a wintertime set point of 35% RH (allowing variations in the range 30 to 40%) and a summertime set point of 55% (50 to 60% allowable range for short-term variation). From a building and operating point of view, this is quite reasonable. Many in conservation accept these limits. A careful reader of the table may note that there is an environment class that is stricter than class A, titled class AA, which is designed for extremely sensitive artifacts such as ivory, and which does not permit seasonal variations. Conrad, it appears, learned a good lesson from Thomson's "second class" mistake.

CHARACTERIZING HUMIDITY

Health researchers have suspected that there is a problem for people who live in damp buildings. Studies discussed in Chapter 9 have found that the people who report that they live in damp conditions have more complaints than those who live in conditions of satisfactory humidity. But a subjective assessment of dampness is usually not very reliable. One would think that we could simply measure humidity to tell if the environment is damp or not. How do we make measurements to distinguish a "wet" environment from a "dry" environment?

Recall from earlier that the paint chemist Browne said there are two kinds of moisture problems that lead to paint peeling: those associated with rainwater and the failure to manage it properly, and those due to elevated moisture levels in buildings and cold surfaces in contact with that humid air. The first set of problems described by Browne (1933) have a cause (e.g., roof leak) and an effect (wet spot on the ceiling) that are directly linked to one another spatially. Where the water gets in, or where it accumulates as it flows downhill by gravity, is where it does its damage. There is no phase change. The second type of problem is quite different. The site of water entry or generation and the site of the effects may be far apart, with only invisible water vapor mediating between these two sites.

The first type of problem is diagnosed and solved by bringing a building professional such as a building inspector or a roofer around to look at the problem. It does not lend itself to measurement unless the inspector wants to probe rather than dismantle. Such problems may have the reputation of being difficult to diagnose and cure, but those involved in such inspections can usually make excellent assessments with little trouble. They are usually associated with funneling, or concentration of rainwater load.

The second type of problem does lend itself to measurement. Most people would have a commonsense grasp of the concept:

- The outdoor air contains a certain moisture concentration.
- Indoor activities such as respiration and transpiration usually add water vapor to the air.
- Ventilation of the indoor air may dilute the indoor concentration.

The net of these three simple effects is indoor air with an absolute humidity higher than the outdoor absolute humidity. How much higher is a good measure of wetness of a space. But such a measure requires quite a bit of qualification.

- A simple snapshot of the temperature and humidity indoors and out will not fairly represent the conditions over time. Instead, spaces should be monitored for a considerable length of time to average out the various contributions and changes in ventilation rate.
- During the winter, this approach may work quite well. But during the summer, when air conditioning or dehumidification mechanically remove humidity from the air, all bets are off.
- Fabrics, wood, upholstery, carpet—hygroscopic materials in the space—will tend to buffer the humidity increment over time, leading to more uniform values than we might have in a glass, aluminum, and plastic environment.

But the net of all this is that we should be able to characterize the wetness of indoor environments. To do this, we take simultaneous long-term measurements of conditions indoors and outdoors, convert those measurements to some value of concentration of moisture in the air (e.g., humidity ratio or vapor pressure), and simply subtract the outdoor value from the indoor. The result is termed the *moisture balance* of an interior environment. Let's take a closer look at moisture generation and ventilation, the factors that deliver moisture balance to a space.

MOISTURE GENERATION

Several researchers have investigated how much moisture is produced in a space. The first contributors were Hite and Bray from Purdue University (1948). Later contributors were Angell and Olson (1988) and Christian (1993).

We discussed above the moisture contribution that is simply the result of metabolism. A relatively inactive person may release about 0.1 lb/hr or 0.05 L/hr. A family of four would produce, from respiration and perspiration, about 5 L/day (11 lb). Normal household activities beyond breathing include washing, bathing and showering, housecleaning, laundry, and cooking. Estimates of the total amount of moisture generated by a family of four vary:

British Research Establishment (UK)	7.5 L/day
Fraunhaufer Institute (Germany)	14.6 L/day
ASHRAE (U.S.)	11.4 L/day

The U.S. estimate amounts to 25 lb of water produced per day by a family of four. This is a modest amount of water. All buildings must be able to accommodate the appropriate humidity contribution in residential or commercial construction. To do otherwise—to fault occupants for excess moisture load—resembles blaming the victim.

Most of the damaging moisture loads are indeed related to construction, not to humidity generation by occupants. The highest loads may be from flashing failure. Jeff Christian (1993) of Oak Ridge National Laboratory assigns the largest load to a Tennessee roof leak of 307 L/day, and 223 L/day for a flooded basement.

Britton (1949a), found that the contribution from an uncovered crawl space was about 100 lb per 1000 ft²/day. His device for calculating the moisture contribution (see Figure 8-2) was quite ingenious. A water level was maintained about 3 ft below the surface, which received different treatments. Water migrated from the source to the surface via capillarity. With this device he was able to determine rates of evaporation from surfaces with different treatments. He found that roofing materials greatly retarded the rate of evaporation. (Polyethylene had not been put to the service of water management in buildings at the time of Britton's research in 1947.) He found that pea gravel was an effective means of reducing evaporation. This finding led to the widespread use of pea gravel in crawl spaces to prevent evaporation. Britton also found that the rate of evaporation from fine soil that had no treatment or cover actually exceeded the rate of evaporation even from the surface of water only. We don't know how clean or contaminated his water surface was, but even the slightest surface film can greatly reduce the rate of evaporation.

Humidifiers are used in buildings and homes to boost the indoor humidity during wintertime dryness. Humidifiers are often controlled by humidistats. Inexpensive humidistats often function poorly. A runaway humidifier can pump large quantities into a building—on the order of 100 lb/day is

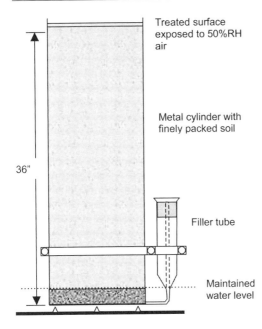

Treated surface
exposed to 50%RH
air

Metal cylinder with
finely packed soil

36"

Filler tube

Maintained
water level

Figure 8-2
Device for measuring the moisture contribution from wet soil, by Britton. Water was poured into the receptacle at the right. Water in the larger tank migrated by capillary action to the surface. Evaporation from the surface equaled the rate at which water had to be replenished.

possible by my estimates. Humidifiers need cleaning and maintenance to prevent mineral and bacterial buildup.

Construction wetness may play an important role in how buildings get started. Concrete contains large quantities of water—green (new) concrete may contain half water by weight. That moisture reacts with the cement, but some water evaporates into the surrounding air. Dimension lumber may be installed at 19% moisture content and go down to about 10%. Gypsum wallboard is usually installed dry (not counting the joint compound), and it should remain dry as the other materials reach equilibrium. For slabs with radiant heat, building occupants may get quite a moisture shock at the rate at which the concrete water is dried into the indoor air. If the contractor is tardy in getting the roof in place, waterlogged materials may take time and effort to dry, especially to dry safely. My colleague Anton TenWolde, originally from the Netherlands, says that in early days there, poor families were moved into houses that had recently been completed so that the eventual occupants would not have to abide the uncomfortable first year as everything dried out.

Swimming pools, we often presume, can bring the air in the pool room to close to 100% relative humidity. This rarely occurs in fact. Treatment chemicals and thin oil films reduce the vapor pressure. The amount of water agitation can increase the evaporation rate. We have found that it is usually possible to maintain air above a swimming pool at between 50 and 60% without excessive ventilation and pretreatment of air. Of course, spas and pools should be covered when they're not in use. Air should be exhausted from pool areas. Wherever chlorine smells pervade, we might expect moisture to travel right along.

VENTILATION

Occupants of buildings need fresh air, of course. But just how much fresh air has been a source of continuing controversy and concern, because conditioned air can be expensive.

Old buildings, medieval buildings say, operated like chimneys, with stale, smoky air exhausted through a hole in the roof or a cupola. Like barns and mill buildings, houses generated so many contaminants and pollutants that ventilation was a necessary part of the design. Benjamin Franklin concerned himself with ventilation, and the Franklin Institute in Philadelphia carried on his work. The aim here was to eliminate *vitiated air,* air that had the "life" taken out of it, presumably the oxygen.

Soon the question became how to tell good air from bad, and in fact, it was easy—by odor. Throughout the first part of the twentieth century, ventilation was driven by odor control. Schools needed to be ventilated. Early ASHRAE studies sought to determine how much fresh air schoolchildren needed. It depended on their frequency of bathing, and that depended on the social class. I recall reading from the 1910s that it is much more effective to wash children with water than with air. The classic study of ventilation requirements for odor control was conducted by Yaglou of the Harvard School of Public Health. Konzo describes Yaglou's research this way:

> His mode of attack on the question "How much fresh air is required for ventilation?" was simple and direct. He was brave enough to place his nose at the outlet of a tight enclosure in which a human "guinea pig" was seated. Yaglou's nose measured the sweetness of the air leaving the box. Although inferior to the capabilities of a plain hound dog, the human nose is one of the most sensitive instruments for detecting odors. When the flow rate out of the enclosure was high, the odor was not perceptible. As the flow diminished, the signal changed to "Wow," and finally to "Holy Cow." (Konzo, 1992)

An updated version replaced Yaglou's nose with a committee of eight noses (according to Konzo) and made use of a portable "sniff car," a van with a ventilation lab inside. Yaglou found that the odor threshold depended not only on the air change rate but also on the amount of space per person. At about 250 ft^3 per person, an acceptable ventilation rate is about 15 ft^3/min for odor control. There are other criteria that drive the need or desire for ventilation. Oxygen is necessary for survival.

Certain contaminants of indoor air may be diluted with ventilation. Fresh carpets and cabinets, for example, may offgas hydrocarbons such as formaldehyde. For such contaminants, only a fixed amount is contained in the materials, so the emission rate necessarily diminishes over time. Combustion products are common contaminants, but they should be removed right at the site of combustion and hardly allowed to enter the indoor air. See the discussion of combustion products below. Mold (see Chapter 9) is sometimes considered a contaminant of indoor air. However, in most seasons and in most locations, outdoor mold spore concentrations are several times higher than indoor concentrations. Higher indoor concentrations usually mean mold growth in the building; this requires fixing the mold problem, not increasing the amount of ventilation.

Is moisture a contaminant requiring dilution with ventilation? In my opinion, no. High indoor humidity requires source control (finding where the water gets in and stopping it before it enters), not ventilation. Ventilation levels necessary for odor control are usually sufficient for moisture control as well. Ventilation may be fine three seasons out of the year. But in the dog days of summer, ventilation would have to move air over our skin quite rapidly to create any sensation at all of comfort. Instead, during those days, humidity comfort may be achieved by locking the building up as tightly as possible and providing dehumidification.

For commercial buildings with air-handling units, having a standard that gives the air exchange rate per occupant is a practical necessity as a starting point for mechanical system design. ASHRAE Standard 62.1 embodies this fresh air requirement for most public buildings. Facilities for smoking, exercise, production of contaminants, and so on, may need different air change rates, but by far the bulk of U.S. commercial and public buildings have a simple design target.

For residential buildings, the benefits of standardized mechanical ventilation are more arguable. Odors in the home are usually taken care of with exhaust fans in the bathroom and kitchen. Furnaces and hot water heaters should take combustion products outside by the most direct route. Items brought into the new home should not be smelly by the time of occupancy. Higher indoor temperatures and air exchange with the outdoors can help new materials to offgas. Smokers shouldn't smoke, at least not in the house. Which leaves moisture. Ventilation for moisture dilution never works, of course, during summertime. During the other seasons it might help. But the strongest argument for ventilation is simple: If the outdoor air is fresh and clean, breathe as much of it as you can.

The cost of providing air at comfort conditions during summer is divided between the cost of reducing the sensible temperature and the cost of removing humidity from the air. In St. Louis, for example, the ratio is 1 : 3 if we wish to hold 60% RH and 1 : 5 if we want 50% RH. This is typical of the entire southeastern quadrant of the United States. See Figure 8-3, calculated to maintain 75°F and 55% RH. Harriman shows the ratio of sensible to latent load for U.S. cities. Clearly, to provide fresh air at comfort

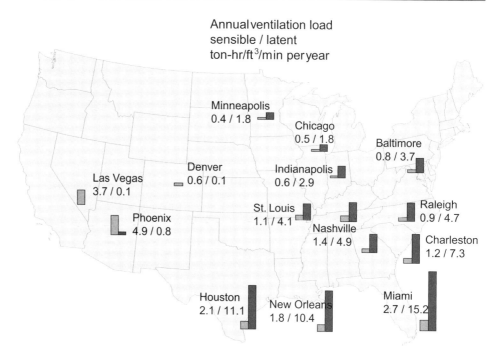

Annual ventilation load
sensible / latent
ton-hr/ft³/min per year

Figure 8-3
Energy cost of preconditioning air from the outdoor conditions for selected U.S. cities through the cooling season to 75°F and 55% RH. Values on the left are the costs for sensible temperature control, on the right for humidity control. Units are ton-hr/(ft³/min) for the entire cooling season. (From Harriman et al., 2001.)

conditions, much more money is spent on humidity removal than on lowering temperature.

Here lies the strength of the argument for airtightness in commercial buildings. Comfort comes with dehumdification for much of the United States, and dehumidification is economical, indeed possible, in a building with a low air change rate with the outdoors.

COMBUSTION

Pure carbon may be ignited and combined with oxygen to form carbon dioxide (and carbon monoxide). Coal contains carbon. Most fuels, however, are hydrocarbons. They react with oxygen to form carbon dioxide and water vapor. The simple combustion reaction for methane, for example, is

$$CH_4 + 2O_2 \rightarrow CO_2 + 2H_2O$$

Table 8-1 gives the moisture production from combustion reactions for different hydrocarbon fuels (alkanes). Note that the moisture produced is greater in both gas volume and weight than the volume or weight of fuel

Table 8-1   Combustion reactions of hydrocarbon fuels

Constituent	Molecular formula	ft^3_{water}/ft^3_{fuel}	lb_{water}/lb_{fuel}
Methane	CH_4	2.0	2.2
Ethane	C_2H_6	3.0	1.8
Propane	C_3H_8	4.0	1.6
Butane	C_4H_{10}	5.0	1.5

From ASHRAE *Handbook—Fundamentals*, 2001, 18.2.

input. For most liquid fuels, such as gasoline, kerosene, and heating oil, the amount of water produced is greater than the amount of fuel used, in both weight and volume. Moisture is just one of the combustion products. Others include particulates, CO_2, CO, and NO_x, the various oxides of nitrogen. None of these products should be contributed to indoor house air.

Chimneys are designed to move combustion air up and out of the building. The theory is simple. Hot air rises, due to its lower density compared to cold air. We can picture this density difference acting at the top of the chimney as if the hot air formed a bubble that would leave the chimney top and move upward until it blended with the surrounding air. As it leaves, it needs makeup air, which it gets from below. The draw of the chimney depends on the temperature difference between the temperature of the exhausting air and the outdoor air. The temperature of the exhausting air depends on the temperature of the chimney liner through which it moves. Think of each foot of length of the chimney as a booster, where the heat of the liner adds its inducement to flow. It also depends on the height of the chimney: A tall chimney produces more momentum in the heated air column, so it exhausts at a higher velocity. It also depends on the kind of airstream into which the combustion air exhausts: turbulent or smooth, with or without a boost from lateral wind flows of air at the top of the chimney.

Anyone who has lit a fireplace knows that the fire must produce some heat before it draws properly. But once the liner is hot, it induces constant and dependable flow. The simplest chimney is simply a vertical column, with a damper to block unwanted flows out of the building. But a more common design for a masonry fireplace is shown in Figure 8-4. This design is used for chimneys located on the outside wall of a building. The chimney wall at the outside is cold, while the inside wall is heated by the interior. This leads to a convective loop that turns at the smoke shelf, and that loop can greatly help getting a fire started. The argument for the smoke shelf is not very compelling for chimneys wholly within a dwelling.

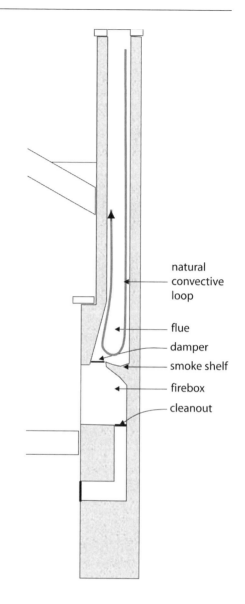

natural convective loop

flue

damper

smoke shelf

firebox

cleanout

Figure 8-4
Chimney at an outside wall. The outside chimney wall is colder while the inside chimney wall is warmer. This leads to a convective loop, and that loop can help induce draft as a fire is started in the fireplace.

Chimneys were designed to operate at high temperatures. The efficiency of a combustion unit is estimated, roughly, from the ratio of the heat used (i.e., minus the heat used to heat the chimney) over the total heat produced. Early units were inefficient by modern standards—around 60%. With the energy crisis, the efficiency of units was improved, so less heat was applied to the chimney, and chimneys began to crumble. The exhaust products from efficient units had the same amount of moisture, but it was delivered to the chimney at a lower temperature. This is a recipe for wetter materials. Wet chimney liners and materials led to rapid corrosion and deterioration of chimneys, until new liners of tile, concrete, or metal were installed. Old chimneys are orphans in buildings with energy-efficient appliances.

Unvented Combustion Appliances

Forty-seven U.S. states now approve for use small heating appliances and "hearth" units that burn propane or natural gas, and that discharge the combustion products directly into the room air. They advertise these units as 99% efficient, because they do not waste any heat in having to deliver combustion products into the chimney—there is no chimney. One may ask if this is a good idea. Chimneys, after all, have been part of the landscape as long as fuel has been burned in buildings.

Unvented gas appliances are advertised as meeting all reasonable safety and health standards when sized and used properly. The basis for this claim seems to be a single report by DeWerth et al. (1996). The authors aimed to compare the impact on indoor air quality (IAQ) of key emissions from vent-free supplemental heating appliances to proposed IAQ guidelines, and to define criteria for proper sizing of a product for its application. Their results are:

> The computer model simulation for 4 hours of continuous use showed that properly installed and used vent-free products for comfort conform to reasonable IAQ Guidelines for CO, NO_2, CO_2, and H_2O vapor. Sizing guidelines have been developed for five DOE heating regions, three types of house construction, and two modes of operation: continuous and cycling. These sizing guidelines can be used by manufacturers, installers, and dealers to qualify and install properly sized vent-free gas heating appliances. The results apply to all vent-free products.

Using these findings, a marketing campaign was undertaken that has successfully promoted the use of these appliances. All research reports contain many qualifying statements that specify the conditions of the test. Marketing campaigns (in my opinion, anyway) tend to quash qualifying statements and aim for broad generalizations that can bring in the largest number of consumers.

The principal assumptions in DeWerth et al.'s work are:

- The air change rate is 0.35 air change per hour for a dwelling. This value is found as a target value for residential ventilation in one or more standards, including ASHRAE 62.2.
- The design outdoor temperature for the model is the 1000-hour temperature. In any year there are 8160 hours. If we measure the temperature every hour over the course of the year and rank them in magnitude, the 1000-hour temperature is the temperature of the

1000th coldest hour. There are 999 hours per year colder than their design outdoor temperature.

- The model was run for four hours only. Some explanations are given in the report as to why such a limitation is reasonable, but the principal reason given seems to be that that is the length of run that the research sponsor asked for.

How reasonable are these assumptions?

- Homeowners do not have air-change-rate monitors in their houses. Some houses have lower air change rates than that, especially in the winter, when supplemental heating may be most desirable. Neither the standard nor this model addresses what happens if the actual air change rate is below this value.

- The model was run for four hours only. Some of the results show climbing levels of contaminants, but the concentration stays below the "acceptable" threshold at the end of the model run. If we were to extrapolate visually, the concentrations exceed the thresholds: say, in hour 5 or 6. Users are not told to use the appliances for four hours only, then wait for the contaminant levels to go back to zero (which is the starting point for each mold run) before turning the appliance back on again.

- If the appliance needs to run for four hours when the temperature outdoors is the 1000-hour temperature, isn't it reasonable to imagine that the appliance might run for more than four hours sometime during the 999 colder hours?

This argument could go on, and reasonable people might find the criticisms posed here either picky or alarmist. This is an example of how one might draw design guidance from research. The model produces numerical output, and that output is compared to some published threshold values. If the results are on the safe side of the threshold, a green light is issued, otherwise a red light or at least a warning is shown. But the assumptions, fine points, footnotes, qualifications, and simplifications are never carried forward into the design guidance or recommendation. A careful industry will scrupulously carry the research findings forward with all of the qualifications.

AIR CONDITIONING

Air conditioning plays a role in regulating summertime humidity. But just how well it does that is the subject of some discussion. The basic element of a refrigeration or air-conditioning system is the coil. The cooling coil is nothing more than a chilled element through which air passes. It lowers the temperature of the air that passes through it, and it removes water from that air. But let's look more closely at how that is done.

Air enters the coil, pushed by the fan, at room temperature. When the unit turns on, the coil fins begin to chill. At first, the temperature of the exiting air is lowered. When the coil surface reaches the dew point temperature, or slightly lower to ensure nucleation, beads of condensation begin to form on the fins. The absolute humidity of the exiting air is reduced. The beads of condensation grow larger and begin to coalesce. As they become larger they begin to work their way down the coil by gravity. They drop from the coil onto the condensate pan. If the pan is clean, the water film on the pan may be small, but if it is dirty or corroded, the materials in the pan will get saturated with water. Once all this material is saturated, the depth of the water in the condensate pan may be enough that water begins to spill down the condensate line. Only then, at that instant, has water been removed from the building. How long does that take? As with everything in engineering, it depends. According to Shirey and Henderson (2004), it takes between 11 and 32 minutes. Now suppose that the unit has been sized to make sure that the building can be cooled quickly. That requires a large cooling unit that can satisfy a thermostat quickly. Suppose that it can satisfy the thermostat before water has begun draining down the condensate line—in that case the building is cooled but with no dehumidification. The resulting air would be cold and clammy.

Any water that remains on the coil as the coil warms up remains as water in the building. If it evaporates from the coil, it evaporates back into the ductwork and back into the building. If there is water on the coil when the unit begins operation, then of course the time to remove condensate is lessened. Units with a high sensible energy rating are units that reduce surface temperature efficiently. However, they may accomplish this at the expense of latent efficiency, that is, at the expense of effective water removal. I consider it unfortunate that the drive toward energy efficiency stresses sensible efficiency and tends to ignore the contribution that humidity removal makes to comfort.

For a unit to deliver comfortable conditions in terms of both temperature and humidity, the unit should not be oversized. A small unit that operates for a longer period of time, or at a colder temperature, is better able to remove water from the air.

The traditional way of controlling both temperature and humidity in an air handler is to cool the air down to the desired dew point temperature, then reheat it back to the desired supply air temperature. Reheating is often considered expensive and wasteful. That has changed recently with technical advances that allow waste heat from the compressor to be used for reheating the air. In museum studies, it may be a good idea to separate the temperature control functions from the humidity control functions, given the difficulty and possible expense in trying to achieve total control from a cooling coil and reheat.

I was once asked to investigate an event in a museum, where flakes from polychrome and gilding had popped off overnight, much to the consternation of the conservators and curators. It was the muggiest part of the summer, and the new museum was putting its glistening new powerful cooling (and dehumidification) system into operation. For a week or two prior to the event, the interior temperature stayed in the low 60°F range as the air handler struggled to remove water from the air. The afternoon before the event, a thermostat was vandalized by an uncomfortable building occupant, causing the temperature to jump quickly by about 15°. When asked to explain how this led to flaking, I compared an artifact to popcorn, with a porous hygroscopic interior and a relatively moisture impermeable exterior skin. How do you optimize the popping of popcorn? Keep it in the refrigerator, so that the interior of the kernel maintains a high moisture content. When the kernel is heated, the sorbed moisture turns to vapor and provides an explosive push from the back side of the skin covering. This "popcorn effect" (Rose, 1994) may have played a part in the unfortunate event.

PLUMBING AND PIPE BURSTING

Plumbing systems are typically composed of three subsystems: water supply, fixtures, and DWV (drain–waste–vent). When freezing temperature surround water supply systems, the water in the pipes turns to ice and causes bursting. Insurance companies paid out around $4.5 billion in the 10-year period 1985–1995 in claims for pipe bursting. The purpose of insurance payouts, of course, is compensation in the case of catastrophic damage. Recently, insurance companies have been hit with claims of mold damage. Pipe bursting is catastrophic; mold is slow, incremental, chronic—not at all catastrophic. Mold remediation has also been quite expensive for insurance companies. The companies have written mold exclusions into most of their policies. So mold damage is rarely covered in claims except when it occurs as a consequence of pipe bursting. Fortunately, the solution to the pipe bursting problem is here, thanks to the research of Jeff Gordon at the University of Illinois. The claims come much more from the southern United States than from the northern states. Texas and Florida were highest on a per capita basis; Minnesota was the lowest. We can attribute this to the surprise factor—Minnesotans build such that freezing pipes are unlikely, whereas southerners may be caught by surprise by an unexpected cold wave.

Gordon began, as all researchers should, with a literature search. His search turned up a Master's thesis at the University of Alaska in Fairbanks under the direction of John Zarling, where the student made pressure measurements of pipes subject to bursting and the results seemed interesting. Jeff mounted water pipes in a freezer and measured pipe temperature and water pressure as the freezer temperature was taken to well below freezing. His results came as a surprise to most people who thought they understood the phenomenon of freezing and bursting pipes.

The common understanding goes something like this: When a pipe that contains water is surrounded by freezing temperatures, the water turns to ice. Ice has a volume that is 8% greater than the volume of water, so the pipe circumference is stretched and ruptures. That's a simple explanation, but it is wrong.

What actually happens is the following, in several phases:

- *Phase 1:* The water pipe is surrounded by freezing temperatures. The temperature of the water goes down. In fact, the water temperature goes several degrees below freezing (see Chapter 2) and remains as a subcooled liquid. Then ice nucleation occurs, forming fernlike crystals of dendritic ice. The formation of those crystals raises the temperature of the water–ice slush back up to exactly freezing temperatures. (Recall that when water evaporates from a surface, the remaining water is cooled by the escape of the higher-energy vapor molecules. By the same token, water that fuses to ice takes the lower-energy molecules out of the liquid state, leaving liquid and solid at a higher temperature.) The formation of ice releases the heat of fusion to the ice–water mix.

- *Phase 2:* Ice begins to grow from the wall of the pipe inward. This is called *annular ice*. As it grows, no stresses are applied to the pipe wall. In fact, the ice may even be seen as protecting the pipe wall from bursting. Throughout this period, water pressure in the line is normal, although the water may seem quite cold coming out the faucet.

- *Phase 3:* The annular ice grows inward and creates a blockage. At first no damage is done. But then the blockage grows in length along the pipe, growing toward the street as well as toward the fixtures. As it grows toward the street, nothing happens, provided that there is no backflow prevention valve. But as it grows toward the fixture, the water pressure begins to rise. This is due, of course, to ice being greater in volume than water. The water pressure in the pipe rises at a constant rate as long as the stresses on the pipe material remain in the elastic range.

- *Phase 4:* As pressure continues to build, the limits of elastic deformation are reached, and the pipe goes into plastic deformation. At first the additional pressure leads to (permanent) relaxation in the pipe wall. Then even the relaxed material is stressed, and it ruptures.

Figure 8-5 shows the measured water pressure broken into four phases as a function of time. The pressure shown here is for copper pipe. In a well-plumbed water supply system, the joints should be stronger than the pipe itself. So in a well-plumbed system it is the pipe rather than a pipe fitting that should fail. Of course, under high pressure the system will fail at its weakest point. If it fails at the pipe, it is likely to fail at the point where the pipe is least ductile (at least in metal pipe), and that is at the coldest point, where the ice meets the water. This is what creates the illusion that it is ice that ruptures the pipe.

There are several solutions. The most obvious is to provide pressure relief downstream from the blockage. An inventor named Augustus in Canada in the 1940s recognized just this, and he invented a faucet that leaked out the base. Gordon wrote up the same idea. *Popular Science* caught notice of this approach and wrote "leave it to a University of Illinois researcher to invent the leaky faucet." Another approach is to use water supply piping that allows 8% volume change without deformation—PEX (cross-linked polyethylene) seems to provide that, provided that the material is not laminated with aluminum. A third approach is to include an air bladder in the system. Water piping systems that included an air chamber (constructed of regular piping material) or a water hammer arrester (a cartridge with a rubber diaphragm separating the air from the water) can provide some protection. A fourth approach is to insulate the pipe. This approach is beneficial not only in helping to keep the water warmer for a longer time but also in retarding the release of the heat of ice formation, thus retarding the rate at which the ice is formed. A fifth approach, certainly the most commonly used, is to allow the pipes to drip during exceptionally cold weather. It is important to keep both the hot and cold water lines dripping (and this may

Figure 8-5

Pressure increase in the confined fluid of a pipe (PSI 1). TCod represents outdoor temperature. Pipe wall temperatures are represented by 1W, 1C, and 1E.

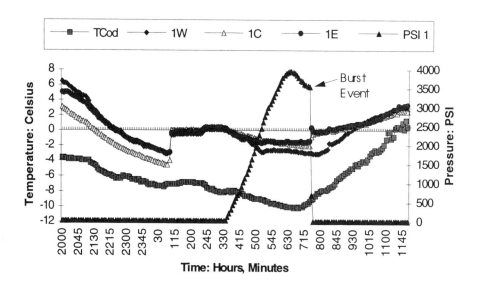

be difficult to assure with a "gearshift-type" faucet), and building users should be aware that it is important to keep the faucets lightly cracked even after the dripping stops, as the ice blockage may still be growing in length.

Plumbers I've met are often stymied as to why the warm water line is the one that requires repair after freezing, much more often than the cold water line. Gordon and associates wondered that as well, until they hit on the very obvious answer—the toilet. The ballcock apparatus in the tank uses a float to permit or prevent water entering and filling the tank. If the water pressure is increased, the valve can simply push the float slightly down in the water and let a few drops of water into the tank. The tank apparatus is a pressure relief valve, all by itself. But a toilet of course protects only the cold water line.

One pressure relief fixture or fitting on each of the cold side and warm side can protect all the fixtures downstream from a site of blockage. They have proven to be so effective that a water supply system can turn to ice and back to water with no rupture in the system.

Rot and Mold

INTRODUCTION

The best dividing line between acceptable and unacceptable building envelope assemblies is this: Building envelopes should not support the active growth of mold and other decay microorganisms. Envelope assemblies that do not support mold growth are, in general, acceptable; those that do fail the test. As mentioned before, surface relative humidity of 80% or more can, under many circumstances, permit mold to grow. Surface humidity above that level can permit high rates of corrosion as well. This line of separation is a rough compromise, of course; numbers that simple always mask complex circumstances that deserve a closer look.

Fungi

My colleague Jeff Gordon describes the beauty and complexity and sexiness of Earth's creatures who are charged by DNA to "be fruitful and multiply." But, he points out, growth is only half of the equation governing living matter; the decay half may be at least as beautiful, complex, and indeed, sexy as the growth half of life's equation. Perhaps if we looked closely enough at mold, fungi, and saprophytes in general, we could find the decay-side equivalents of orchids, redwoods, peacocks, and giraffes. At the very least we should expect surprises. There are molds that walk, individual fungi the size of several counties of lower Michigan, and molds that reproduce with sperm similar to the sperm of mammals. They are endlessly fascinating organisms.

Fungi reproduce by spores. The spores may travel by air or water, sometimes by insects, and sometimes by the transportation of infected materials. In any sample of outdoor air or outdoor soil, there may be a significant concentration of spores of various fungi. If conditions on building surfaces are suitable for the growth of molds or rotting fungi, inoculation is not automatic but depends on chance that mold spores of individual species will encounter the welcoming surface. The more common types of mold spores, such as *Penicillium, Alternaria,* and *Cladosporium,* have a high likelihood of initiating growth. The less common fungi may require days or months before inoculation.

Basidiomycetes

The fungi that cause wood decay, rather than simple wood surface discoloration, are the basidiomycetes. They are the most complex fungi, and they include mushrooms. Wood and wood products, including paper (which provides a facing for gypsum wallboard) are composed largely of cellulose and lignin. The fungi that attack primarily lignin leave the surface looking bleached, due to the remaining cellulose. Common white-rot fungi include *Polyporus versicolor, Poria nigrescens,* and *Peniphora mollis.* Brown-rot fungi attack the cellulose and leave the surface looking brown, often with checking in the wood surface. An example of a brown-rot fungus is *Poria monticola.*

Dry Rot

What is dry rot? There are at least three different meanings. At its most specific, dry rot in North America refers to the fungus *Poria incrassata.* Verrall (1968) describes *P. incrassata* as producing large, tough, water-conducting strands called *rhizomorphs,* which can conduct water several feet away from a constant and abundant supply of moisture. Once it is established, it can rapidly attack flooring, walls, woodwork, and furniture. Control is quite simple—remove the water supply.

The fungus (Figure 9-1) is extremely sensitive to drying. One study showed that if it is detached from its water source, it dies in 1 day at 30% RH, 5 days at 65%, and 10 days at 90%. But it also has shown an interesting ability to make use of *metabolic water,* the water that is formed when cellulose degrades to H_2O and CO_2. *P. incrassata* is often found where wood is in direct contact with wet soil, such as where wood formwork for concrete is not removed from the soil, or in some crawl spaces. Oliver (1997, p. 86) states that in Great Britain the true dry rot fungus is *Serpula lacrymans,* formerly called *Merulius lacrymans.* By virtue of its ability to transport water and nutrients several feet, the organism may "wet up" conditions that are otherwise marginal for growth. The organism produces a substantial amount of acid (oxalic acid), and if it accumulates and drops the pH to about 3, growth of the rot will cease. Unfortunately (fortunately for the organism), calcium can neutralize the effect of the acid and calcium is readily found in masonry materials.

Figure 9-1
Poria incrassata mycelium on a door that was kept in storage. (From FPL, 2000.)

A second use of the term *dry rot* refers to any of the brown-rot fungi described above. The resulting surface may be dark brown. The checking pattern of cracks both with the grain and perpendicular to the grain leaves the look of small rectangles on the surface. In fact, the surface may look so dry as to look burned.

A third use of the term *dry rot* may refer to decay of the wood by any basidiomycete. While water is present, the fungi can attack and severely weaken the wood. But if the water source dries up, the fungi may die or become inactive. The look of the wood may still be the look of decay, with weakened, discolored, desiccated wood and perhaps the appearance of mycelia or fruiting bodies, and it will be dry. Some may even use the term *dry rot* simply as a loose term for *rot*.

I would argue against the use of the term *dry rot* at all. It seems to create the impression that dryness can lead to rotting, which is simply not true—all rotting requires water. Call it *rot*, or *decay*, or *brown-rot infestation*, or be specific as to the type of fungus or the particular fungus infesting the wood. If one term such as *dry rot* can have several meanings, the inevitable resulting arguments are rarely helpful in understanding or communicating observations about real buildings.

MOLD

Mold is a fungus that affects the surfaces of materials, mostly organic materials, if conditions are right. Wet surfaces with the right nutrients may support a succession of fungal colonizers, with different species preferring different conditions. Even under dry conditions, mold spores and fragments of mold organisms are found in the air, on surfaces, and in building cavities, often at high concentrations. Mold growth (or *amplification*) occurs under conditions of wetness.

In some ways, mold is like dirt. It is unsightly. It is everywhere, but is usually more common outdoors than indoors. There are traces of dirt everywhere, but some places are dirtier than others and some places are unacceptably dirty. Dirt in the air may affect respiratory health—think of the Dust Bowl conditions during the Depression. Dirt may be toxic for people who eat dirt. If we find dirt, we clean it up. Dirt particles in the air may accumulate on surfaces and in building cavities. Some surfaces are easier to clean than others. The only surfaces totally free of dirt are those that are scrubbable and are recently scrubbed. The idea of making a room or a building "dirt-free" is either a clinical imperative such as in operating rooms, or hype such as for marketing cleaning products. Mold is much like dirt in each of these regards.

Mold is unlike dirt, of course, in one significant respect. Mold is a living organism, a member of the fungus kingdom that may grow under the right conditions; dirt is mostly inorganic.

Mold spores are the principal means of mold reproduction. Most mold spores are transported in the air, in order to find new sites for colonization. Spores may carry toxins capable of disposing of previous colonizing organisms. *Penicillium* mold, for example, may poison bacteria in the neighborhood with penicillin. *Stachybotrys* spores may (or may not) contain toxins such as tricothecenes to wipe out the indigenous local bacteria or simpler fungi.

All organisms digest food; mold does its digestion outside the organism itself. It excretes enzymes capable of breaking down long-chain hydrocarbons. Those enzymes need to travel by diffusion in a thin water film to the food molecules, which they break down into simpler sugars and starches. These water-soluble simpler compounds then diffuse outward from the site where they were created, and some of them migrate back to the hungry mold organism. Mold relies to a great extent on having a thin film of water several molecules thick that can transport the enzymes outward, but not too far, and transport the broken-down compounds back to the organism. The film, of course, is nothing like a flat membrane because the surface of materials at the microscopic level is mountainous and cavernous. The mold organism grows hyphae, which are thin strands the tips of which are capable of conducting the same reactions where they touch the upholstery on which the organism resides. The strands of hyphae form a mat called a *mycelium*. The mycelium creates a buffer that helps to regulate the wetness of the surface. It retards evaporation of the surface, helping to guarantee a stable moisture film necessary for digestion. Mold needs an edible substrate, air, and a multimolecular film at the surface. Does condensation lead to mold? No, condensation creates liquid water, and liquid water would, in effect, drown the mold, deprive it of oxygen, and turn any attempts at digestion into wasted effort.

The conditions for initial mold growth on a surface may be quite different from the conditions under which growth continues, or under which growth recurs on affected but scrubbed surfaces. Generally, initial growth requires higher levels of moisture than is required for continued growth. Mold continues to grow on surfaces:

- Where the moisture content of the substrate provides a dependable water source
- Where the air humidity is high. This ensures that the water film is thick enough to permit diffusion of enzymes outward and simple hydrocarbons back to the organism
- Where there is no water flow on the surface
- Where sufficient food can be found
- Where there are no significant inhibiting chemicals or treatments

Different organisms require different thicknesses of films. The phylloplane (leaf-inhabiting) fungi, such as *Penicillium* and *Cladosporium,* get by with rather thin films. They can thrive where the relative humidity in the air is 80% or greater. *Stachybotrys* requires more water and a thicker film; it requires a surface relative humidity around 95% or greater. Biologists use surface water activity (a_w) as the measure of available water, which is expressed as a decimal less than 1. For purposes here, water activity corresponds to surface relative humidity. The IEA, Annex 14 (1991) has put forth a threshold value of 80% surface relative humidity ($a_w < 0.8$) as an average monthly value, below which mold growth is unlikely and above which it can be expected to occur. This is very helpful because it permits nonbiologists (e.g., designers, engineers, building scientists) to design and construct physical conditions with some expectation of mold control. Recall from Chapter 3 that transient modeling normally has, as one of its outputs, surface relative humidity. Thus, we can use modeling to predict the likelihood or not of mold growth on building surfaces.

MOLD MEASUREMENT

The buildings we design and build should smell fresh and they should look fresh. They should not support the growth of mold organisms. That is, the surfaces should remain at a surface relative humidity below the threshold that permits mold to propagate. Building science should aim at designing and constructing buildings that keep surface relative humidity below that threshold, usually considered to be 80% surface relative humidity. In Chapter 3 we showed how transient modeling allows us to predict surface relative humidity, thus allows us to estimate the potential for mold growth in any building envelope assembly.

In actual buildings, mold may be estimated by visual assessment or by sampling.

Visual Assessment

Guidelines for the visual estimation of mold are given in EPA *Mold Remediation in Schools and Commercial Buildings* (2001) and the New York City Department of Health's *Guidelines on Assessment and Remediation of Fungi in Indoor Environments* (2002). These two documents describe visual assessment of mold. They outline several levels of severity of mold problems, with different approaches for remediation in each case. The levels are determined by noting the size of the affected area. From the NYC *Guidelines:*

- *Level I:* small isolated areas (10 ft² or less; e.g., ceiling tiles, small areas on walls)
- *Level II:* midsized isolated areas (10 to 30 ft²; e.g., individual wallboard panels)
- *Level III:* large isolated areas (30 to 100 ft²; e.g., several wallboard panels)
- *Level IV:* extensive contamination (greater than 100 contiguous square feet in an area)
- *Level V:* remediation of HVAC systems (small areas and large areas)

Techniques of remediation that apply to each level are found in the report, which is available online; a general discussion of remediation is given later in this chapter. Techniques for remediation are under constant study. Despite the subjective interpretation possible in estimating surface area that is affected by mold, the approach described here is most helpful and conducive to improvement in buildings. There is something inherently correct in an approach that begins with the experience and observation of a mold problem and goes directly to the steps to correct the problem.

Neither of the two recognized guidelines for mold remediation, the New York City Department of Health's *Guidelines on Assessment and Remediation of Fungi in Indoor Environments* and the USEPA's *Mold Remediation in Schools and Commercial Buildings,* calls for environmental sampling for routine mold problems. Both guidelines discourage environmental sampling in most cases. This opinion is summarized on the Center for Disease Control Web site:

Generally, it is not necessary to identify the species of mold growing in a residence, and CDC does not recommend routine sampling for molds. Current evidence indicates that allergies are the type of diseases most often associated with molds. Since the susceptibility of individuals can vary greatly either because of the amount or type of mold, sampling and culturing are not reliable in determining health risk. . . . Reliable sampling for mold can be expensive, and standards for judging what is and what is not an acceptable or tolerable quantity of mold have not been established. (CDC, 2000b)

Sampling Techniques

There are common techniques for taking mold samples in buildings. Samples may be taken in the air or on surfaces. The aim of sampling is to find an estimate of the concentration of viable mold spores or mold material per unit area of surface or per unit volume of air. One common form of air sampler passes a measured quantity of air through a petri dish, which is sent to a laboratory to culture. The cultured spores allow individual species to be determined, and the results are reported out as colony-forming units (CFUs) per cubic meter. Different species grow in different agars, so the selection of agar can influence the outcome regarding the species reported. A second common form of air sampling draws an airstream so that material is impinged on a sticky plate. Spores and other material are counted and reported on a volume basis. Surface wipes and bulk samples can report the amount of material per surface area or mass of the bulk sample. Recently, PCR methods (DNA sampling) have been used for very precise and accurate estimates of quantity as well as species of mold material in samples.

All measured data must be reported with an estimate of the total error, to a certain confidence interval. The American Society of Heating, Refrigerating, and Air-Conditioning Engineers (ASHRAE) publishes a *Guide for Engineering Analysis of Experimental Data*, which provides recommended procedures for applying basic statistical methods to experimental data. This guide says that all data must be reported not with one number but with three: mean of x, $\pm y$, to z% confidence. In a mold investigation, the critical value is the mean concentration in the space that we study; the laboratory number is simply a means to arrive at that mean value. The lab number is not an answer in itself. There are many possible sources of error and bias in mold sampling measurements, including those due to:

1. Equipment selection and operation
2. Intralaboratory differences

3. Interlaboratory differences
4. Time of day
5. Season
6. Disturbance of settled material
7. Sampling location
8. Other simple random errors

According to the National Academy of Science Institute of Medicine (IOM, 2004), no rigorous estimate has been made of the impact of these different errors on the significance of reported sampling output to date. The IOM report, for example, notes (citing Heederik et al., 2003) that even within a home, a variance ratio of 3 to 4 may not be uncommon for airborne sampling of viable microorganisms. This implies that 27 to 36 samples per home would be required to estimate the average exposure reliably without less than 10% bias in the relationship between some health endpoint and the exposure.

Simple scientific curiosity propels mold measurement. So does the interest in using mold growth prevention (and its hygrothermal physical correlates) as a limit state in building science. Interest in personal exposure limits, clearance criteria, and correlations with health outcomes require pursuit of mold measurements. However, those enterprises may take a lot of time and effort. Not all scientific concerns lend themselves to good measurement. We use nonscientific terms quite freely without imposing measurability requirements: beauty, freedom, virtue. If we were looking for a semiempirical quality that is difficult to measure, we might try the terms *clean/dirty*. Standards do exist for cleanliness, and nothing is perfectly clean. The dirt analogy for mold deserves consideration. What we "know" about mold is based largely on its biochemical behavior in the laboratory where concentrations of isolates can be manipulated to achieve effects. In the house environment, dose and exposure to mold products (spore, mycotoxins) may not simply be not quantified but may indeed be not quantifiable over time, across several seasons and years. It is only by careful attention to measurement techniques that a researcher may arrive at useful data. We can imagine the difficulty in applying sampling to diagnosis, to litigation, and heaven forbid, to legislation.

DRY DEPOSITION OF MOLD MATERIAL

Outdoor air typically contains more mold spores and other mold material than does indoor air. If indoor air contains more than outdoor air, it is strong evidence of active mold growth in the building. However, indoor air comes from outdoor air. So, in a typical building with a lower mold spore count indoors than outdoors, something must remove the mold material. In a commercial building, filters placed in the airstream of the fresh air intake can be specified so that the remove almost all of the airborne mold material. In a residence, the filters are placed in the return airstream for buildings with forced-air systems. Once outdoor air enters the building, contaminants and all, it may be cleaned as it is circulated from the return-air system to the supply system. But even houses with hydronic heating show this phenomenon of lowered concentration of mold material indoors than outdoors. It can be explained quite simply—the building envelope acts as a filter.

Take, for example, a wood frame building. Fresh air enters the building through the building envelope. It passes through cracks and cavities. The pathway is often tortuous because of the many layers of materials and offsets in the joints among those materials. The cavity, especially if it contains fiberglass (which is porous to airflow and which, of course, serves as a filter in forced-air systems) is a collector of most of the particulates that might enter a house, including mold material. So we would expect building cavities to be natural accumulators of mold material. Is this okay? I would argue that it is fine; indeed, it is desirable, because the alternative is a higher concentration in the indoor air.

But not all mold investigators view it that way. There is a debate over the health effect of molds (see below) and a side argument over the health effect of mold materials in cavities. If a high concentration of mold material in a building cavity is the result of active visible mold growth in that cavity (visible after opening), that is undesirable. But if a high concentration of mold material in a cavity is a result of dry deposition, we should be grateful for the cavity effect. One more mold spore in the cavity is one less mold spore in the lung of an occupant.

Dry deposition was the only way I could explain a finding at one very historic house by Frank Lloyd Wright. The original wood paneling was removed from one corner, and mold samples in the air showed a spike in concentration 200 times higher after exposure than before. As you might imagine, there were some water problems in this Frank Lloyd Wright building, but not at these cavities. The paneling material showed clearly that there had never been a water problem at any time in this cavity. I should mention that this argument proceeds by common sense and an understanding of physical processes in building envelopes. This argument regarding dry deposition has not yet appeared in the mold literature.

HEALTH EFFECTS OF MOLD

Mold has health effects on humans. Humans have a zealous concern for anything affecting health. Zeal can mask deliberative thought and can overtake caution. So the response to alarms of threats from mold contains some deliberative search for facts and some hype. Public health occupational health and epidemiology all work with statistics for the common good; individual health zealously pursues longevity and the survival of one organism at a time. Deliberation and zeal are both evident in how the "mold crisis" has played out.

Stachybotrys Chartarum

Science is not unlike law. We look for causes of unwelcome events, and the search may at times be zealous. We may suspect certain causes, but causal factors must remain innocent until proven guilty, even though particular suspects may be tarred in the press. In Cleveland in 1993–1994 there were eight cases of infants with idiopathic pulmonary hemosiderosis (bleeding lung disease), including several deaths (CDC, 1994). The disease is termed *idiopathic* to indicate that the cause of the disease is not established. The fact that it affected infants indicates that it is not allergic, as allergic diseases are immune responses and infants have no developed immune systems. The cases seemed to occur in a rather small geographic location, characterized by older homes, poverty, and an African-American population. Dearborn, a pulmonologist, and his fellow researchers noted that the homes of the case infants had suffered major water damage in the prior six months. Aggressive air sampling showed a high concentration of the mold, which was then termed *Stachybotrys atra*, now *S. chartarum*. They also noted that environmental tobacco smoke was a factor correlating with the cases.

Dearborn was well aware of the record that *S. chartarum* had. Russian researchers determined that an infestation of this organism in straw and grain had led to the deaths of thousands of horses in Ukraine and Eastern Europe in the 1930s. The disorder, termed *stachybotyrotoxicosis*, was shown to affect not only animals but also humans who handled or were in close contact with infested hay. Toxins from *S. chartarum* were isolated and shown to be potent in very small doses. In 1986, Croft et al. reported an outbreak of toxicosis in a Chicago home that he associated with tricothecenes, a toxin produced by *S. chartarum*, which Croft found in the home. The home had had a chronic moisture problem. When the water and mold problems were corrected, the symptoms associated with tricothecene toxicosis disappeared.

I visited one of the homes where one of the Cleveland infants had died. The home had been repaired, and I was invited to view a video of the condition in the home prior to remediation. The home was in a 90-year-old neighborhood that was originally built for immigrant workers and was blighted with poverty. Like most of the cities around the Great Lakes, Cleveland had built a combined sanitary and storm sewage disposal system. (Sanitary disposal systems in low-lying flat areas cannot use steep slopes in the lines, so they compensated by adding stormwater for its flushing effect.)

The house had a basement, and the basement floor contained a floor drain. The city of Cleveland has maintained a statute that mandates that all roof rainwater conductors must be deposited into below-grade stormwater conductors. The rationale for this is consistent with the design of a combined system requiring flushing water, but the low-fire clay pipes installed in the early part of the century had mostly failed, collapsed, or clogged. So rainwater tended to saturate the soil in contact with the foundation instead. Cleveland, too, has a curious heating system design for these homes called the *Cleveland drop*. This is a simple vertical piece of ductwork that extends from a grate in the floor separating the basement or crawl space from the first floor, and extending downward to a point about 6 in. above the basement or crawl space floor. The intent of the Cleveland drop is to serve rather like the drop tube in a hot water heater, and it is part of the use of the basement as a plenum return for the furnace, originally a gravity warm air furnace. In the 1960s and 1970s, basements were turned into "rec" (recreation) rooms, with paneled walls and trim.

The video revealed the following: The team doing the investigation-demolition was dressed in protective clothing covering and full respiration protection equipment. They removed the paneling and exposed gypsum wallboard that was covered with a dark blackish coating. They removed the gypsum wallboard and showed a cavity that was about 2 ft deep. There was a floor drain in the area behind the paneled wall and a horizontal line of coating indicating that the combined sanitary-storm floor drain had backed up, flooding the basement to a depth of more than a foot and leaving the surfaces coated with waste. The corners were black, indicating that there was chronic wetness in the locations of the downspouts. The Cleveland drop was found in the cavity, so that the contaminated conditions in that cavity had a direct air feed up to the first floor. It is not hard to imagine that occupants of the house would have health disorders, given the conditions in the cavity. These conditions might not have been apparent in a casual observation of the finished surfaces. I was left with the impression that the soup of contaminants present in this building did not argue strongly for the identification of any single one as the culprit.

When Dearborn and his colleagues published their findings in several articles, there were responses in the news media and in professional circles. The news media hyped the "toxic mold," "black mold," and "killer mold." Building occupants with health complaints began to wonder if their building has "got Stachy." A "mold is gold" movement began at the initiative of some underemployed trial lawyers familiar with asbestos litigation. Meanwhile, professionals began to consider mold and its health effects with a new seriousness. Some considered mycotixicosis as a hypothesis that merited very serious consideration. Others, such as Harriet Burge of the Harvard School of Public Health, were skeptical, questioning how spores that big could reach alveoli that small. A similar CDC study (unpublished, cited in CDC 1997) of seven pulmonary hemorrhage cases in Chicago between 1992 and 1995 was unable to detect *Stachybotrys* in any of the case homes, while identifying that mold in 35% of control homes. This Chicago study found a different fungus, *Trichoderma*, in significantly more case homes than control homes. The Chicago study formed no conclusions on either mold regarding causality.

The Centers for Disease Control, which had been involved in Dearborn's original work, undertook a review of the possible association between pulmonary hemosiderosis and *S. chartarum* in the indoor environment. Their results were published in CDC (2000a). This report noted that an epidemiologic association was hampered by a lack of several items, including a lack of consistent criteria for defining water damage and the absence of a standardized protocol for inspecting and gathering data on the presence of fungi from individual homes. The CDC working group in 1999 did not reject the possible relationship between *S. chartarum* and the condition here called *acute idiopathic pulmonary hemosiderosis* (AIPH; to distinguish it from classic pulmonary hemosiderosis). But the 2000 CDC report was more critical, saying that the conclusions of association "are not substantiated adequately by the scientific evidence. . . . The associations should be considered not proven; the etiology [causality] of AIPH is unresolved" (CDC, 2000b).

Researchers continue to pursue links between *S. chartarum* and health. *Stachybotrys* spore material has been found in the nasal washing of a child with AIPH. Professional organizations have sought to summarize the findings to date. There is a consensus, for the present at least, that "current scientific evidence does not support the proposition that human health has been adversely affected by inhaled mycotoxins in home, school or office environments" (ACOEM, 2002).

Of course, toxins are most clearly harmful when ingested. The purple amanita mushroom is a case in point. The mold *Aspergillus flavus* can produce aflatoxin, which has caused several deaths in those who ate aflatoxin-affected fruit.

Allergy, Asthma, and Infection Associated with Mold and Dampness

Damp and moldy buildings lead to complaints of respiratory symptoms and other health effects. Research in this area is most difficult, so the results are often weak and inconclusive. In many cases it has been difficult to distinguish those effects that are caused by mold and those that are not. One problem is that high levels of humidity in the air may lead to growth of molds on surfaces (amplification) but will also lead to increased stickiness of the surfaces and reduction in dust levels. Indoor environments are very complex. Contaminants differ room to room, from morning to evening, and from summer to winter. Dragging feet on carpets and plopping on upholstery can drastically change the contaminant mix in a room. Not only that, but occupants are widely different, with varying sensitivities to respiratory effects. Crafty litigators are on the lookout for the "eggshell defendant," the one most likely to have ill effects from small contaminations or concentrations. In one study we began, we had hoped to study indoor environments over 18 months, in order to measure indoor conditions in the same season, both pre- and postremediation. Unfortunately, we discovered that the average length of time that residents remained at the same address was eight months. We have already discussed the difficulty in making measurements of indoor humidity (Chapter 8) and mold (this chapter). The list of real-life difficulties does not stop here; this gives only a sampler of the difficulties inherent in doing environmental health studies.

Still, there is a growing sense that dampness causes health problems, and part of those problems may be associated with mold. A study by Brunekreef et al. (1989) of 4625 children found significant relationships between rates of hay fever and "mold" or "dampness" in homes; the conditions of mold or dampness were based on self-reports by the occupants. Most dampness studies have used self-reporting. Studies using investigators have occurred occasionally (Koskinen et al., 1999); studies using objective measures for humidity are getting under way.

The National Academy of Science Institute of Medicine classified the strength of association between damp and/or moldy environments and health effects. Their findings are shown in Table 9-1. This table indicates that there are no health effects for which dampness and mold are considered causal factors. There is evidence of association for several health effects, notably triggering asthma and allergy, and respiratory infection in immunocompromised persons. These findings provide good perspective for building professionals who seek an understanding of the possible health impacts of moisture and mold-related events. However, people whose family members have compromised health may read these findings differently, and their concerns cannot be ignored.

Nocebo Effect

The medical research community makes convincing progress in the development of medical treatments because of their use of double-blind controlled experiments. In these experiments the population (e.g., the entire market for a pharmaceutical) is divided into three groups: those who have no involvement in the study (population), those who are given the test treatment (case), and those who are given a placebo (control). The sample size is determined using statistics that need to show, to a predetermined

Table 9-1   Summary of findings regarding the association between health outcomes and exposure to damp indoor environments and the presence of mold or other agents

Findings	Dampness	Mold
Sufficient Evidence of a Causal Relationship	(no outcomes met this definition)	(no outcomes met this definition)
Sufficient Evidence of an Association	Upper respiratory (nasal and throat) tract symptoms	Upper respiratory (nasal and throat) tract symptoms
	Cough	Cough
	Wheeze	Wheeze
	Asthma symptoms in sensitized asthmatic persons	Asthma symptoms in sensitized asthmatic persons
		Hypersensitivity pneumonitis in susceptible persons
Limited or Suggestive Evidence of an Association	Dyspnea (shortness of breath)	Lower respiratory illness in otherwise-healthy children
	Lower respiratory illness in otherwise-healthy children	
	Asthma development	
Inadequate or Insufficient Evidence to Determine Whether an Association Exists	Airflow obstruction (in otherwise-healthy persons)	Dyspnea (shortness of breath)
	Mucous membrane irritation syndrome	Airflow obstruction (in otherwise-healthy persons
	Chronic obstructive pulmonary disease	Mucous membrane irritation syndrome
	Inhalation fevers (nonoccupational exposures)	Chronic obstructive pulmonary disease
	Lower respiratory illness in otherwise-healthy adults	Inhalation fevers (nonoccupational exposures)
	Acute idiopathic pulmonary hemorrhage in infants	Lower respiratory illness in otherwise-healthy adults
	Skin symptoms	Acute idiopathic pulmonary hemorrhage in infants
	Gastrointestinal tract problems	Skin symptoms
	Fatigue	Gastrointestinal tract problems
	Neuropsychiatric symptoms	Fatigue
	Cancer	Neuropsychiatric symptoms
	Reproductive effects	Cancer
	Rheumatologic and other immune diseases	Reproductive effects
		Rheumatologic and other immune diseases

confidence level, that the characteristics of the sample represent the characteristics of the population. The case and control groups are treated identically in every way, so that participants in the study will not know which of the two groups they are in. If the case group shows improvement over the control group, to a statistical assessment of odds, the treatment can be considered a success. The case group is not compared to the population as a whole but to the control group, to account for what is called the placebo effect, that is, the salutary effect of being given a treatment, even an ineffective one.

We may think of contaminants in the indoor environment as a "sick pill," a treatment that leads to worsened health rather than improved health. Suppose we want to know, with the same level of scientific confidence as that we established for pharmaceuticals and other medical treatments, how bad an environment is for us. In theory, we would once again need to divide the population into three groups: those not involved in the study (the population as a whole), those in a control group, and those in the "treatment" group. The participants in the last two groups would not know whether or not they are subject to the contaminant. Tests of contaminant concentration would be taken for both groups as well as tests for health outcomes. If such tests lead to suspicions that something is wrong, that effect would be accounted for in the control group as well. In an experiment with proper controls, the health of subjects who were surrounded by contaminants would be compared not to the public at large, but to other people who were having their buildings and their health tested.

Placebo is Latin for "I shall please." The name given to the second effect is *nocebo,* Latin for "I shall annoy or bother." The scenario painted above is theory. In practice, we simply cannot confirm or deny the nocebo effect, because it involves intentional harm to subjects. Some versions of nocebo testing have taken place. Subjects were given aspirin, and half were told it could have gastric side effects and half were not given this information. Those who were told of the side effects had the effects in greater proportion to those who were not told.

The purpose here is not to confirm or deny such effects. I really don't know how strong the power of suggestion is, for good or ill. If you wish to share my appreciation of epidemiology, public health research, and occupational health research related to moisture, see IOM (2000) and IOM (2004).

MOLD REMEDIATION

The New York City Department of Health's *Guidelines* (2002) describe mold remediation in general as follows:

> The size of the area impacted by fungal contamination primarily determines the type of remediation. The sizing levels below are based on professional judgement and practicality; currently there is not adequate data to relate the extent of contamination to frequency or

severity of health effects. The goal of remediation is to remove or clean contaminated materials in a way that prevents the emission of fungi and dust contaminated with fungi from leaving a work area and entering an occupied or non-abatement area, while protecting the health of workers performing the abatement. The listed remediation methods were designed to achieve this goal, however, due to the general nature of these methods it is the responsibility of the people conducting remediation to ensure the methods enacted are adequate. The listed remediation methods are not meant to exclude other similarly effective methods. Any changes to the remediation methods listed in these guidelines, however, should be carefully considered prior to implementation.

Non-porous (e.g., metals, glass, and hard plastics) and semiporous (e.g., wood, and concrete) materials that are structurally sound and are visibly moldy can be cleaned and reused. Cleaning should be done using a detergent solution. Porous materials such as ceiling tiles and insulation, and wallboards with more than a small area of contamination should be removed and discarded. Porous materials (e.g., wallboard, and fabrics) that can be cleaned, can be reused, but should be discarded if possible. A professional restoration consultant should be contacted when restoring porous materials with more than a small area of fungal contamination. All materials to be reused should be dry and visibly free from mold. Routine inspections should be conducted to confirm the effectiveness of remediation work.

The field of mold remediation is under development: Standards are being written and refined, and practitioners are trying to find the right balance point between doing too much and doing too little. The NYC *Guidelines* chart a good commonsense course.

SUMMARY AND FINAL COMMENTS

Buildings should be dry and healthful. They should smell good and feel dry. They should not support the growth of microorganisms that can emit offensive odors and cause allergic reactions in sensitized persons. The indoor humidity should be sufficiently low that skin can dry to the indoor air in a reasonable time and clothes do not stick to the skin.

Buildings should last a long time. They should be able to resist acute catastrophic damage from fire, earthquake, or windstorm, and they should be able to resist chronic damage as well, most of which is mediated by the presence of excess water.

Corrosion and mold growth are surface phenomena. Surface phenomena are governed by heat and moisture conditions in the air and in the substrate. There is a constant exchange of heat and moisture across surfaces as the air and the substrate tend toward equilibrium in changing environments. If we need to choose a physical threshold that distinguishes acceptable from unacceptable building envelope assemblies, it is this: Avoid average surface relative humidity in excess of 80% (or water activity in excess of 0.8) on a monthly basis. This threshold value comes from the IEA, Annex 14 (1991).

The greatest source of water in building envelopes is leakage of rainwater. This occurs through the roof, especially at areas of water concentration and at penetrations. Rainwater leakage occurs in walls due to wind-driven rain. Windows, balconies, corners, and other details that require flashing are the major source. All cladding materials permit some water leakage and some permit water sorption. Water that enters through the cladding and flashing should escape back to the outdoors through designed drainage or other openings that permit ventilation or diffusion drying. Some drying may need to occur toward the interior as well.

On the building site, rainwater should be managed so that the soil in contact with the building foundation is not allowed to become saturated with water. If that is achieved, water leakage into foundations is prevented and the only exchange that occurs at the basement is by capillarity and vapor transport, both of which are slow and rarely problematic. Rainwater may be harvested at the site or allowed to percolate to replenish the aquifer. Rainwater that goes to storm drainage into waterways is of little benefit.

Foundations should be clean and dry. They should not be flooded and the surfaces and any cavities should be inspectable and cleanable.

Wall assemblies should be designed using good engineering. That is, they should be considered allowable only if, for the climate, they are able to resist water and humidity loads from both outside and inside and maintain surface relative humidity in the safe range throughout the year. The old tool for making this assessment—the profile method—remains useful especially for compact "sandwich" building envelope assemblies. Assemblies with cavities are more complex, and assemblies with airflow are even more so. Transient analysis (time dependent, using computer programs) is capable of analyzing building envelopes with cavities and with materials that store moisture. They cannot yet perform good analysis of envelopes that permit airflow through or within the envelope.

Hygrothermal building science of the last 50 years has required its professionals to master the following concepts:

Psychrometrics, the characterization of temperature and moisture concentration in air samples. Understanding psychrometrics requires an understanding of vapor pressure, relative humidity, absolute humidity, humidity ratio, wet-bulb temperature, and dew point temperature.

Diffusion of Water Vapor through Building Materials. The kinetic nature of gases permits active vapor molecules to penetrate materials that are porous and hygroscopic. The permeability of materials used in construction can be measured, although this property is very dependent on the moisture content of materials

Profile Method. Thermal conductivity and vapor permeability values of building materials are selected from tables. Design values of indoor and outdoor conditions are selected to represent extreme conditions. From these inputs, two profile curves—saturation vapor pressure from temperature and estimated vapor pressure—are derived. They are corrected to bring actual vapor pressure in line with saturation wherever it is found to exceed saturation, although this important step is often neglected by users of the method. Rates of water accumulation for at-risk surfaces are estimated, and that is used, subjectively, to determine the acceptability or not of building assemblies. If the lines cross in a profile analysis, that condition is often called "condensation"—an imprecise use of the term.

Rainwater Management at the Outside of the Building. Joints in all materials—roof covering, flashing, cladding, weather-resistant barriers, flanges on windows, and accessories—all need to be installed with correct shingle-style lapping to shed water to the outside. The design for indoor humidity presumes 100% success with the exterior rainwater management, so vapor control in walls is centered around preventing wetting rather than permitting drying.

Moisture Control Regulations. There is a reflexive reliance on prescriptive requirements for crawl space venting, attic venting, and indoor vapor barriers. The basis for these requirements is obscure, so alternative proposals do not have a fair basis for consideration.

A new generation of building scientists should be familiar with all of the work of the preceding generation. But in addition, they should master the following concepts:

Airflow through Building Envelopes. Building envelopes are never perfectly airtight. Occupants need fresh air, and in many buildings air infiltration through building envelopes provides ventilation air. If the indoor space is conditioned, there is an energy penalty with infiltration. In simple buildings, the energy penalty of air movement may be offset by the potential for drying incidental moisture that enters the envelope. During seasons with air conditioning in operation, there is no benefit to air exchange because it adds to the latent load. Buildings with air-handling units require tight building envelopes for pressure control.

Sorption. Most building materials are porous and hygroscopic. They have an equilibrium moisture content that correlates most closely with relative humidity in the surrounding air. They exchange heat and water vapor with the air that surrounds them. The water vapor binds to the surfaces of the pores with varying strength. Those molecules in closest proximity to the molecules of the material are held tightly and are called *adsorbed;* those held less tightly in the matrix of the material rather than directly on the surface are called *absorbed.*

Contact Angle. Surfaces may be *hydrophobic* (water-repellent) or *hydrophilic* (attracting water). The contact angle measures the attraction of water for a surface. The contact angle for any material or surface indicates the strength of capillarity that permits absorbed water to distribute in the matrix of a material. Water always moves from larger to smaller pores, never from smaller to larger pores.

Suction. Porous and hygroscopic materials often contain more water than the quantity they exchange with the surrounding air. The attachment of water to a material may be measured by suction, that is, by the amount of pressure necessary to remove it from the material. The water in porous materials may be drainable (low suction pressure), capillary (medium suction pressure), or sorbed (high suction pressure).

Transient Modeling. Since moisture can be stored in materials, its transport cannot be characterized by steady-state modeling, only by transient or time-dependent modeling. A first generation of transient hygrothermal models such as MOIST from NIST is successful within a limited range of applications.

Moisture Engineering. Hygrothermal building performance can be analyzed, and the resulting estimates can be used to investigate assemblies outside the confines of the prescriptive regulations of the past. The moisture loads to a building envelope come from both inside and out, and both can be included in a transient model. Transient analytic tools are capable of accounting for diffusion, latent effects due to phase change, capillary transport, and material properties that are dependent on moisture content and temperature. One of the outputs of transient models can be surface relative humidity; this allows us to determine the potential for mold growth and corrosion, two effects that often serve as thresholds that distinguish acceptable from unacceptable building envelope assemblies.

Mold. Despite media reports, health risks from mold in buildings are largely restricted to those people allergic to mold. Nevertheless, building envelopes should be designed and constructed to avoid mold growth. Mold may grow on any wetted surface that contains food and lacks inhibiting chemicals. The moisture conditions for inoculation may be more severe than the conditions for continued growth. With our present understanding, keeping building component surfaces at a surface relative humidity level lower than 80% for the term of a month or so appears to keep surfaces satisfactorily dry and free of mold growth.

For many designers, water has been considered a nuisance. However, water is becoming a scarce resource, and the nuisance outlook must give way to an outlook of appreciation and conservation. We may begin by rejecting the moisture villain image of a generation ago, and making a serious study of the mechanics (and poetics) of water.

ASHRAE Coefficients to Calculate Saturation Water Vapor Pressure from Temperature

The following is a program written in Basic language that may be used to calculate vapor pressure in pounds per square inch (psi) from temperature in degrees Fahrenheit.

```
Function SaturationVaporPressure (Temperature, RH)
    'units for RH must be 0 < rh < 1, not 0 < rh < 100
    'convert Fahrenheit temperature to absolute (Rankine) temperature
T = Temperature + 459.67
    'constants over ice from ASHRAE Handbook of Fundamentals, Chapter 6
c1 = -10214.16462
c2 = -4.89350301
c3 = -0.00537657944
c4 = 0.000000192023769
c5 = 3.55758316E-10
c6 = -9.03446883E-14
c7 = 4.1635019

    'constants over water
c8 = -10440.39708
c9 = -11.2946496
c10 = -0.027022355
c11 = 0.00001289036
c12 = -0.000000002478068
c13 = 6.5459673
```

```
'lnSVP is the natural log of the saturation vapor pressure
If Temperature < 32 Then
    lnSVP = c1 / T + c2 + c3 * T + c4 * T ^ 2 + c5 * T ^ 3 + c6 * T ^ 4 + c7 * Log(T)
Else
    lnSVP = c8 / T + c9 + c10 * T + c11 * T ^ 2 + c12 * T ^ 3 + c13 * Log(T)
End If


svp = Exp(lnSVP)
VaporPressure = svp * RH
    'Output is in psi
End Function
```

For output in other units, see the unit conversion section in Appendix B. For use with standard permeance measurements in inches of mercury (in.Hg), the results in psi must be multiplied by 2.036 to find units of in.Hg.

Unit Conversions

Dimension, Area, Volume

1	in.	=	2.54	cm
1	ft	=	0.3048	m
		=	30.48	cm
1	mile	=	1.609	km
1	ft^2	=	0.0929	m^2
10	ft^2	$\cong$	1	m^2 (the symbol "$\cong$" means "equals about")
1	ft^3	=	28.32	L
1	m^3	=	1000	L
1	quart	=	0.94	L

Mass, Force, Density

1	lb_m (mass)	=	453.6	g
1	kg	=	2.2	lb_m
1	N	=	1	kg·m/s^2
1	lb_f (force)	=	4.45	N
1	lb	=	7000	grains
1	lb/ft^3 (density)	=	16	kg/m^3

1 L of water has mass of 1 kg

Pressure

1	Pa	=	1	N/m^2
1	atm	=	29.921	in.Hg
		=	407	in. of water
		$\cong$	33	ft of water
		=	760	mmHg
		=	14.7	psi
		=	101,325	Pa
		=	101.325	kPa
		=	1.01325	bar

1	psi	=	6.9	kPa
1	in. water	=	248.84	Pa
		$\cong$	250	Pa

Temperature

°F	=	°C · 1.8 + 32
°C	=	(°F − 32)/1.8
°R (absolute)	=	°F + 459.67
K (absolute)	=	°C + 273.15

Work, Heat, Energy

1	J	=	1	N · m
1	Btu	=	1.055	kJ
1	kWh	=	3.60	MJ
1	therm	=	12,000	Btu

Power

1	Btu/h (Btuh)	=	0.2931	W
1	T, refrigeration	=	12,000	Btuh

Rate of Heat Transfer

1	Btu/hr-ft^2	=	3.155	W/m^2

Thermal Conductivity, k

1	Btu-in./hr-ft^2-°F	=	0.1442	W/(m ·K)
1	Btu/hr-ft-°F	=	1.731	W/(m ·K)

Overall Heat Transfer Coefficient, U

1	Btu/hr-ft^2-°F	=	5.678	W/m^2 ·K

Thermal Resistance, R

1	ft^2-hr-°F/Btu	=	0.176	m^2 ·K/W

Permeability

1	perm	=	1	grain/hr-ft^2-in.Hg
1	perm	=	57.45	ng/h ·m^2 · Pa

References

The reference list contains some material that is hard to find but is important in recounting the history and background of some moisture control provisions. The hard-to-find references are noted with an asterisk*.

*Abramovitz, M., et al., 1949. *Proceedings of the University of Illinois Conference on Architectural Education,* Department (now School) of Architecture, University of Illinois at Urbana–Champaign, February 21, 22, 23.

ACOEM, 2002. *Adverse Human Health Effects Associated with Molds in the Indoor Environment.* American Council of Occupational and Environmental Medicine Evidence-Based Statement. Available at *http://www.acoem.org/guidelines/article.asp?ID=52.*

Allen, E., 1980. *How Buildings Work.* Oxford University Press, New York.

Angell, W. J., and W. W. Olson., 1988. Moisture sources associated with potential damage in cold-climate housing. Originally published by Cold Climate Housing Information Center, University of Minnesota, St. Paul, MN. CD-F0-3405-1988. Reprinted in J. Merrill and K. Parrot, eds., 1988. *Condensation and Related Moisture Problems in the Home.* Building Research Council, University of Illinois at Urbana–Champaign, Champaign, IL.

Anon. (L. V. Teesdale.), 1938. Condensation. *Architectural Forum.* April.

ASHRAE, 1994. *Recommended Practices for Controlling Moisture in Crawl Spaces.* ASHRAE Technical Data Bulletin, Vol. 10, No. 3. American Society of Heating, Refrigerating, and Air-Conditioning Engineers, Atlanta GA. Includes I. Samuelson, Moisture control in crawl spaces.

ASHRAE, 1999. *Handbook–Applications.* American Society of Heating, Refrigerating, and Air-Conditioning Engineers, Atlanta, GA.

ASHRAE (2001). The ASHRAE *Handbook,* updated annually, includes four volumes: *Fundamentals, Applications, Refrigeration,* and *HVAC Systems and Equipment.* Material in this volume makes extensive use of ASHRAE *Handbook, Fundamentals* 2001, American Society of Heating, Refrigerating, and Air-Conditioning Engineers, Atlanta, GA.

ASHVE, 1937. *Proceedings of the 43rd Annual Meeting* (p. 23, Initial appointment of Insulation Committee). American Society of Heating and Ventilating Engineers (now ASHRAE), Atlanta, GA.

Beall, C., 1999. *Thermal and Moisture Protection Manual: For Architects, Engineers, and Contractors.* McGraw-Hill, New York.

Bell, A. P., and G. F. Roper, 1876. Residence of L. Ward. *The Building News*, xxxii.

*BOCA, 1948. *Abridged Building Code.* Building Officials Conference of America, Washington, DC. Adopted September 16.

Bohren, C., and J. Walker, 1987. *Clouds in a Glass of Beer.* Wiley, Hoboken, NJ.

*BRAB, 1952. *Proceedings: Condensation Control in Buildings as Related to Paints, Papers, and Insulating Materials.* Building Research Advisory Board, National Research Council/National Academy of Sciences, Washington DC. Contains T. S. Rogers, Opening of the conference.

BRAB, 1963. *Final Report: Design Criteria for Residential Slabs-on-Ground.* Building Research Advisory Board Report 17R. Publication 1077, National Academy of Sciences–National Research Council, Washington, DC.

Brewster, D., 1931. Air conditioning as applied to furniture, fixtures and other interior woodwork, *ASHVE Journal.* January, pp. 65–69.

*Britton, R. R., 1948. *Condensation in Walls and Roofs.* Technical Papers 1, 2, 3, 8, and 12. Housing and Home Finance Agency, Washington, DC.

*Britton, R. R., 1949a. *Crawl Spaces: Their Effect on Dwellings—An Analysis of Causes and Results—Suggested Good Practice Requirements.* Technical Bulletin 2. Housing and Home Finance Agency, Washington, DC, January.

*Britton, R. R., 1949b. *Condensation Control in Dwelling Construction: Good Practice Recommendations.* Technical Bulletin 10. Housing and Home Finance Agency, Washington, DC, May–June.

Brown, J. P., and W. Rose, 1996. Humidity and moisture in historic buildings: the origin of building and object conservation. *APT Bulletin*, 27(3). *http://palimpsest.stanford.edu/byauth/brownjp/humidity1997.html#fn16*

Browne, F. L., 1933. *Some Causes of Blistering and Peeling of Paint on House Siding.* Report R6 U.S. Forest Products Laboratory, Madison, WI.

Brunekreef, B., Q. W. Dockery, F. E. Speizer, J. H. Ware, J. D. Spengler, and B. G. Ferris, 1989. Home dampness and respiratory morbidity in children. *American Review of Respiratory Diseases*, 140:1363–1367.

Buchan, Lawton, Parent Ltd., 1991. *Survey of Moisture Levels in Attics.* Report submitted to the Research Division, Canada Mortgage and Housing Corporation, Ottawa, Ontario, Canada.

CDC, 1994. Acute pulmonary hemorrhage/hemosiderosis among infants: Cleveland, January 1993–November 1994. *Morbidity and Mortality Weekly Report (MMWR)*, 43:881–883.

CDC, 1997. Update: pulmonary hemorrhage/hemosiderosis among infants: Cleveland, Ohio, 1993–1996. *MMWR*, 46:33–35.

CDC, 2000a. Update: pulmonary hemorrhage/hemosiderosis among infants: Cleveland, Ohio, 1993–1996. *MMWR*, 49(9):180–184.

CDC, 2000b. Questions and answers on *Stachybotrys chartarum* and other molds. *http://www.cdc.gov/nceh/asthma/factsheets/molds/default.htm*, March 9.

Christian, J. E., 1993. A search for moisture sources. In *Bugs, Mold and Rot II*, W. Rose and A. TenWolde, eds. National Institute of Building Sciences, Washington, DC.

CMHC, 1996. *Best Practice Guide: Brick Veneer Steel Stud.* Canada Mortgage and Housing Corporation, Ottawa, Ontario, Canada.

CMHC, 1997. *Best Practice Guide: Brick Veneer Concrete Masonry Unit Backing.* Canada Mortgage and Housing Corporation, Ottawa, Ontario, Canada.

CMHC, 1999a. *Attic Venting, Attic Moisture and Ice Dams.* About Your House Series: CE 19. Canada Mortgage and Housing Corporation, Ottawa, Ontario, Canada. Available at: http://www.cmhc-schl.gc.ca/en/burema/gesein/abhose/abhose_ce13.cfm.

CMHC, 1999b. *Best Practice Guide: Wood Frame Envelopes.* Canada Mortgage and Housing Corporation, Ottawa, Ontario, Canada.

CMHC, 2001. *Best Practice Guide: Flashing.* Canada Mortgage and Housing Corporation, Ottawa, Ontario, Canada.

Conrad, E., 1995. A table for classification of climatic control potential in buildings. Landmark Facilities Group, CT.

Courtauld Institute of Art, 1934 (or 1935). *Some Notes on Atmospheric Humidity in Relation to Works of Art.* London.

Croft, W. A., B. C. Jarvis, and C. S. Yatawara, 1986. Airborne outbreak of tricothecene toxicosis. *Atmospheric Environment,* 20(3):549–552.

Denny, M. W., 1993. *Air and Water: The Biology and Physics of Life's Media.* Princeton University Press, Princeton, NJ.

DeWerth, D. W., R. A. Borgeson, and M. A. Aranov, 1996. *Development of Sizing Guidelines for Vent-Free Supplemental Heating Products.* GRI 96-0093. American Gas Association Research Division, Arlington, VA.

Dutt, G. S., and D. T. Harrje, 1979. Forced ventilation for cooling attics in summer. In *Summer Attic and Whole-House Ventilation,* M. H. Reppert, ed. National Bureau of Standards, Washington, DC, July.

EPA, 2001. *Mold Remediation in Schools and Commercial Buildings.* EPA 402-K-01-001. U.S. Environmental Protection Agency, Office of Air and Radiation, Indoor Environments Division (6609-J).

Erhardt, D., and M. Mecklenburg, 1994. Relative Humidity Re-examined, in A. Roy and P. Smith, eds., *Preventive Conservation: Practice, Theory and Research. Preprints of the Contributions to the Ottawa Congress,* International Institute for the Conservation of Artistic and Historic Works (IIC), London, 28–31.

*FHA, 1942. *Property Standards and Minimum Construction Requirements for Dwellings.* Federal Housing Administration, Washington, DC.

Forest, T. W., and M. Y. Ackerman, 1999. *Basement Walls that Dry.* Canada Mortgage and Housing Corporation, Ottawa, Ontario, Canada.

Forest T. W., and I. S. Walker, 1993. *Attic Ventilation and Moisture.* Canada Mortgage and Housing Corporation, Ottawa, Ontario, Canada.

FPL, 2000. *Wood Handbook: Wood as an Engineering Material.* Agriculture Handbook 72. Forest Products Laboratory, U.S. Department of Agriculture, Forest Service. U.S. Government Printing Office, Washington, DC. Available at: http://www.fpl.fs.fed.us/documnts/FPLGTR/fplgtr113/fplgtr113.htm.

Frank, H. S., and Wen, W. Y., 1957. Ion–solvent interaction. III. Structural aspects of ion–solvent interaction in aqueous solutions: a suggested picture of water structure. *Disc. Faraday Society,* Vol. 24, 133.

*French, H. F., 1865. *Farm Drainage: The Principles, Processes, and Effects of Draining Land with Stones, Wood, Plows, and Open Ditches, and Especially with Tiles: Including Tables of Rain-Fall.* Orange Judd., New York.

Frye, N., 1973. *Anatomy of Criticism.* Princeton University Press, Princeton, NJ.

Gould, R. F., ed., 1964. *Contact Angle: Wettability and Adhesion.* American Chemical Society, Washington, DC.

Gratwick, R. T., 1974. *Dampness in Buildings.* Halsted Press, New York.

Gutman, R., 1988. *Architectural Practice: A Critical View.* Princeton Architectural Press, Princeton, NJ.

Gwosdow, A. R., J. C. Stevens, L. G. Berglund, and J. A. J. Stolwijk, 1986. Skin friction and fabric sensations in neutral and warm environments. *Textile Research Journal,* 56:574–580.

Hanks, R. L., 1992. *Applied Soil Physics: Soil Water and Temperature Applications.* Springer-Verlag, New York.

Harriman, L., G. Bundrette, and R. Kittler, 2001. *Humidity Control Design Guide for Commercial and Industrial Buildings.* American Society of Heating, Refrigerating, and Air-Conditioning Engineers. Atlanta, GA.

Heederik, D., J. Douwes, and P. S. Thorne, 2003. Biological agents—evaluation. In *Modern Industrial Hygiene,* J. Perkin, ed., ACGIH, Cincinnati, OH.

*HHFA, 1949. *Condensation Control in Dwelling Construction.* Housing and Home Finance Agency, Washington, DC.

*HHFA, 1954. *Moisture Migration from the Ground.* Housing and Home Finance Agency, Washington, DC.

Hillel, D., 1982. *Introduction to Soil Physics.* Academic Press, San Diego, CA.

Hinrichs, H.S., 1962. *Comparative Study of the Effectiveness of Fixed Ventilating Louvers.* ASHRAE Transactions 1791. American Society of Heating, Refrigerating, and Air-Conditioning Engineers, Atlanta, GA.

*Hite, S. C., and J. L. Bray, 1948. *Research in Home Humidity Control.* Engineering Experiment Station Research Series 106. Purdue University, West Lafayette, IN.

Hutcheon, N. B., and G. O. P. Handegord, 1989. *Building Science for a Cold Climate,* Construction Technology Centre Atlantic, Inc., Fredericton, New Brunswick, Canada.

IEA, Annex 14, 1991. *Condensation and Energy,* Vol. 2, *Guidelines and Practice.* International Energy Agency, Laboratrium Bouwfysica, Leuven, Belgium.

IEA, Annex 24, 1996. *Heat, Air and Moisture Transfer in Insulated Envelope Parts.* International Energy Agency, Laboratrium Bouwfysica, Leuven, Belgium. Contains four reports: Vol. 1, *Modeling* (various authors); Vol. 2, *Environmental Conditions* (C. Sanders); Vol. 3, *Material Properties* (M. K. Kumaran); *Symbols and Terminology* (M. K. Kumaran).

IOM, 2000. *Clearing the Air: Asthma and Indoor Air Exposures.* Institute of Medicine, National Academy Press, Washington, DC. Available at: http://www.nap.edu/books/0309064961/html/.

IOM, 2004. *Damp Indoor Spaces and Health.* Institute of Medicine, National Academies Press, Washington, DC. Available at: http://www.nap.edu/books/0309091934/html/.

Jaffe, B., 1976. *Crucibles: The Story of Chemistry.* Dover, New York.

Jordan, C. A., E. C. Peck, F. A. Strange, and L. V. Teesdale, 1948. *Attic Condensation in Tightly Built Houses.* Technical Bulletin 6. Housing and Home Finance Agency, Washington, DC, September, pp. 29–46.

Kavanau, J. L., 1964. *Water and Solute–Water Interactions.* Holden-Day, San Francisco.

Konzo, S., ed., 1939. *Winter Air Conditioning: Forced Warm-Air Heating.* National Warm Air Heating and Air Conditioning Association, Columbus, OH.

Konzo, S., 1992. *The Quiet Indoor Revolution.* Building Research Council, University of Illinois, Champaign, IL.

Koskinen, O. M., T. M. Husman, T. M. Meklin, and A. I. Nevalainen, 1999. The relationship between moisture or mould observations in houses and the state of health of their occupants. *European Respiratory Journal*, 14(6):1363–1367.

Kumaran, M. K., et al., 2002. *A Thermal and Moisture Transport Database for Common Building and Insulating Materials: Final Report from ASHRAE Research Project 1018-RP*. American Society of Heating, Refrigerating, and Air-Conditioning Engineers, Atlanta, GA.

Künzel, H., 1995. *Simultaneous Heat and Moisture Transport in Building Components: One- and Two-Dimensional Calculation Using Simple Parameters*. IRB Verlag, Stuttgart, Germany.

Labs, K., J. Carmody, R. Sterling, L. Shen, Y. J. Huang, and D. Parker, 1988. *Building Foundation Design Handbook*. University of Minnesota Underground Space Center, Minneapolis, MN.

Latta, J. K., 1973. *Walls, Windows and Roofs for the Canadian Climate*. National Research Council Canada, Ottawa, Ontario, Canada.

Leeds, L. W., 1868. *Lectures on Ventilation*. Originally published by Wiley, New York. Published in 1976 by the American Life Foundation, Watkins Glen, NY.

Li, D.-W., and B. Kendrick, 1995. A year-round comparison of fungal spores in indoor and outdoor air. *Mycologia*, 87(2):190–195.

Lstiburek, J., 1999. *Builder's Guides*. Building Science Corporation, Westford, MA.

Lstiburek, J., and J. Carmody, 1994 (and later). *Moisture Control Handbook*. Van Nostrand Reinhold, New York.

Massari, G., and I. Massari, 1985. *Damp Buildings, Old and New*. ICCROM, Rome.

McCabe, J., 1931. Humidification and ventilation in art museums. *Museum News*, September 1 pp. 7–8.

McGee, H., 1984. *On Food and Cooking: The Science and Lore of the Kitchen*. Scribner, New York, NY.

Michalski, S., 1993. Relative humidity: a discussion of correct/incorrect values. *Preprints, ICOM Committee for Conservation 10th Triennial Meeting, Washington, DC*, Vol. II. ICOM Committee for Conservation, Paris, pp. 624–629. Reprinted in *Bugs, Mold and Rot II*, National Institute of Building Sciences, Washington DC.

Nakaya, U., 1954. *Snow Crystals, Natural and Artificial*. Harvard University Press, Cambridge, MA.

*NAS, 1960. *Documentation of Building Science Literature*. Publication 791. National Academy of Sciences–National Research Council, Washington, DC.

NBS, 1979. *Summer Attic and Whole-House Ventilation*. NBS Special Publication 548. National Bureau of Standards, now National Institute for Standards and Technology, Washington, DC.

Nelkin, D., 1971. *The Politics of Housing Innovation*. Cornell University Press, Ithaca, NY.

New York City Department of Health and Mental Hygiene, Bureau of Environmental and Occupational Disease Epidemiology, 2002. *Guidelines on Assessment and Remediation of Fungi in Indoor Environments*. Available at: http://www.ci.nyc.ny.us/html/doh/html/epi/moldrpt1.html.

Nicholas, D. D., ed., 1973. *Wood Deterioration and Its Prevention by Preservative Treatments*. Syracuse University Press, Syracuse, NY.

NRCA, 2001. *Roofing and Waterproofing Manual*. National Roofing Contractors Association, Rosemont, IL.

Oliver, A., 1997. *Dampness in Buildings.* Blackwell Science, Oxford.

Oxley, T. A., and E. G. Gobert, 1981. *Dampness in Buildings: Diagnosis, Treatment, Instruments.* Butterworths, London.

Pirages, S., 2003. Mold and health issues. *Proceedings: Ventilation, Humidity Control and Energy.* Air Infiltration and Ventilation Centre and National Institute of Building Sciences, Washington, DC.

Plenderleith, H. J., 1956. *Conservation of Antiquities and Works of Art.* Oxford University Press, New York.

Pugin, A. W., 1853. St Augustine's, Ramsgate. *The Builder* xi:377.

Ramsey, C. G., and H. R. Sleeper, 1951. *Architectural Graphic Standards, 4th ed.* Wiley, Hoboken, NJ.

Rogers, T.S., 1938. Preventing condensation in insulated structures. *Architectural Record,* March, pp. 109–119.

Rogers, T. S., 1951a. *Design of Insulated Buildings for Various Climates.* Roberts Printing Company, Toledo, OH.

Rogers, T. S., 1951b. Design of Insulated Buildings for Various Climates. *Architectural Record.*

Rogers, T. S., 1964. *Thermal Design of Buildings.* Wiley, Hoboken, NJ.

Rose, W., 1987. Moisture damage to homes in Champaign County, IL. *Proceedings of the BTECC Symposium on Air Infiltration, Ventilation and Moisture Transfer.* National Institute of Building Sciences, Washington, DC.

Rose, W., 1994. Effects of climate control on the museum building envelope. *Journal of the American Institute for Conservation,* 33(2).

Rose, W., 1997. Details for a dry foundation. *Fine Homebuilding.* August–September.

Rose, W., 2001. Measured values of sheathing and shingle temperatures for residential attic and cathedral ceilings. In *Thermal Envelopes of Buildings VIII.* National Institute of Building Sciences, Washington, DC.

Rose, W., 2003. The rise of the diffusion paradigm in the U.S. *Proceedings of the 2nd International Conference on Research in Building Physics,* September.

Rowley, F.B., 1938. *A Theory Covering the Transfer of Vapor through Materials.* ASHVE Transactions 1134. American Society of Heating, Refrigerating, and Air-Conditioning Engineers, Atlanta, GA, July.

Rowley, F. B., A. Algren, and C. Lund, 1939. *Condensation of Moisture and Its Relation to Building Construction and Operation.* ASHVE Transactions 1115. American Society of Heating, Refrigerating, and Air-Conditioning Engineers, Atlanta, GA.

Russell, W. A., 1954. *Moisture Migration from the Ground.* Housing Research Paper 28. Housing and Home Finance Agency, Washington, DC.

Schwartz, T. A., ed., 1990. *Water in Exterior Building Walls.* American Society for Testing and Materials, West Conshohocken, PA.

SHC, 1959. *Crawl Spaces in the Home.* Circular Series, Vol. 4, No. 2. Small Homes Council, University of Illinois at Urbana–Champaign.

Shermer, M., 2002. *Why People Believe Weird Things.* Henry Holt, New York.

Shirey, D. B., and H. I. Henderson, 2004. Dehumidification at part load. *ASHRAE Journal* Vol. 6 no. 4. April.

Skarr, C., 1988. *Wood–Water Relations.* Springer-Verlag, New York.

SMACNA, 2004. *Architectural Sheet Metal Manual.* Sheet Metal and Air Conditioning Contractors of North America, Hauppauge, NY.

Stamm, A. J. 1964. *Wood and Cellulose Science.* Ronald Press, New York.

Teesdale, L. V., 1937. *Condensation in Walls and Attics.* U.S. Department of Agriculture, Forest Service, Madison, WI.

TenWolde, A., and W. B. Rose., 1999. Issues Related to Venting of Attics and Cathedral Ceilings. ASHRAE Transactions, Vol. 105, Pt. 1. American Society of Heating, Refrigerating, and Air-Conditioning Engineers, Atlanta, GA.

Teulon, S. S., 1854. Cottages for the crown labourers of Windsor Great Park. *The Builder,* xii:99.

Thomson, G., 1978. *The Museum Environment.* Butterworths, London.

Thomson, G., 1986. *The Museum Environment, 2nd ed.,* Butterworths, London.

Tobiasson, W., 1986. Vents and vapor retarders for roofs. *Proceedings of the Symposium on Air Infiltration, Ventilation, and Moisture Transfer,* BTECC-National Institute for Building Sciences, Washington, DC, p.187–197.

*Tobiasson, W., J. Buska, and A. Greatorex, 1994. Ventilating attics to minimize icing at eaves. *Energy and Buildings,* 21:229–234.

Trechsel, H., ed., 1994. *Moisture Control in Buildings.* ASTM Manual Series MNL 18. American Society for Testing and Materials, West Conshohocken, PA.

Trechsel, H. R., ed., 2001. *Moisture Analysis and Condensation Control in Building Envelopes.* American Society for Testing and Materials, West Conshohocken, PA.

Trechsel, H., and M. Bomberg, eds., 1989. *Water Vapor Transmission through Building Materials and Systems.* ASTM STP 1039. American Society for Testing and Materials, West Conshohocken, PA. Includes M. Taos, Results of the 1985 round-robin test series using ASTM E96–80.

Verrall, A. F., 1968. Poria incrassata *Rot: Prevention and Control in Buildings.* Technical Bulletin 1385. U.S. Department of Agriculture, Forest Service, Washington, DC.

Viollet-le-Duc, E.-E., 1872. *Lectures on Architecture.* Dover Publications, New York.

Vogel, S., 1994. *Life in Moving Fluids.* Princeton University Press, Princeton, NJ.

Zumdahl, Stephen S., 1997. *Chemistry.* Houghton Mifflin Company, New York.

Index

Abramovitz, M., 3–4, 5
Absolute humidity, 48, 50, 249
Absorption, 82, 136, 250
Academie de Beaux-Arts, 19
Accessibility, 161
ACI (American Concrete Institute), 169
ACOEM (American Council of Occupational and Environmental Medicine), 244
Activity:
  dynamic, 29
  kinetic, 29, 39, 62, 69, 249
Adsorption, 8, 9, 54, 71, 82, 136, 250
A-horizon, 148
AIPH (acute idiopathic pulmonary hemosiderosis), 242, 244
Air barrier, 177
Air conditioning, 176, 204, 226–228
Air film, 77, 117
Air flow, *see* Flow, air
Air gap, 170
Airtightness, 164, 176, 199
Analysis, 90–92. *See also* Modeling
Angell, W. and Olson, W., 217
Animism, 9
Annular ice, 229
Architecture, 18–19
  design, 3, 6, 206
ASHRAE, 10, 17, 28, 57, 62, 73, 74, 209
  Crawl space symposium, 162–163
  Experimental Data Guide, 239
  Handbook, Fundamentals, 42, 76, 77, 79, 80, 83, 140, 162, 174, 175
  museums, 216
  Standard 160P, 89–94

  Standard 55, 211–212
  Standard 62, 220, 225
Asphalt shingle(s), 100, 110, 191
  service life, 198, 203
Aspiration, 49
Assembly:
  cavity, 178–179, 181, 182, 189, 249
  compact, 178–179, 181, 189, 206, 249
ASTM, 10, 73, 74, 75, 131
Attic, 159, 189–207
Attic ventilation, xi, 57, 60, 64, 65, 69, 72, 83, 95, 114, 115, 190–205, 206, 250
  cooling effect, 204
  mechanical, 193, 202
  ratio, 190, 194–197, 198
Avogadro number, 25, 42

Backfill, 148
Balcony, 177
Band joist, 166
Basement, 152–158
Basidiomycetes, 234–235
Beall, C., 2
Belly board, 163, 164
Bernoulli, 29
BOCA, 73
Boltzmann constant, 38, 43
  hydrogen bond, 35
Bound water, 30, 51–55, 122
Boyle's Law, 42
BRAB (Building Research Advisory Board), 17, 18, 58, 81, 167
  Condensation Conference, 68–69
Brewster, D., 213–214

265